W9-ANT-282

WordPerfect for Windows Answers:
Certified Tech Support

Mary Campbell

Osborne **McGraw-Hill**
Berkeley · New York · St. Louis
San Francisco · Auckland · Bogotá
Hamburg · London · Madrid · Mexico
City · Milan · Montreal · New Delhi
Panama City · Paris · São Paulo
Singapore · Sydney · Tokyo · Toronto

Osborne **McGraw-Hill**
2600 Tenth Street, Berkeley, California 94710, USA

For information on software, translations, or book distributors outside of the U.S.A., please write to Osborne McGraw-Hill at the above address.

**WordPerfect for Windows Answers:
Certified Tech Support**

1234567890 DOC 9987654

ISBN 0-07-882053-7

Contents at a Glance

Contents

Foreword

Few things are as frustrating as having a computer problem that you can't solve. Computer users often spend hours trying to find the answer to a *single* software question! That's why the tech support experts at Corporate Software Incorporated (CSI) have teamed up with Osborne/McGraw-Hill to bring you the **Certified Tech Support Series**—books designed to give you all the solutions you need to fix even the most difficult software glitches.

At Corporate Software, we have a dedicated support staff that handles over 200,000 software questions every month. These experts use the latest hardware and software technology to provide answers to every sort of software problem. CSI takes full advantage of the partnerships that we have forged with all major software publishers. Our staff frequently receives the same training that publishers offer their own support representatives and has access to vendor technical resources that are not generally available to the public.

Thus, this series is based on actual *empirical* data. We've drawn on our support expertise and sorted through our vast database of software solutions to find the most important and frequently asked questions for WordPerfect for Windows. These questions have also been checked and rechecked for technical accuracy and are organized in a way that will let you find the answer you need quickly—providing you with a one-stop tech support solution to your software problems.

No longer do you have to spend hours on the phone waiting for someone to answer your tech support question! You are holding the single, most authoritative collection of answers to your software questions available—the next best thing to having a tech support expert by your side.

We've helped millions of people solve their software problems. Let us help you.

Randy Burkhart
Senior Vice President, Technology
Corporate Software Inc

Acknowledgments

I would like to thank all the staff at Corporate Software who enthusiastically committed so much time and knowledge to this effort. So many of them spent time on weekends and after hours to search their data banks for the best questions and answers. They also spent untold hours reviewing manuscript and pages and responding to all of our requests for help. Without all of their hard work, this book would not exist. I would like to personally thank each of the following people for their assistance.

Alice P.
Florentine L.
Jacqueline G.
Ken M.
Marion M.
Michael L.
Stephen A.
Todd B.
Tracy G.

Special thanks to:
Christian P.
Jan R.
Jennifer L.
John S.
Kim A.
Loretta B.
Lori F.
Margaret M.

The staff at Osborne was also an important part of this book. Without exception, everyone did more than their share to insure that we met all the important deadlines. I would like to extend special thanks to: Larry Levitsky, Publisher, for the idea to do the series and all of his work with Corporate Software to make the idea a reality; Scott Rogers, Acquisitions Editor, who took the time to read each chapter and made excellent suggestions for improvements; Kelly Vogel, Editorial Assistant, who helped to organize all the components of the project; Claire Splan, Project

Editor, who managed the editorial process and helped to polish the manuscript; and all of the Production staff, who each did everything possible to make this book the best source of technical support available.

I would also like to especially thank my assistants, Gabrielle Lawrence and Elizabeth Reinhardt. They contributed extensively to the book's contents and art work. They also proofread the final manuscript to help catch technical and grammatical errors.

Introduction

There is no good time to have a problem with your computer or the software you are using. You are anxious to complete the task you started and do not have time to fumble through a manual looking for an answer that is probably not there anyway. You can forget about the option of a free support call solving your problems since most software vendors now charge as much as $25 to answer a single question. *WordPerfect for Windows Answers: Certified Tech Support* can provide the solutions to all of your WordPerfect problems. It contains the most frequently asked WordPerfect questions along with the solutions to get you back on track quickly. The questions and answers have been extracted from the data banks of Corporate Software, the world's largest supplier of third-party support. Since they answer over 200,000 calls a month from users just like you, odds are high that your problem has plagued others in the past and is already part of their data bank. *WordPerfect for Windows Answers: Certified Tech Support* is the next best thing to having a Corporate Software expert at the desk right next to you. The help you need is available seven days a week, any time you have a problem.

WordPerfect for Windows Answers is organized into 14 chapters. Each chapter contains questions and answers on a specific area of WordPerfect. Within each chapter you will find the simplest questions at the beginning, progressing to intermediate and advanced questions as you move through the chapter. With this organization, you will be able to read through questions and answers on particular topics to familiarize yourself with them before the troubles actually occur. An excellent index makes it easy for you to find what you need even if you are uncertain which chapter would cover the solution.

Throughout the book you will also find the following elements to help you sail smoothly through your WordPerfect tasks whether you are a novice or a veteran user:

- **Frustration Busters:** Special coverage of WordPerfect topics that have proven confusing to many users. A few minutes spent reading each of these boxes can help you avoid problems in the first place.

- **Tech Tips and Notes:** Short technical helps that provide additional insight to a topic addressed in one of the questions.

- **Tech Terrors:** Pitfalls you will want to steer clear of.

Top Ten Tech Terrors

Every computer user experiences technical problems at some time. We've tapped the data banks and consultant expertise at Corporate Software and identified the ten most common WordPerfect problems. These are problems that *thousands* of users have encountered. You may find it worthwhile to read through this list as a preventive measure, to avoid these problems altogether. Then, if you do happen to encounter them, you'll know how to fix them.

1

I'm tired of changing the font each time I create a document. How can I change the initial (default) font for the printer?

WordPerfect documents remember which printer is selected while you create and edit them. The initial font a document uses depends on which printer you have selected. To change the current initial font for a printer:

1. Choose Select Printer from the File menu.

2. Select the printer driver whose initial font you want to change.

3. Choose Initial Font.

4. Select the desired font face, size, and style from the Font Face, Font Size, and Font Style list boxes in the Printer Initial Font dialog box, as shown in Figure 1-1.

5. Choose OK to close the dialog box and confirm your choices.

FIGURE 1-1   Printer Initial Font dialog box

6. Choose <u>S</u>elect to make this printer your current one or choose <u>C</u>lose to close the dialog box without selecting a new printer.

2 How can I set a default document directory to tell WordPerfect where to look when saving and opening my documents?

WordPerfect's default document directory determines where WordPerfect first looks for documents. To specify a default document directory:

1. Choose Pr<u>e</u>ferences from the <u>F</u>ile menu.

2. Choose the <u>F</u>ile icon and the D<u>o</u>cuments/Backup radio button.

3. Type the directory or pathname for your documents in the D<u>e</u>fault Directory text box.

4. Choose OK and <u>C</u>lose to close the File Preferences dialog box and save your changes.

Keep in mind that if you change to another location to look for files, WordPerfect will remember that new location. The next time you look at files during the same WordPerfect session, WordPerfect will show the files in the new location, not those in the default directory. However, if you exit and reenter the program, the default directory will be selected once again.

Tech Terror: Information specifying the default directory is contained in a file called WPCSET.BIF. If you delete or rename that file, you will lose your customized default directory setting and other customized settings. WordPerfect will then generate a new WPCSET.BIF file with all the preset defaults.

3 How do I change the unit of measure WordPerfect uses?

WordPerfect can measure distances in inches, centimeters, millimeters, points (1/72 of an inch), and 1200ths of an inch. The measuring system WordPerfect uses sets the display of the distances on the Status Bar, the units you use to type entries, and other measurements. To change the units of measure:

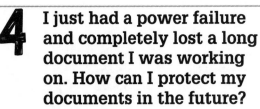

1. Choose Preferences from the File menu, then choose the Display icon.

2. Choose the Document radio button, then the Units of Measure or the Status/Ruler Bar Display pop-up button.

   The Units of Measure option sets how WordPerfect measures distances in dialog boxes and in the codes that you see when you reveal codes. The Status/Ruler Bar Display option sets how WordPerfect measures distances indicated in the Status Bar and Ruler Bar.

3. Select any of the following options from the pop-up lists:
   Inches (")
   Inches (i)
   Centimeters (c)
   Millimeters (m)
   Points (p)
   1200ths of an inch (w)

4. Choose OK to accept the changes and Close to return to your document.

4 I just had a power failure and completely lost a long document I was working on. How can I protect my documents in the future?

Timed backups are the best way to help prevent losing work due to a power failure or a machine "crash." Timed backup files are written to disk when WordPerfect is exited from improperly, and are saved with special filenames. If WordPerfect finds these specially named files when it starts, it allows you to restore these backups. To set backup options:

1. Choose Preferences from the File menu by using the File icon.

2. Choose the Documents/Backup radio button.

3. Select Timed Document Backup.

4. Specify the number of minutes between backups in the text box. WordPerfect will make backups at the specified intervals.

5. Choose OK and Close to confirm your choices and to close the File Preferences dialog box.

Tech Note: Although this is a good method of recovering work that might otherwise be lost, there is no guarantee that everything will be completely recovered. Be sure to actually save your work as frequently as possible.

I need to insert different characters into my document that aren't on the keyboard? Where do I find them?

WordPerfect provides the ability to insert special characters that are not available on your keyboard, such as typographical symbols, letters used in other languages, and icons. To insert WordPerfect's special characters:

1. Place your insertion point where you want the character to appear in your document.

2. Choose Characters from the Insert menu or press the CTRL+W shortcut key.

3. Select the appropriate set of characters from the Character Set pop-up button, then select a character from the Characters list box.

4. Choose Insert to add the special character without closing the dialog box, or choose Insert and Close to insert the character and close the dialog box.

The following illustration shows a document with several special characters that were added this way:

Survey Responses			
Question	Yes	No	Undecided
❶	¼	¼	½
⇨ ❷	½	⅛	⅜
❸	⅜	¼	⅜
⇨ ❹	⅝	⅛	¼
⇨ ❺	½	⅛	⅜

Tech Tip: Use CTRL+W to add a special character in prompts where you cannot use the menu command, such as when you are making an entry in a text box.

All of my documents are formatted for 8 1/2 by 11-inch paper regardless of the size of paper I put in my printer. How can I use legal and other paper sizes?

The paper definition sets the size of paper your document is formatted for. You will want your definition to agree with the paper in your printer. You can switch paper size definitions within a document when you want to switch paper sizes or print sideways. To select a paper definition:

1. Move the insertion point to the page in your document where you want to specify a different paper definition.

2. Choose <u>P</u>age from the <u>L</u>ayout menu, then choose Paper <u>S</u>ize.

3. Select the paper definition you want to use in the Paper Size dialog box, then choose <u>S</u>elect to confirm your choice and return to your document. The page size chosen remains in effect for the rest of the document.

7 Even though I have created directories for different types of documents, it is still difficult to locate files I use frequently. Are there any other options in WordPerfect that can help?

You can use the QuickList to define directories and files that you use frequently. You can use QuickList items to easily select a file you want to work with. To add or edit a QuickList item, follow these steps:

1. Choose Save As or Open from the File menu.

2. Select the QuickList pop-up button and choose Show QuickList.

3. Select the QuickList pop-up button, then Add Item or Edit Item.

4. Type the directory and file information in the Directory/Filename text box and a description in the Description text box as shown in the following illustration. If you are editing a QuickList item, you can modify the existing entries.

```
┌─────────────────────────────────────────┐
│ ═        Add QuickList Item              │
├─────────────────────────────────────────┤
│ Directory/Filename:          ┌────────┐  │
│ c:\wpwin60\person\        □   │   OK   │  │
│                              └────────┘  │
│                              ┌────────┐  │
│ Description:                 │ Cancel │  │
│ Personal Files               └────────┘  │
│                              ┌────────┐  │
│                              │  Help  │  │
│                              └────────┘  │
└─────────────────────────────────────────┘
```

5. Select OK to finish adding or editing the QuickList item. At this point, you can continue opening or saving a file before you choose OK or you can select Cancel to leave the dialog box without opening or saving a file.

To use the QuickList item you just created or edited, select the QuickList item from the QuickList list box. All files selected by the QuickList item appear in the Filename list box. The QuickList list box will remain in dialog boxes that you use to select a file until you select the QuickList pop-up button and choose Show Directories.

Tech Tip: WordPerfect has several QuickList items already defined for you. These include files in the default document directory, macros, templates, and graphics. The file locations these QuickList items represent are set with the Preferences command in the File menu.

I am concerned about other users looking at confidential documents that I have created. Is there anything I can do to prevent this?

WordPerfect allows you to assign passwords to documents. If you password-protect a document, no one will be able to open or look at it without first supplying the correct password. It's a good idea to use password protection to safeguard information in important documents that you do not wish anyone else to see. To add password protection to a document:

1. Open the document you want to password-protect.

2. Choose Save As from the File menu and click the Password Protect box.

3. Choose OK, type a password, and again choose OK.

4. Retype the password and choose OK.

Since the password does not appear onscreen, you are prompted to type it twice to ensure that the file uses the correct one. After you select OK a second time, WordPerfect saves the password-protected file. The next time you open the document, you are prompted to enter the password as shown here:

```
┌─────────────────────────────────────────────┐
│ ▬              Password                       │
├─────────────────────────────────────────────┤
│  Enter password for file:          ┌────────┐│
│  C:\WPWIN60\WPDOCS\JUNK.WPD         │   OK   ││
│                                     └────────┘│
│  ┌──────────────────────────┐      ┌────────┐│
│  │ ••••••                    │      │ Cancel ││
│  └──────────────────────────┘      └────────┘│
│                                     ┌────────┐│
│                                     │  Help  ││
│                                     └────────┘│
└─────────────────────────────────────────────┘
```

Tech Terror: Remember your password!
If you forget it, you cannot open the file.

9 **If I want to change a macro do I need to record it all over again or can I edit it?**

You can edit the macro to make changes. To do this, select Macro from the Tools menu, and click Edit. From the Edit Macro dialog box, select the name of the macro to edit and click Edit. The macro displays in a window that includes a Macro Edit Feature Bar like the one shown here:

10 **Why do I receive the error message "Invalid QCode Received by Printing Process"?**

The error message "Invalid QCode Received by Printing Process" is caused by an error in WordPerfect's code. If you receive this message when sending a file to print from within WordPerfect, follow these steps:

1. Open the file SH_SH_.ENV, located in the WPC20 directory, in WordPerfect.

2. Turn on reveal codes by pressing ALT+F3, and delete the HRt code at the end of the line of text.

3. Resave the file as an ASCII text file and restart WordPerfect for Windows.

Installation and Startup

Installing WordPerfect for Windows is easy, because the WordPerfect installation program handles most of the work for you. The installation process consists of inserting the first installation disk into your drive, selecting Run from the File menu, typing **A:\INSTALL**, selecting OK, and following the instructions. If your WordPerfect installation disk is in a different drive, you will substitute the appropriate drive letter for A:\. After WordPerfect is installed, you can start it by selecting the WPWin 6.0 icon in the Program Manager. The following box highlights steps you can take to fine-tune WordPerfect's performance after installation.

FRUSTRATION BUSTERS!

If you are unsatisfied with WordPerfect's performance on your system, consider using some of the following options to help the program run faster.

- Use Draft view rather than Page view or Two Page view.

- Close the WordPerfect documents that you are not currently working on.

- Divide a large document into smaller ones.

- Close other applications you are running.

- Remove any RAM drives unless you have at least 8MB of RAM.

- Increase the RAM on your computer.

- Add a Windows graphics card if your monitor's resolution is more than 800 x 600 or you are using a 256 color mode.

- Make sure your Windows swap file is a permanent swap file using the Windows Control Panel.

- Use a disk cache such as SMARTDrive, which comes with DOS.

- Reduce the numbers in the SMARTDRV line in your AUTOEXEC.BAT file.

- Change your buffers set in CONFIG.SYS to a higher or lower number.

- Set the Desktop wallpaper to None in the Windows Control Panel.

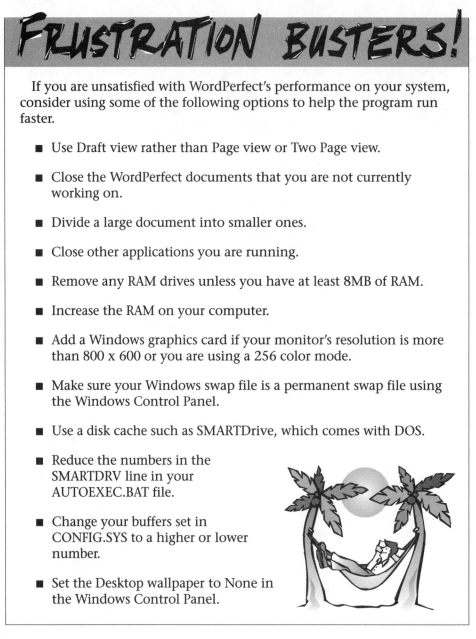

Tech Tip: Some of these optimization options require changing DOS and Windows settings. If you are unfamiliar with these DOS or Windows settings, you might want to refer to *DOS Answers: Certified Tech Support* (Osborne/McGraw-Hill, 1994) or *Simply Windows 3.1* (Osborne/McGraw-Hill, 1993) for tips about these features. You can also check the Windows or DOS help for an explanation of these features.

What does WordPerfect require to run on my computer?

WordPerfect Corporation recommends the following system requirements for WordPerfect 6.0 for Windows:

- A personal computer using a 386 processor or better
- 6-8MB RAM (4MB is the minimum)
- A hard disk with at least 32MB of free disk space (10.5MB minimum)
- A VGA graphics adapter and monitor or better
- Microsoft Windows 3.1 running in enhanced mode (WordPerfect can run on Windows 3.0, but it is not recommended)
- A mouse (highly recommended)

Why does WordPerfect 6.0 for Windows have five installation options?

WordPerfect has five installation options to allow you to select the WordPerfect features you want to install. The following list describes the five options, shown in Figure 2-1. While the Standard installation is recommended for most users, you can choose whichever best meets your needs.

- **Standard**—Installs all of WordPerfect.
- **Custom**—Installs only the WordPerfect features that you select, such as the Learn, Speller, Thesaurus, and sound

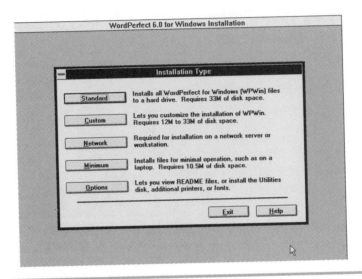

FIGURE 2-1   WordPerfect installation options

driver files. You also can use the Custom option to add WordPerfect features that were not initially installed.

■ **Network**—Installs a shared copy of WordPerfect on a network file server or workstation.

■ **Minimum**—Installs only those files needed to run WordPerfect.

■ **Options**—Provides other choices besides installing WordPerfect. You can view the README files, install additional printer drivers, install the WordPerfect utility disk, install Bitstream TrueType fonts that WordPerfect provides, or install language modules.

Why does WordPerfect for Windows create a WPC20 and a WPWIN60 directory?

WordPerfect uses files that other WordPerfect Corporation products can use. Rather than each product having its own copy of the common files, these applications have a shared directory where all common files are placed. If you have more than one WordPerfect Corporation product for Windows

installed, these applications probably are using some of the
same files in the shared directory and saving disk space. The
shared directory is WPC20. The WPWIN60 directory contains
only the program files specific to WordPerfect 6.0 for Windows.

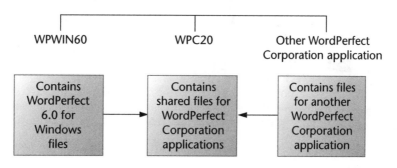

What can I do to save disk space when I install WordPerfect 6.0?

A full installation of WordPerfect 6.0
for Windows requires 32MB of free
disk space. A custom installation
allows you to choose the options you
want. The space requirements for a
custom installation range from 12MB to 32MB, depending on
the WordPerfect features you install. You can perform a
minimum installation, which only requires 10.5MB of disk space.
If a minimum installation is run, only the files necessary to run
WordPerfect 6.0 for Windows are installed. Therefore, the
Speller, Grammatik, Thesaurus, macros, and conversion filters
are not installed. If you later want to use any of these additional
features, run a custom installation.

I just received the message that I do not have enough room to install WordPerfect. What do I do?

When you see this message, the WordPerfect installation
program is prompting you to decide whether to continue with
the installation process even though your hard disk does not
have enough room for all of the WordPerfect files. Usually, when
you see this message, you will select <u>N</u>o. Then leave the
installation program, delete files to free up sufficient space, and

restart the installation process. If you select Yes and you are installing WordPerfect on top of an existing copy of WordPerfect 6.0 for Windows, you probably can continue without running into problems. This situation occurs when you are reinstalling WordPerfect after accidentally deleting files. If you select Yes and you really do not have enough room for all the files WordPerfect's installation program will copy to your disk, the installation program will continue until it runs out of free disk space for its files.

Tech Tip: If you do not have enough room to install all of WordPerfect on your computer, use the custom installation to select the parts of WordPerfect you will install. Skipping over parts of WordPerfect reduces the hard disk space requirement.

Why would I receive the error message "File in Use or is Read-Only" when trying to open my document?

When you open a document, WordPerfect tries to open the document exclusively, which means that only WordPerfect can save changes to that file. When WordPerfect cannot open a document exclusively because it is already being used by some other application, you will see a message like this:

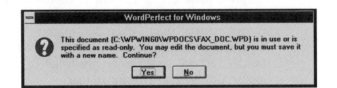

At this point, you can select Yes to open the file. If you do this, however, you will not be able to save it using the same filename because WordPerfect does not have it exclusively. You can also select No to cancel the command.

One reason for getting a "read-only" message about a file you open is that the file has the read-only attribute. You can check this with the Windows File Manager or with WordPerfect. To view or set the file attribute in WordPerfect, follow these steps:

1. Select Open from the File menu.

2. Highlight the file to check the attributes in the Filename list box.

3. Select the File Options pop-up button or right-click the file, and select Change Attributes.

4. WordPerfect opens a dialog box like the one shown here indicating which file attributes the highlighted file has.

Change File Attributes		
Current Dir: c:\wpwin60\wpdocs		**OK**
Filename: c:\wpwin60\wpdocs\fax_doc.wpd		**Cancel**
Attributes		**Help**
☒ Archive ☐ Read-Only		
☐ Hidden ☐ System		

5. Select Cancel twice if you only want to view the attributes, or change which check boxes are selected and select OK and Cancel if you want to change the file attributes.

This error message commonly occurs on a network when one user has a document open and a second user attempts to access the file. The second user can open the document, but if any changes are made to the file, the second user must use a new filename to save the document. The problem can also occur if you are not on a network when you use the file in more than one application or when you open the document in more than one WordPerfect document window.

In WordPerfect 5.2 for Windows, I had a WP{WP}.SET file. Where is this file in WordPerfect 6.0 for Windows?

Tech Note: The .BIF extension for your settings file stands for binary initialization file.

WordPerfect 6.0 for Windows uses files with a .BIF extension to store the default settings which in previous versions were stored in the WP{WP}.SET file. The WPCSET.BIF file is stored by default in your Windows subdirectory. It can be in a different location if you add **/PI-*path*** to the command line that starts WordPerfect for Windows or if the WP_WP_.ENV file in the WPWIN60 directory has the line **/pi=*path***. In either case, *path* represents the drive and directory containing your WPCSET.BIF file. This file contains a user's private initialization instructions, including any of the settings stored under Preferences in the File menu.

I ran a minimum installation and parts of WordPerfect won't work. Do I have to install the complete version of WordPerfect?

The minimum installation option omits several features such as the Speller, Thesaurus, Grammatik, graphics files, macros, and templates. When you want to install one of these, follow these steps:

1. From the Windows Program Manager, select <u>F</u>ile and then <u>R</u>un.

2. Type **C:\WPWIN60\INSTALL.EXE** in the <u>C</u>ommand Line text box and select OK. Replace C:\WPWIN60 with the drive and path where the WordPerfect 6.0 for Windows installation program is located if it is not in C:\WPWIN60.

3. From the WordPerfect Installation screen, select <u>C</u>ustom and <u>F</u>iles.

4. Select the <u>U</u>nmark All button to remove all of the check boxes.

5. Highlight the item to install in the <u>S</u>elections list box and press the SPACEBAR, or click its check box.

6. Select OK.

7. Select Start <u>I</u>nstallation.

8. Type the location of the drive containing the original WordPerfect installation disks (usually A:\) and select OK. WordPerfect will start copying the files. You may be prompted to switch which disk is in the drive.

9. Select the group to hold the WordPerfect icons and OK. The installation program will only create new icons if you are installing parts of the program that you did not install before.

10. Select <u>N</u>o to skip over the README files.

11. Select OK to finish with the installation program.

The options of WordPerfect you have selected are now installed.

I just deleted some of my WordPerfect program files. How do I get my files back?

If you delete WordPerfect program files, you can recover these files one of two ways, depending on how quickly you realize your mistake. If you realize the mistake shortly after deleting the file, you can try using MWUNDEL in DOS 6 for restoring deleted files in Windows or another utility that restores deleted files. If you cannot restore the deleted files, you can recover them by reinstalling them from the WordPerfect installation disks. If you know the WordPerfect feature that the deleted files were used for, you can selectively install WordPerfect as described in the previous question. You can always run through the standard installation option for WordPerfect to reinstall all of your files.

Tech Terror: If you are using an undelete utility designed to run from the DOS prompt, do not try running it from a DOS prompt application window within Windows. Windows and other active applications probably have many temporary files that you do not want to damage.

What does the error message "Cannot find SHWINB20.DLL" mean?

This error message occurs because the WP_WP_.ENV file is pointing to the wrong shared applications directory. This shared applications directory is where WordPerfect installs files shared with more than one WordPerfect Corporation application. To fix this problem, edit the WP_WP_.ENV file which is located in your WordPerfect 6.0 for Windows directory and change the line "/WPC=*path*" to point to the correct directory for the WordPerfect 6.0 for Windows shared applications directory.

Why do I get the message "The directory '*path*' referred to by the '/WPC' switch in the WP_WP_.ENV file does not contain the shared application files?"

This error message occurs because the WP_WP_.ENV file is pointing to the wrong shared applications directory. You can use Windows Notepad to open the WP_WP_.ENV file, which is located in the WPWIN60 directory. Change the /WPC= parameter to point to the correct drive and directory.

Is there a way to load WordPerfect before loading Windows?

You can load WordPerfect for Windows directly from a DOS prompt as you load Windows. To do this, type **WIN C:\WPWIN60\WPWIN.EXE** and press ENTER. This assumes you have your WPWIN60 files in a directory called C:\WPWIN60. If your directories are set up differently, modify the command line to replace C:\WPWIN60 with the proper drive and directory.

I entered the wrong license number when I installed WordPerfect 6.0 for Windows. Can I fix this?

You can change the WordPerfect license number from within WordPerfect. Select About WordPerfect from the Help menu, and select Edit License Number. After the number has been edited, select OK twice.

What startup options does WordPerfect have?

WordPerfect has many startup options that change how WordPerfect runs. To use these startup options only one time, start WordPerfect by selecting Run from the File menu, type **C:\WPWIN60\WPWIN** followed by the startup options you want in the Command Line text box, and select OK. If you want to continue using a startup option, select the WordPerfect icon, select Properties in the File menu or press ALT+ENTER, and add the startup options to the end of the entry in the Command Line text box. Table 2-1 summarizes the startup options available.

Startup option	Effect
:	Starts WordPerfect without displaying the startup screen (the picture of the pen).
/d-*path*	Stores temporary and overflow files in the drive and directory set by *path* rather than the drive and directory set by DOS's TEMP environment variable.
filename	Opens the named document in WordPerfect once WordPerfect is loaded. Includes the path information when the file is not in the default document directory.

TABLE 2-1　　WordPerfect 6.0 for Windows Startup Options

Startup option	Effect
filename /bk-*bookmark name*	Opens the named document in WordPerfect once WordPerfect is loaded and moves to the named bookmark.
/fl	Helps correct display problems by sending text directly to the screen. Prevents application errors from occurring when you're using a 256-color graphic card driver.
/l-*language code*	Selects the language .DLL file to use and the entry in the Language Resource File (WP.LRS) based on the *language code*.
/la-*login alias*	Replaces requests for the user name with the name supplied as the *login alias*.
/li	Displays the screen's contents using logical inches rather than real inches, making screen elements larger so the screen is easier to read.
/m-*macroname*	Plays the named macro once WordPerfect is loaded. If this macro file is not in the directory where WordPerfect looks for macros, you must include the path information.
/mt-*macroname*	Plays the named macro stored in the default template once WordPerfect is loaded.
/nb	Prevents WordPerfect from backing up a document as it saves its newer version. This is especially useful if you need to conserve disk space.
/ni-*path*	Sets the path where WordPerfect looks for the public binary information file (WPCNET.BIF) rather than in the Windows directory.
/nt	Tells WordPerfect to be aware that a network is operating so that it can make use of the network settings.
/pi-*path*	Sets the path where WordPerfect looks for the personal WordPerfect Corporation binary information file, rather than in the Windows directory, which is the default. (The personal binary information file is called WPCSET.BIF in a stand-alone environment, or *XXXX####*.BIF in a network environment, where *XXXX* are the first four characters of your network ID and #### is a hash value unique to each user.)
/pn-*filename*	Sets the name of the personal binary information file to use in place of the default (WPCSET.BIF when you are not on a network).
/restore	Regenerates documents that are not functioning properly.
/sa	Tells WordPerfect to run in stand-alone mode, which ignores any network.
/sn	Sets WordPerfect to use the default personal WordPerfect Corporation binary information file (WPCSET.BIF).

TABLE 2-1   WordPerfect 6.0 for Windows Startup Options (*continued*)

Startup option	Effect
/sp	Sets WordPerfect to use the personal WordPerfect Corporation binary information file rather than the public WordPerfect Corporation binary information (WPCNET.BIF).
/u-*name*	Sets the user initials which WordPerfect uses to allow multiple users to run WordPerfect on a network, and which WordPerfect uses to create unique temporary files on a network.
/unr-*path*	Sets the path for the user name reconciliation files when you are on a network.
/wpc-*path*	Sets the path to the shared directory for WordPerfect Corporation shared code files (default is \WPC20).
/x	Starts WordPerfect using the default values for WordPerfect customizations made through the Preferences command in the File menu.

TABLE 2-1   WordPerfect 6.0 for Windows Startup Options (*continued*)

I keep getting the error message "Not enough Global Memory to execute request" when I try to install WordPerfect 6.0 for Windows. What is wrong?

This message appears because you do not have enough memory of any type to install WordPerfect 6.0 for Windows. The error message is created by Windows. Making more memory available to Windows will eliminate this problem. You can increase your memory by performing these four steps, trying to install WordPerfect after completing each one:

1. Look at your CONFIG.SYS file and make sure that it has HIMEM.SYS, EMM386.EXE, and DOS=HIGH in that order. These lines may have other entries on these lines, such as DOS including a comma and UMB and EMM386.EXE including multiple switches. These commands require DOS 5 or DOS 6. If you are using an earlier version of DOS, you need to have a separate memory manager program for extended memory.

2. Make sure you are running with the correct version of DOS: 5 or 6 if you are using DOS to handle extended memory management.

3. Edit your AUTOEXEC.BAT and place REM in front of any TSRs not needed.

4. Run Chkdsk or ScanDisk to check for any hard disk damage.

5. Run MemMaker if you are using DOS 6. This DOS utility organizes how programs and drivers are placed in memory. Running this utility does not increase the memory you have, but it does rearrange how the memory is used to leave more for other purposes.

I installed WordPerfect 6.0 files to a WordPerfect 5.2 directory and now neither version of WordPerfect will run. What's wrong?

When you install WordPerfect 6.0 files to a WordPerfect 5.2 directory, neither version of WordPerfect will run because the files have become mixed. WordPerfect 5.2 is trying to use some files designed specifically for WordPerfect 6.0 and WordPerfect 6.0 is trying to use some files designed specifically for WordPerfect 5.2. These mixed files include the WPWIN.EXE file and several environment files located in the program directory. Make sure that when installing WordPerfect 6.0, you install it to a different directory than the WordPerfect 5.2 directory.

Can I set WordPerfect to use different default directories by starting WordPerfect with different icons?

You can set WordPerfect to look for documents in different locations by loading WordPerfect with a different icon that selects a different .BIF file. To set up several different WPWin 6.0 icons, with each icon loading WordPerfect documents from a different subdirectory as the default, follow these steps:

1. Copy the WPCSET.BIF file from the program directory to each subdirectory.

2. Create a new program item in the Windows Program Manager by following either set of options:

   ■ Select New in the File menu, the Program Item radio button, and OK.

   ■ Hold down the CTRL key while you drag the WordPerfect icon to another location. This creates a duplicate of the icon so you only need to change the program item's properties that need to change. Click the new icon, then select Properties from the File menu or press ALT+ENTER to modify the icon's settings.

3. Type a description of the icon in the Description text box.

4. Type **C:\WPWIN60\WPWIN.EXE /PI-*path*** in the Command Line text box where *path* is the subdirectory containing a copy of the WPCSET.BIF file.

5. Select OK.

6. Repeat steps 2 through 5 for each icon.

Tech Tip: Setting the default directory used when you start WordPerfect with a specific icon does not prevent you from opening files in other directories. All you are doing is selecting the location of files WordPerfect initially uses when started with that icon.

The first time you load WordPerfect for Windows with each of these new icons, select Preferences from the File menu, the File icon, and the Documents/Backup radio button, and enter the default subdirectory in the Default Directory text box. Select OK. Every time you start WordPerfect with that icon, WordPerfect looks for documents in that location instead of the locations that other WordPerfect startup icons use. You can see here several WordPerfect icons used to choose which group of files you will work with once you start WordPerfect:

When I start WordPerfect, I see the message "The directory path for the shared code is invalid." How do I start WordPerfect?

When you are running WordPerfect on a network, the message "ERROR: The directory path for the shared code is invalid" indicates that you are not mapped to the same drive letter that was indicated during the installation. All users must use the same drive mapping. To verify the correct mapping, open the file WP_WP_.ENV in the WPWIN60 directory. The settings are listed there. The /WPC line specifically contains the path to the shared code files.

Can I start WordPerfect by double-clicking a document file in the File Manager the same way I start other applications by double-clicking their data files?

Double-clicking a file in the Windows File Manager will load the file's application as well as the selected file, as long as the document extension is listed in the [EXTENSIONS] section of the WIN.INI file. If the WordPerfect document extension is missing from this section and you double-click a WordPerfect for Windows file, however, you will receive the following message:

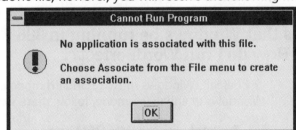

This message indicates that the WordPerfect 6.0 for Windows document extension is not included in WIN.INI. Edit the [EXTENSIONS] section of the WIN.INI file to include the following statement:

    WPD=C:\WPWIN60\WPWIN.EXE ^.WPD

WIN.INI is a text file, so you can use Notepad or Windows' SysEdit utility. When you save your WordPerfect files with the .WPD extension, you can double-click them in the File Manager

Tech Tip: If you have some WordPerfect documents you work with frequently, add the files as program items in the Program Manager. Selecting the icon will open WordPerfect as well as the selected document. The same file extension association that works for the File Manager also works for the Program Manager.

Tech Terror: You cannot open another session of WordPerfect with an attachment such as electronic mail if you already have one open. This is a limitation of WordPerfect for Windows rather than a limit of the File Manager or Windows.

to start WordPerfect with the selected files. You do not need to supply the .WPD extension yourself each time you name a WordPerfect file, because WordPerfect saves documents with this extension by default. You can see that Windows has an association between the .WPD extension and an application by the icon next to the file. The following illustration shows two files listed in the File Manager window. MAGAD is not associated with an application, so it is empty. FAX_DOC.WPD is associated with WordPerfect, so it has a different icon.

📄 fax_doc.wpd
📄 magad

 When I try to run WordPerfect under OS/2 version 2.1, I get the error message "WordPerfect 6.0 for Windows requires that Windows be running in 386 Enhanced Mode." How do I run WordPerfect?

By default, Windows runs in standard mode in OS/2. To run Windows in enhanced mode, follow these steps:

1. Right-click the WIN-OS/2 icon.
2. Select Open, then Settings.
3. Click the Session tab, and select WIN-OS/2 Full Screen. If this option is grayed out and you cannot select it, click the Program tab. Under Path & Filename, enter an asterisk. At this point you can click the Session tab and select WIN-OS/2 Full Screen.
4. Select the WIN-OS/2 Settings button.
5. Select WIN_RUN_MODE under Setting.

6. Select 3.1 Enhanced Compatibility under Value.

7. Select Save.

8. Select About Program Manager from the Help menu in Windows to be sure you are in enhanced mode. Once you are in enhanced mode, WordPerfect will run fine.

When I run BIFED20.EXE located in WordPerfect's WPC20 directory, I get the error message "No Resource Language Information - Reinstall." How do I correct this problem?

This error message appears when Windows cannot access the BIFED20.EXE file that you use when you work with WordPerfect for Windows on a network. To eliminate this problem, open the WIN.INI file located in the Windows directory by double-clicking on the file in the File Manager. This opens the file into Notepad. Locate the [WPCorp] section. Make sure that the following lines are present in this section:

```
[WPCorp]
spwin20=US
thwin20=US
WPWin60=g:\wpwin60\
BIFED20=US
WPWin60US=g:\wpwin60\
```

These lines assume WPWIN60 is the main directory of WordPerfect 6.0 for Windows and G is the network drive where the application is located. Make the appropriate changes to this section, then select Save from Notepad's File menu, then Exit from the File menu. The average network user does not use this file. The above procedure is usually performed by a network administrator or supervisor.

When I installed WordPerfect on my server, two additional icons were created: a WPCNET Flagging icon and a WPCNET Settings icon. What are these icons for?

Select the WPCNET Settings icon to edit the default settings of WordPerfect. The settings that you change are saved in the file WPCNET.BIF, which is stored in the WPCNET directory. This file is the equivalent of the WP{WP}.SET Master Set file in the previous version of WordPerfect. For any new user who logs into WordPerfect, a personal .BIF file is created based on the settings in this WPCNET.BIF file.

Select the WPCNET Flagging icon to update existing personal .BIF files for changes made to the WordPerfect defaults (saved in the WPCNET.BIF file). Double-click the WPCNET Flagging icon, choose the options that you want to update, and choose Override Private .BIF. Now when an existing user logs into WordPerfect, the settings made in the WPCNET Flagging icon cause WPCNET.BIF to update that user's personal .BIF file. (This procedure is the equivalent of running NWPSETUP.EXE in the previous version of WordPerfect.)

Formatting

Formatting is a way to make changes in the appearance of your WordPerfect documents. The most common kinds of formatting changes are changes to the font, spacing, or size of text. You can tailor your formatting to the mood and impact you are trying to achieve with a document. For example, creating an invitation to a 1920s theme fund raiser using basic fonts does not provide as much impact as creating the same invitation using 1920s style fonts, thus adding an element of visual excitement. Changing formats can lead to some surprising results; we'll guide you through the process.

When you need to format a document quickly, you can use WordPerfect's default styles. *Styles* are stored sets of format settings. When you apply a style to text, those formatting features are put into effect for that text. By editing or changing the style itself, you change the formatting applied to each section of text formatted with that style. In a sense, styles let you paint by numbers. You can apply style A to headings, style B to normal text, and style C to footnotes or endnotes. Later, if you decide you want to change the way these elements look, you can simply edit the style once, and the formatting applied to all headings, normal text, or footnotes will change. As you may imagine, styles can greatly increase your productivity.

To apply a style:

1. Select the text you want to format.
2. Select Styles from the Layout menu, click the Styles Button Bar button, or press ALT+F8.
3. Highlight the style you want to use in the Name list box.

   By default, this list box displays the styles saved in the current document or template. You can also display the *system styles*. System styles are those that WordPerfect uses to format different elements in your document, such as the header and footer, tables of contents, or footnotes.
4. Select Apply.

To display the system styles in the Style List dialog box:

1. Open the Style List dialog box by selecting Styles from the Layout menu, clicking the Styles Button Bar button, or pressing ALT+F8.
2. Select Setup from the Options pop-up list.
3. Select the System Styles check box and OK. The Name list box in the Style List dialog box now displays the system styles as well as the document and template styles.

To create a style:

1. Open the Style List dialog box by selecting <u>S</u>tyles from the L<u>a</u>yout menu, clicking the Styles Button Bar button, or pressing ALT+F8.

2. Select C<u>r</u>eate.

3. Enter a name for the style in the <u>S</u>tyle Name text box.

4. Enter a description of the style to precisely identify its purpose in the <u>D</u>escription text box.

5. Select the type of style you want to create from the T<u>y</u>pe pop-up list.

6. Select <u>C</u>ontents and enter the formatting codes you want the style to use. You can enter them using either key combinations or the menus. Enter the formatting codes the same way you would enter them to format text in the document.

7. Select OK to save the style, adding it to the <u>N</u>ame list box in the Style List dialog box. The style will be saved as part of the current document.

How can I change the font for existing text in my document?

You can change fonts in one of two ways. Either you can insert the code for the new font preceding the text, or you can select all of the text that you want to change, and insert paired codes that turn the font on and off. When you insert a font code in front of text, the rest of the document uses that font until you insert the next font code. If you select the text before inserting the font codes, only the selected text is affected, because two codes are inserted, one turning the font on and the other turning the font off. Both methods produce the same results. If you have used Windows for a while, you may find it easier to select the text before selecting the font. If you are just starting to use Windows with WordPerfect for Windows, you may find it easier to insert font codes without selecting the text. To change the font for existing text:

1. Either put your insertion point in front of the text you want to reformat or select the text you want to reformat.

2. Select <u>F</u>ont from the <u>L</u>ayout menu or press F9.

3. Select the font settings you want to use, including the font face itself, any attributes affecting its appearance, and its size or position, using the Font dialog box. Then select OK.

 **Tech Tip:** To make your document as effective as possible, limit the number of fonts that you use. As a rule of thumb, don't use more than three distinctive text formats on a single page. Text can be made to look distinctive by changing its size or other font attributes.

 ## How do I change the default font of the currently selected printer?

Each document uses the default font for the currently selected printer. To change the default font for all new documents using your currently selected printer:

1. Choose Se<u>l</u>ect Printer from the <u>F</u>ile menu.

2. Choose Initial <u>F</u>ont.

3. Use the <u>F</u>ont Face, Font <u>S</u>ize, and F<u>o</u>nt Style list boxes to select the new default font.

4. Select OK, then <u>C</u>lose to return to the document.

Unless you switch printers, all new documents will use the new font.

 ## Are there any keyboard shortcuts I can use to select text in a document?

WordPerfect offers several keyboard shortcuts for selecting text in a document.
To select:

- *One word*—put the insertion point at the beginning of the word, and press CTRL+SHIFT+RIGHT ARROW.

- *One character*—press SHIFT+RIGHT ARROW or SHIFT+LEFT ARROW.

- *Text from the insertion point to the end of the line*—press SHIFT+END.

- *Text from the insertion point to the beginning of the document*—press CTRL+SHIFT+HOME with the WPWin 6.0 keyboard; or SHIFT+HOME, HOME, UP ARROW with the WPDOS Compatible keyboard.

- *Text from the insertion point to the end of the document*—press CTRL+SHIFT+END with the WPWin 6.0 keyboard; or SHIFT+HOME, HOME, DOWN ARROW with the WPDOS Compatible keyboard.

I have both soft and hard page breaks in my document. They look the same on the screen. How can I tell which is which?

Soft and hard page breaks display as solid lines in both Page and Two Page view. However, in Draft view, soft page breaks display as single lines, and hard page breaks display as double lines. Both types of page breaks extend all the way across the document window, as shown here:

Soft Page Break

Hard Page Break

You can also tell the difference between soft and hard page breaks by selecting Reveal <u>C</u>odes from the <u>V</u>iew menu or pressing ALT+F3. Hard page breaks appear as HPg codes, and soft page breaks appear as SRt-SPg or HRt-SPg codes.

How can I get more than one bullet on a line in a bulleted list?

You probably created your bulleted list by selecting Bullets & <u>N</u>umbers from the <u>I</u>nsert menu. This feature, only inserts bullets or numbering at the beginning of the line, followed by an indent. If you need to insert a bullet later in the line, you will have to do so manually. You can do this by inserting a character from one of the WordPerfect character sets, or by copying a bullet from Windows' Character Map and pasting it into your document. You can add these bullet characters even if you do not want to create a bulleted list by selecting Bullets & <u>N</u>umbers from the <u>I</u>nsert menu.

To insert a bullet from one of the WP character sets:

1. Position the insertion point where you want to insert the bullet.

2. Select <u>C</u>haracter from the <u>I</u>nsert menu or press CTRL+W.

3. Select the WordPerfect character set you want to use from the Character <u>S</u>et pop-up list.

4. Highlight the character you want to insert in the Cha<u>r</u>acters box as shown in Figure 3-1.

5. Select <u>I</u>nsert then <u>C</u>lose, or Insert <u>a</u>nd Close to insert the bullet you selected and return to the document.

To use the Character Map accessory to copy and paste a bullet:

Character
Map

1. Select the Character Map program icon, shown here, in the Accessories program group of the Program Manager. (The Character Map application is installed in the Accessories program group by default. If you can't find it

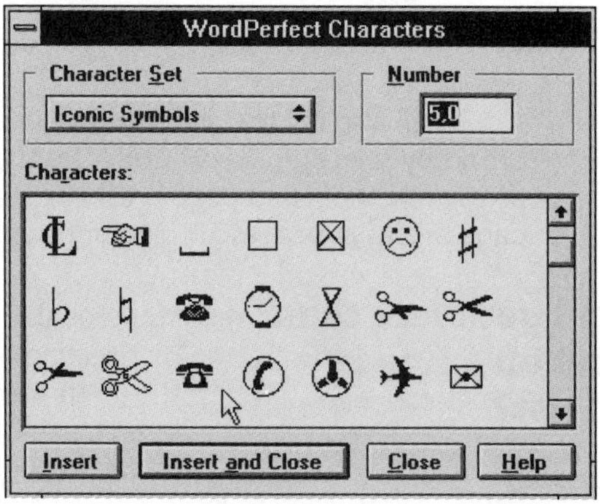

FIGURE 3-1   The WordPerfect Characters dialog box

there, check the other program groups. If you can't find the icon at all, select Run from the File menu, then Browse. Select the CHARMAP.EXE file in your \WINDOWS directory and OK to run the application.)

2. Highlight the bullet you want in the grid. If you want to see the bullets offered by a different font, select that font in the Font drop-down list box.

3. Choose Select to transfer the bullet to the Characters to Copy text box.

4. Select Copy, then Close.

5. Return to your Word Perfect document and put your insertion point where you want to insert the bullet.

6. Select Paste from the Edit menu.

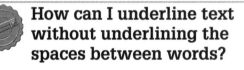

How can I underline text without underlining the spaces between words?

You can allow WordPerfect to underline spaces between words when it underlines words, or tell it not to. The default is to underline these spaces, but you can turn this feature off. To turn it off:

1. Select Font from the Layout menu.

2. Clear the Spaces check box in the Underline Options area of the dialog box and select OK.

Tech Tip: Underlining spaces as well as words can be useful in creating a signature line or other type of line. Simply tell WordPerfect to underline a series of spaces, and your line appears.

I want to space the characters in my document title evenly between the left and the right margins. How do I do this?

Fortunately, WordPerfect offers a feature that can space the characters automatically. To do so:

1. Select the text you want to space between the margins.

2. Select Justification from the Layout menu.

3. Select All.

Selecting All spaces the characters evenly between the left and right margins, as shown in Figure 3-2. You would not want to select Full from the Justification submenu for two reasons. First, full justification extends lines between the left and right margins by adding spaces between the words instead of characters. Second, full justification does not affect the last line in a paragraph that contains the hard return. Lines containing the hard return use left justification. Since titles are usually one line, full justification would not have an effect on the spacing in your title.

Tech Terror: Don't use All spacing for normal text. If you do, the last line of every paragraph, which is usually a little shorter than the width of the paragraph, will be evenly spaced between the two margins. This looks very odd and makes normal text difficult to read.

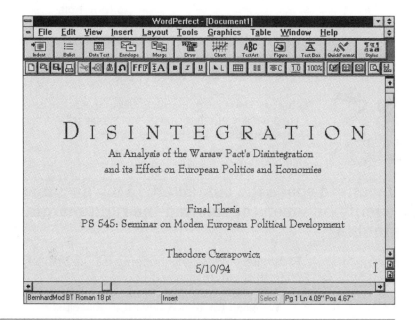

FIGURE 3-2   Spacing characters evenly between the margins

Tech Tip: You can set an upper limit to the amount of space that <u>F</u>ull or <u>A</u>ll justification can enter between words. To do so, select <u>T</u>ypesetting from the <u>L</u>ayout menu, then <u>W</u>ord/Letterspacing. Change the entries in the <u>C</u>ompressed To and <u>E</u>xpanded To text boxes to limit how much WordPerfect can expand or compress words to align them with the margins. Select OK when you are done.

Can I insert special characters into my document?

Yes, there are two ways to insert special characters into your document. You can choose special characters from the more than 1,500 characters and special symbols contained in the WordPerfect character sets, or you can insert special characters from any of the fonts available on your system. You can use special characters as icons or bullets in your document. You can also call up special mathematical or linguistic characters that you do not have access to with the keyboard. For example, Figure 3-3 shows how special characters in a flyer add visual interest and divide areas.

To insert characters from the WordPerfect character sets:

1. Select <u>C</u>haracter from the <u>I</u>nsert menu or press CTRL+W.

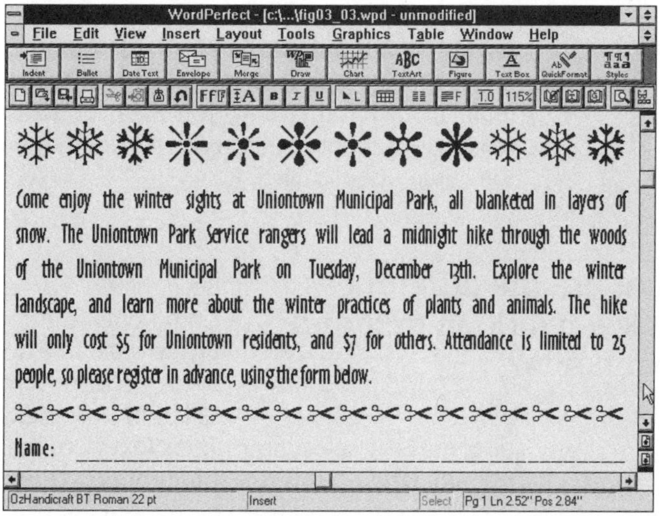

![WordPerfect screenshot showing a winter flyer with snowflake characters across the top, body text inviting people to enjoy winter sights at Uniontown Municipal Park, and a row of scissor characters above a Name field.]

FIGURE 3-3   Using special characters in your document

2. Select the character set containing the appropriate character from the Character Set pop-up list.

3. Highlight the character you want to use from that character set in the Character box.

4. Select Insert and Close to insert the one character and return to your document. You can also select Insert, then repeat steps 2 and 3 to select and insert several characters before selecting Close to return to the document.

This character can now be formatted for the desired font size, just like any other character.

You can also use the Windows' Character Map application to copy special characters, such as mathematical or linguistic symbols, bullets, or icons, to the Clipboard and then paste this character into your WordPerfect document. Using the Character Map is described under the question "How can I get more than one bullet on a line in a bulleted list?" earlier in this chapter.

I inserted a new document into my current document. Why didn't the inserted document keep its own Initial Codes Style?

When you insert a document into an active document, the inserted document uses the Initial Codes Style of the active document instead of using its own Initial Codes Style. There is no way to prevent this. If you want the inserted document to retain its own formatting, you will need to apply formatting manually, or apply other styles that do not base themselves on the Initial Codes Style.

What are the differences between hidden text and Comments?

Both the hidden text format and the Comments feature let you insert unseen text in a document. However, these features were designed for different purposes. Hidden text can be displayed (by selecting Hidden Text from the View menu) and printed; when displayed, it may affect page numbering. It is best used for concealing text you might later want to add to your document, because adding it is as simple as removing the format.

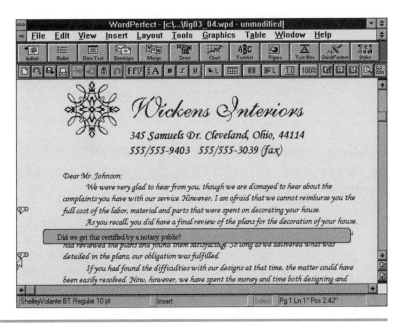

FIGURE 3-4   Displaying comments in a document

Comments, on the other hand, cannot be treated like regular document text. They cannot be printed and do not affect your page numbering. Comments are actually a separate unit of text that is not part of your actual document but can be displayed within your document. You can think of Comments as sticky-notes for printed documents. However, unlike sticky-notes, it is fairly easy to convert Comments into document text. Use Comments for making notations in a document you are sharing with other users. In Figure 3-4, you can see that comments look like small icons in the margin until you choose to display them. When you display them, they look like the balloons you see in comics that display dialog.

How can I insert hard returns and tabs in a style I am creating?

When you create a style, you use the Styles Editor. You can access the Styles Editor by selecting <u>S</u>tyles from the <u>L</u>ayout menu, then selecting C<u>r</u>eate, or edit a style by highlighting a style in the <u>N</u>ame list box and selecting <u>E</u>dit. In the <u>C</u>ontents box, you will enter the complete contents of the style, which can include tabs or hard returns. To insert a tab code at the insertion point's position in the <u>C</u>ontents box, press CTRL+TAB. To insert a hard return, press SHIFT+ENTER.

I added page numbers to my document. I don't see them on the screen, though they do appear when I print the document. What is wrong?

Most likely, you are displaying your document in Draft view instead of Page view. Page numbers will not appear on the screen in Draft view, even though they have been inserted. To switch to Page view, select <u>P</u>age from the <u>V</u>iew menu. Figure 3-5 shows a page using page numbers.

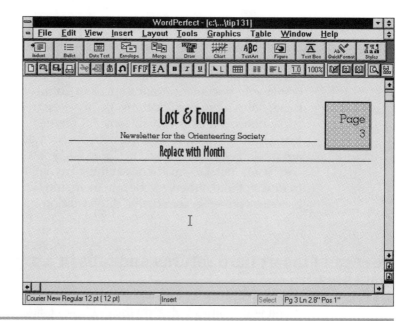

FIGURE 3-5   Using page numbers in your document creatively

What does the QuickFormat feature do?

The QuickFormat feature copies attributes of selected text, such as boldfacing or italics, and quickly applies these attributes to other text. For example, you may want to underline several words in a paragraph. You can first underline one word, then select that word and click the QuickFormat button in the Button Bar, shown below, or choose QuickFormat from the Layout menu. Your mouse pointer becomes a paint roller. You can now "paint" the underlining onto other words by dragging the mouse over them. To turn off the quick formatting, click the QuickFormat button or select QuickFormat from the Layout menu again.

QuickFormat can copy more than just font attributes. If you select an entire paragraph before turning the QuickFormat feature on, you can also copy the paragraph formatting, such as tab settings or line spacing. If you select no text before turning the QuickFormat feature on, WordPerfect displays the following dialog box, to let you select which types of formatting you want to copy.

I want to use a different font for envelopes than for the document. Can I do this?

Yes, you can use different fonts for envelopes created within a document than for the document itself. You can choose different font faces, sizes, and attributes such as bold and italics. You can even use different fonts for the return and mailing addresses. To change these fonts for your envelopes:

1. Select Envelope from the Layout menu.

2. Select the Font button to set the font for return addresses or the Font button to set the font for mailing addresses.

3. Select the font, size, and appearance for these addresses from the Font dialog box that appears.

4. Select OK then Close to return to the document with your new font settings for the envelopes.

What is the difference between absolute and relative tabs?

WordPerfect supports two types of tabs: absolute and relative. The difference between absolute and relative tabs comes from the way WordPerfect measures where they start. Absolute tabs are measured from the left edge of the paper. Relative tabs are measured from the left margin. Since relative tabs are measured from the margin, changing the margin changes where the tab stop falls on the page. Absolute tabs, on the other hand, always fall at the same position on the page, as shown in Figure 3-6.

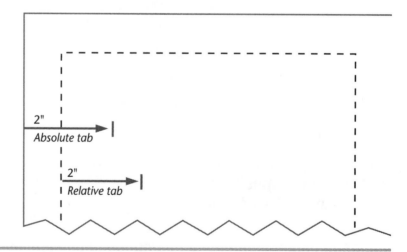

FIGURE 3-6   Absolute and relative tabs are measured from different locations

Can I create a style using existing text that I have already formatted?

Yes, you can use existing text to create a style. To do so:

1. Position the insertion point within the text you have formatted.

2. Select Styles from the Layout menu.

3. Select QuickCreate, opening the Styles QuickCreate dialog box.

4. Enter the name for your style in the Style Name text box.

5. Enter a description of your style in the Description text box.

6. Select either the Paragraph or Character radio button in the Style Type area for the type of style you are creating.

   Paragraph styles affect the entire paragraph the style is applied to, while character styles only affect selected text.

7. Select OK, then Close to return to your document. You can now apply this new style the same way you would apply any other styles.

Every time I change my printer, I have to reset the default font. Is there a way to make WordPerfect keep the same default font, regardless of which printer I use?

Yes, you can set a default font that does not depend on the currently selected printer by using the Initial Codes Style. To do so:

1. Select Document from the Layout menu.

2. Select Initial Codes Style.

3. Select Font from the Layout menu with your insertion point in the Contents box.

4. Select the font the way you normally do, by selecting a typeface, a font size, and font attributes or positions.

5. Select OK to return to the Initial Codes Style dialog box.

6. Select the Use as Default check box and OK to return to your document.

You need to select the Use as Default check box before closing the dialog box to ensure that all new documents use the new initial font, and not just the current one. When you do this, the new initial font is saved in the template used to create new documents.

You can also edit the Initial Codes Style for the template directly. Most of the time, changing the default font with the initial codes is easier. However, you may want to know the steps involved since they are the steps you perform to alter the settings stored in the default template. To do so:

1. Select Template from the File menu or press CTRL+T.

2. Select Standard from the Document Template to Use list box.

3. Select Edit Template from the Options pop-up menu.

4. Select the Initial Style button from the Template Feature Bar, opening the Styles Editor dialog box.

5. Select Font from the Layout menu or press F9, and select the desired font face, size, and attributes.

6. Select OK twice.

7. Select the Exit Template button from the Template Feature Bar, and Yes when prompted about saving changes to STANDARD.WPT.

 I accidentally typed a whole paragraph in uppercase and don't want to retype it. Is there an easy way to change how text is capitalized?

Yes, you can easily change the case of your text. You can change selected text to all lowercase, all uppercase, or initial capitalization, in which the first letter in every word is capitalized. To change the case of a word or selected text:

1. Select the text.

2. Select Convert Case from the Edit menu.

3. Select the desired case: Lowercase, Uppercase, or Initial
Capitals.

Why are my tab setting codes deleted when I insert a justification code in front of them?

If you insert a center or full justification code before a tab setting code in your document, the tab setting code may be deleted. There is no way to prevent this from happening. You need to insert the justification code in a different place, or just reenter the tab settings after changing the justification.

I am inserting bullets in my document, but when I press ENTER, another bullet doesn't automatically appear. How come?

The next bullet does not automatically appear because the New Bullet or Number on ENTER check box was not selected in the Bullets & Numbers dialog box. To have WordPerfect automatically insert a bullet into your document when you press ENTER:

1. Select Bullets & Numbers from the Insert menu.

2. Select the New Bullet or Number on ENTER check box and select OK.

I inserted bullets into my document, using the Bullets & Numbers option from the Insert menu. Is there an easy way to insert another bullet or number?

Yes. WordPerfect offers an easy shortcut to inserting the last bullet or number again. You can do this by pressing CTRL+SHIFT+B, wherever you want that bullet inserted. Figure 3-7 shows a document using the Bullets & Numbers feature to create a list.

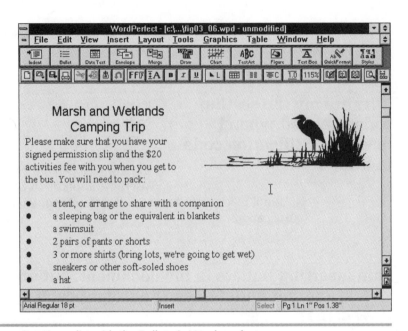

FIGURE 3-7 Creating a list with the Bullets & Numbers feature

Is there some easy way to print a sample of all of the available fonts?

Yes, there's an easy way to print a sample of each of the fonts available to WordPerfect on your system. WordPerfect comes with a macro named ALLFONTS.WCM, which creates a list of all the fonts available to WordPerfect, along with sample text for each font.

To use this macro:

1. Open a new document by selecting New from the File menu.

2. Select Macro from the Tools menu, then Play, or press ALT+F10.

3. Enter **ALLFONTS.WCM** in the Name text box, then select Play.

The ALLFONTS.WCM macro may take several minutes to run depending on the number of fonts installed and your computer's speed. Once the list of available fonts is created in the document you can save or print the document, just like any other document you create.

How can I create reversed text (white text on a black background) in my documents?

To create reversed text, you must use a graphics text box. To create the reversed text box:

1. Put your insertion point where you want the reversed text to appear.

2. Select Text from the Graphics menu.

3. Select Border/Fill from the Graphics Box Feature Bar.

4. Select 100% Fill from the Fill Style drop-down list, then select OK.

5. Select Font from the Layout menu or press F9.

6. Select Color, then choose a light color from the color palette and select OK.

7. Type the text you want reversed.

8. Select Close from the Graphics Box Feature Bar or click anywhere in the document outside the graphics box to return to the document.

To print your reversed text, you must be using a printer that has graphics capability. Reversed text is not sent to the printer as text, but as a graphic image.

Also, reversed text can be difficult to read unless you take into account a few issues. Use the lightest possible color for the font, usually white, to get the highest level of contrast. Use a sans serif font with heavy lines. Otherwise, the thin lines that create serifs or the letters will simply disappear into the background, being too thin to stand out well. Use larger fonts to make the text easier to read. Since reversed text is harder to read than normal text, use it only for headings or other short sections of text. The headings in Figure 3-8 use reversed text with a large, sans serif font to make them easier to read.

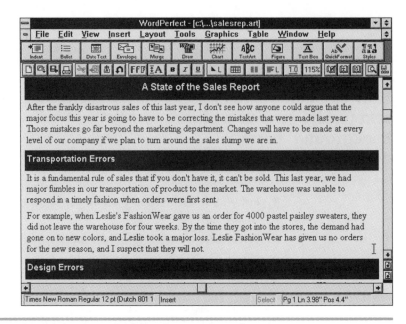

A State of the Sales Report

After the frankly disastrous sales of this last year, I don't see how anyone could argue that the major focus this year is going to have to be correcting the mistakes that were made last year. Those mistakes go far beyond the marketing department. Changes will have to be made at every level of our company if we plan to turn around the sales slump we are in.

Transportation Errors

It is a fundamental rule of sales that if you don't have it, it can't be sold. This last year, we had major fumbles in our transportation of product to the market. The warehouse was unable to respond in a timely fashion when orders were first sent.

For example, when Leslie's FashionWear gave us an order for 4000 pastel paisley sweaters, they did not leave the warehouse for four weeks. By the time they got into the stores, the demand had gone on to new colors, and Leslie took a major loss. Leslie FashionWear has given us no orders for the new season, and I suspect that they will not.

Design Errors

FIGURE 3-8   Reversed text emphasizing short sections of text

I edited the Initial Codes Style in one document. Now I want to use that Initial Codes Style in all of my documents. How can I do this?

To use the Initial Codes Style of one document for all future documents, you need to copy it to the default template used to create all future documents. You can place tabs, fonts, margins, justification, and column settings in the Initial Codes Style.

1. Select Document from the Layout menu.

2. Select Initial Codes Style, opening the Styles Editor dialog box.

3. Use the menus in the Styles Editor dialog box with the insertion point in the Contents box to create the style you want to use for all future documents.

4. Select the Use as Default check box, and OK.

All future documents will use the Initial Codes Style that you created to set the default formatting.

You can edit the Initial Codes Style at any time from anywhere in the document by choosing <u>D</u>ocument from the <u>L</u>ayout menu, then Initial Codes <u>S</u>tyle. However, unless you select the <u>U</u>se as Default check box, only the current document's default formatting is selected.

Does WordPerfect offer an easy way to transpose two characters?

Yes, you can switch two characters using the WordPerfect macro named TRANSPOSE.WCM, which will transpose, or reverse, the two characters to the left of the insertion point. To use this macro:

1. Put your insertion point to the right of the two characters you want to transpose.

2. Select <u>M</u>acro from the <u>T</u>ools menu, then <u>P</u>lay, or press ALT+F10.

3. Enter **TRANSPOSE.WCM** in the <u>N</u>ame text box, and select <u>P</u>lay.

Times New Roman is my default font. However, when I set the font size to Extra Large, I want to change to the Arial font as well as increase the font size. Is this possible?

Yes, you can switch fonts when you apply a different relative font size. WordPerfect's Font Map feature lets you do this. To change the setting:

1. Select <u>F</u>ont from the <u>L</u>ayout menu or press F9.

2. Select the Font <u>M</u>ap button.

3. Select the <u>A</u>utomatic Font Change radio button in the Item to Map area of the dialog box.

4. Select the item from the A<u>u</u>tomatic Font Change list box that you want to change. For example, you can select Extra Large Print.

5. Select your default font from the Font drop-down list. This is the font you want to change when the Extra Large Font size is applied to it.

6. Select the font you want to use—Arial, for example—from the Face drop-down list. This is the font you want to use when you apply the Extra Large font size to the font selected in the Font drop-down list.

7. Select OK twice to save this new setting and return to the document.

What you have done is specified that when you apply the Extra Large font size to Times Roman text, the text will be formatted with the Arial font, in the larger size. If you ever want to return to using WordPerfect's automatic font mapping, you can open this dialog box again, and select the Automatic Selection check box before selecting OK.

I wanted to change the name of my bullets and numbers style, but the option is unavailable. How come?

You cannot change the name of the original bullets and numbers styles, though you can edit them. To edit a bullet and numbers style:

1. Select Bullets & Numbers from the Insert menu.

2. Select Edit to open the Styles Editor dialog box.

3. Edit the description, contents, and type of style. However, the Style Name text box is grayed out, making it unavailable.

4. Select OK twice to return to the document.

Why do my subdocuments print differently when I print them alone, or as part of the expanded master document?

Subdocuments use the formatting for the current printer. Therefore, if you print subdocuments as part of a master document that uses a different printer, they will be re-formatted to use that printer's default formats.

Why don't my Windows fonts appear in the Font dialog box?

If your Windows fonts do not appear in the Font dialog box, you probably have a WordPerfect printer driver selected, and must choose a Windows printer driver. You cannot use the TrueType or Adobe Type Manager fonts that come with Windows when you use the WordPerfect driver. To select a Windows printer driver:

Tech Note:
WordPerfect drivers have a WordPerfect logo to the left of them. Windows drivers have a Windows emblem to the left of them.

1. Choose Select Printer from the File menu.
2. Highlight a Windows printer in the Printers list box.
3. Choose Select and Close.

Your Windows fonts will now appear in the Font dialog box or when you select the Font Face button in the Power Bar.

All of a sudden, the text on my screen got smaller, even though the zoom didn't seem to change. I can't get the text to look the regular size anymore. What's wrong?

If the display pitch of a font changes on screen, causing the text to appear larger or smaller, you need to press CTRL+F3 to redraw the screen. The display pitch changes most often when a document uses a bold or table definition code. One way to work around this problem is to use a font that contains the bold attribute such as Courier Bold, and to use as few tables as possible.

Is there some way to create the mean symbol in WordPerfect for Windows?

Yes, WordPerfect does provide a way to create a mean symbol, which is a bar over a letter. To do so:

1. Select Equation from the Graphics menu.

2. Type **X** or another letter you want to use, a space, and **BAR**.

3. Select Close from the File menu.

The mean symbol will be inserted into your document in a graphics box. A mean symbol is a bar over a letter, as shown here:

Tech Tip: If you want to incorporate the mean symbol into a paragraph, add an inline equation style graphics box. You add this graphics, box style by selecting Custom Box from the Graphics menu, selecting Inline Equation from the Style Name list box, and selecting OK. Then start WordPerfect's Equation Editor by selecting Content from the Graphics Box Feature Bar and selecting Edit. At this point, you can enter the mark that you want to appear. When you leave the Equation Editor, the graphics box is treated as a character in the current paragraph.

When I insert a date time or code, I want the month to be all uppercase. How can I do this?

To change date codes and date text to uppercase, you need to edit the WP.LRS file. To do so:

1. Retrieve the WP.LRS file into WordPerfect.

2. Search for the United States section, which has a heading of "US English - United States" and appears on page 58.

3. Select the month in the listing and change it to uppercase by selecting Convert Case from the Edit menu, then Uppercase.

4. Save the WP.LRS file, replacing the old version.

Is there some way to combine the characters from my WordPerfect character sets to create one character?

Yes, you can combine characters in the WordPerfect character sets, creating an overstrike character in which one character appears directly on top of another. To do so:

1. Put the insertion where you want to insert the overstrike character.
2. Select Typesetting from the Layout menu, then Overstrike.
3. Type the characters that you want printed on top of each other without spaces in the Characters text box.

    It doesn't matter in which order you type the characters. If you want to use WordPerfect characters, press CTRL+W and insert them as normal using the WordPerfect Characters dialog box.

4. To change font size or attributes for the characters you are going to overstrike, click the button beside the Characters text box, and select the attribute you want to apply.
5. Choose OK to insert the overstrike character and return to the document.

Tech Tip: You can use the Overstrike option to create characters that do not exist as part of your font sets. For example, you can use Overstrike to create a yen symbol, like the one shown here, even if you do not have a yen symbol in any of your fonts.

¥

Layout

Layout features control where text appears in your document and include options such as headers and footers, tab settings, columns, and more. Your layout choices are very important because they help determine how effective your document will be as a communication medium. Sloppy layouts can turn readers off to your text and make your document more difficult to read. An imaginative and effective layout, however, actually increases your document's effectiveness by making it more interesting to look at and easier to read. Once you identify layouts that are effective for each type of document you create, you will want to save them for future projects as described in the Frustration Box that follows.

Normally, it is best to create and edit your entire document before concerning yourself with layout. Making sure that the text of the entire document is finished before beginning the layout process will prevent you from having to design a document twice.

However, if you are creating a standard document, such as a letter or frequently used report, you might want to use a predefined WordPerfect template or create a standard layout yourself before creating the document, since you already know what the final layout should look like. See Chapter 11, "Macros and Templates," to learn about the WordPerfect templates that you can use.

Can I insert the path and filename of my document into the header or footer?

You can insert the path and filename of a document into the header or footer to serve as a reminder of the document's origin. This is especially useful when exchanging drafts of a document with other writers or reviewers as it helps insure that they have the correct version.

To insert the path and filename into the header or footer:

1. Create the header or footer.

2. Select Other from the Insert menu in the header or footer.

3. Select Filename or Path and Filename.

The path and filename will not appear until the document is saved the first time.

I often work on long documents that are edited frequently. Can I prevent the first or last line of a paragraph from appearing at the top or bottom of a page by itself?

Yes, you can prevent these single lines from appearing by themselves. Individual lines at the top or bottom of pages, called *widows* and *orphans*, can make it harder for readers to follow the meaning of your document, because they have to turn the page in the middle of a thought. This makes your documents appear unprofessional. You can avoid having widows or orphans by using Widow/Orphan control. To activate this feature:

1. Select Page from the Layout menu.

2. Select Keep Text Together.

3. In the Widow/Orphan area of the dialog box, select the Prevent the first and last lines of paragraphs from being separated across pages check box.

4. Select OK to return to your document with this feature in effect.

Now, when a soft page break causes a single line of a paragraph to appear by itself at the top or bottom of a page, WordPerfect adjusts the soft page break so that the line appearing by itself is joined by one or two more lines from that paragraph.

I want to have several different headers and footers in my document. How many different headers and footers can I have and how do I change them?

You can have as many different headers or footers as you want in a document. However, if you insert more than one header or footer on one page, only the first one will appear on your printed page.

To change your header or footer on a certain page, go to that page and create a new header or footer. To do this, select Header/Footer from the Layout menu, select the radio button for the new header or footer you want to create, then select Create.

Is there a shortcut for editing tab settings?

You can edit tab settings using the Ruler Bar as a shortcut. To do so:

1. Select <u>R</u>uler Bar from the <u>V</u>iew menu or press ALT+SHIFT+F3 to display the ruler, shown here:

2. To delete a tab setting, drag it down off the Ruler Bar.

3. To move a tab setting, drag it to a new position.

4. To set a new tab, click the Ruler Bar where you want it. This will, by default, create a left-aligned tab. To change the alignment of the tab, right-click the triangle tab setting and select the alignment you want from the Quick Menu.

When you move or add a tab, a vertical dotted line is displayed indicating the tab's position. This helps you see the exact measurement on the Ruler Bar when lining up text further down the page.

Tech Note: When you modify tabs with your Ruler Bar, be aware of where your insertion point is positioned. A Tab Set code is inserted at this position and these tabs will be in effect from that point on. To turn on Reveal Codes, press ALT+F3.

How can I change the character used to line up text when using a decimal tab?

To change the decimal/align character:

1. Place the insertion point where you want to change the decimal/align character.

2. Choose <u>L</u>ine from <u>L</u>ayout menu.

3. Choose <u>T</u>ab Set.

4. Enter a new character in the Cha<u>r</u>acter text box in the Align Character area and choose OK.

Can I turn tabular columns into a table?

You can convert columns created with tabs into tables. To do so:

1. Make sure you have the same number of tabs between each column. Press ALT+F3 to turn on Reveal Codes to verify this.

2. Select all of the text that you want to convert into a table.

3. Select Create from the Table menu.

4. Select the Tabular Column radio button in the Convert Table dialog box and choose OK.

Tech Tip: See Chapter 7, "Tables," for further information on working with tables.

You can also convert tabular columns to a table by clicking the Power Bar's Table Quick Create button, then selecting Tabular Columns.

Tech Tip: When turning tabular columns into a table, make sure that you have the same number of tabs between the columns in each row. If you don't, the results will not be correct.

Tech Note: When you create a table from tabular columns, you may need to adjust the column widths by selecting Format from the Table menu and choosing the Column radio button.

Is there a shortcut for creating columns?

WordPerfect offers a shortcut for formatting your document with columns.

1. Display the Power Bar, if it is not already displayed, by selecting Power Bar from the View menu.

2. Click the Columns Define button in the Power Bar, shown in the margin.

3. Select 2, 3, 4, or 5 Columns from the menu to format your document with that many columns. By default, the columns will be formatted as newspaper-style columns.

You can open the Columns dialog box by selecting Define from this menu, or by selecting Columns from the Layout menu, then Define. In the Columns dialog box, you can specify the type and number of columns to use, the spacing between columns, and the column widths. Select OK to close the Define dialog box and format your document with the column settings you specify.

Why can't I access the Header/Footer command in the Layout menu?

You are probably in Page view and have put your insertion point at the very top or very bottom of the page. When your insertion point is already in the header/footer area in Page view, WordPerfect "grays out" or dims the Header/Footer command in the Layout menu, making it unavailable. Look at the application window's title bar, which usually displays "WordPerfect" and the name of your document. If you are in the header/footer area of your document, the title will also display "Header A/B" or "Footer A/B." When your insertion point is in the header/footer area, you can simply type or format text as you normally do to edit the header or footer.

I want to restart numbering with a different number at a certain point in my outline. How do I do this?

To restart numbering in an outline:

1. Position the insertion point where you want to start the renumbering.

2. Choose Outline from the Tools menu.

3. Select Set Number from the Options pop-up list in the Outline Feature Bar.

4. In the Paragraph Number text box, type the number you want to begin renumbering with, then choose OK.

How can I insert tabs and back tabs in an outline?

Normally, pressing TAB in an outline heading changes the heading to the next level, while pressing SHIFT+TAB changes the heading to the previous level. To actually move text to a tab stop in an outline, you must either use the Indent feature or insert a hard tab. To use the Indent feature, select Paragraph from the Layout menu, then Indent or press F7. To insert a hard left tab, press CTRL+TAB. To insert a hard back tab, press CTRL+SHIFT+TAB.

Tech Tip: You only need to insert hard tabs or indents in an outline when you want the code to appear immediately after the outline number. If you want to use a tab or indent later in the outline heading, the TAB key will work normally.

I want to call attention to the long quotes in my document by indenting them. Is there a quick way to do this?

You can quickly indent text using the Indent button on the Button Bar. Before typing the quote, click the Indent button, which indents the current paragraph. Pressing ENTER, which inserts a hard return at the end of the paragraph, will turn off the indentation. Your next paragraph will be normally aligned. You can press F7 instead of selecting the Indent button.

To indent a quote that you have already typed in, put your insertion point at the very beginning of the quote and click the Indent button, or press F7. Only the current paragraph is indented.

Tech Tip: Some style books require that long quotes be indented from both the left and the right margin. To do this, put your insertion point at the beginning of the paragraph that contains or will contain the quote, and select P̲aragraph from the L̲ayout menu, then D̲ouble Indent. You can also position your insertion point, then press CTRL+SHIFT+F7.

What is the difference between a column break and a page break, and how do I insert them?

Tech Tip: Notice that if your insertion point is not in a column and you press CTRL+ENTER, you will insert a page break.

Column breaks end one column and move the insertion point to the beginning of the next column. If you insert a column break in the last column on a page, the insertion point moves to the top of the next column, which is the first column on the next page. Hard page breaks start a new page in the document. If your document is formatted to have three columns, and you insert a hard page break in the second column, the third column is left blank and the insertion point moves to the beginning of the first column on the next page.

To insert a column break, press CTRL+ENTER with the insertion point in a column. To insert a hard page break with the insertion point in a column, select P̲age Break from the I̲nsert menu, or press CTRL+SHIFT+ENTER.

I changed the margins in my document, but when I view my document, I see that the headers and footers do not use the new margins. Why?

Both the document and its headers and footers use the default margins set by the document's initial codes. When you change the margin settings for the document, however, the margin settings for headers and footers do not automatically change to match. Instead, the headers and footers still use the default margin codes. If you want to use the same margins for the document and the headers and footers, you can change the margin settings either in the document's initial settings or in the header or footer itself.

To change the margin settings for headers and footers separately:

1. Select Header/Footer from the Layout menu.

2. Select the radio button for the header or footer for which you want new margin settings.

3. Choose Edit.

4. Select Margins from the Layout menu or press CTRL+F8.

5. Enter the margin settings you want to use, then select OK.

To modify the margins in the document's initial codes, which affect both the document and the headers and footers:

1. Select Document from the Layout menu.

2. Select Initial Codes Style.

3. Select Margins from the Layout menu.

4. Enter the margin settings you want to use, then select OK twice to return to the document.

Can I center text vertically on my labels?

You can use vertical centering for the text on your labels. To do so:

1. Put your insertion point on the physical page where you want to start centering text on labels.

2. Select Page from the Layout menu.

3. Select <u>C</u>enter.

4. Select either the Current <u>P</u>age or Current and <u>S</u>ubsequent Pages radio button, then choose OK.

- *Current Page* centers the text on the current label only.

- *Current and Subsequent Pages* centers the text on the current label, and all later labels in the document.

I want to print labels but can't fit all my information on one label. Is there any way to get more information onto each label?

Yes, you can get more information onto each label by using a smaller font. A smaller font lets you fit more lines of text on each label and more characters on each line. Change the font for the document by choosing <u>F</u>ont from the <u>L</u>ayout menu. Select Initial Font, then select a new font size from the Font <u>S</u>ize list box. Select OK twice to return to the document.

Tech Tip: Some fonts are naturally a little smaller than others. For example, most fonts with "Times" in their name are narrower than other fonts of the same height. Thus, you can fit more text into the same amount of space. Times fonts are based on a font designed for *The New York Times* newspaper, which was meant to fit the most text into the smallest possible space so the newspaper could print more news on the same number of pages.

Where are the paper definitions stored?

WordPerfect paper definitions can be stored in two locations:

- When using a Windows printer driver, the paper definitions are stored in the user's .BIF file.

- When using a WordPerfect printer driver, the paper definitions are kept in the .PRS file.

What is the difference between logical and physical pages?

A physical page is an entire piece of paper that is specified with the height and width settings of the paper size definition. In other words, it is the page that you are going to put through your printer. Logical pages are smaller areas of the page that make up a physical page. Logical pages are not separate sheets of paper, but a way you can divide up one sheet of paper so that WordPerfect treats different parts of it as separate pages. You can specify logical pages using the Subdivide Page or Labels command. For example, Figure 4-1 shows a document with labels created by selecting La_bels from the _Layout menu. Each label is one logical page, and all the labels together make up a physical page. You can select _Page from the _Layout menu, then Subdi_vide, to create two logical pages on each 8 1/2 x 11-inch page to create a booklet, as shown in Figure 4-2.

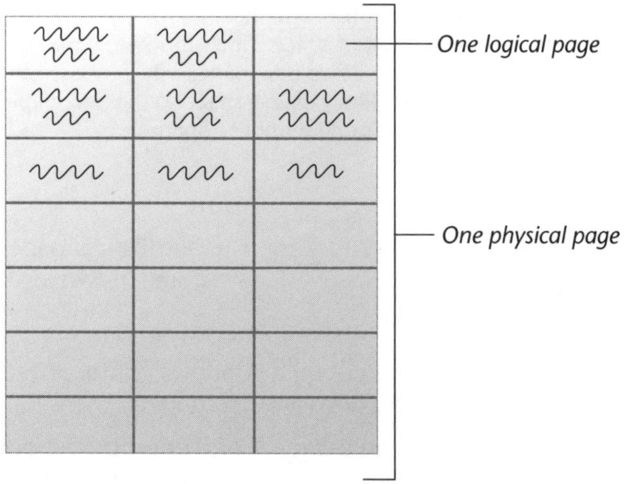

One logical page

One physical page

FIGURE 4-1 Many logical pages can appear on a single physical page

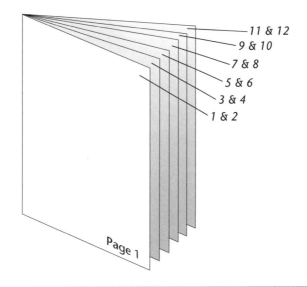

FIGURE 4-2   You can use logical pages to create a booklet

I am using the Block Protect feature to keep some text together. I have several consecutive protected blocks, but WordPerfect is treating them like one large protected block of text. How do I separate them?

When you use the Block Protect feature on consecutive blocks of text, those blocks need to be separated by at least one hard or soft return. Otherwise, the individual blocks of text are treated as one large block of text.

What is the difference between newspaper columns and balanced newspaper columns?

Newspaper columns are continuously running columns of text. When a page or column break is inserted in a newspaper column, the text flows to the top of the next column. Therefore, the last column may be shorter than the preceding ones. Balanced newspaper columns are also continuously running columns of text. However, when a page or

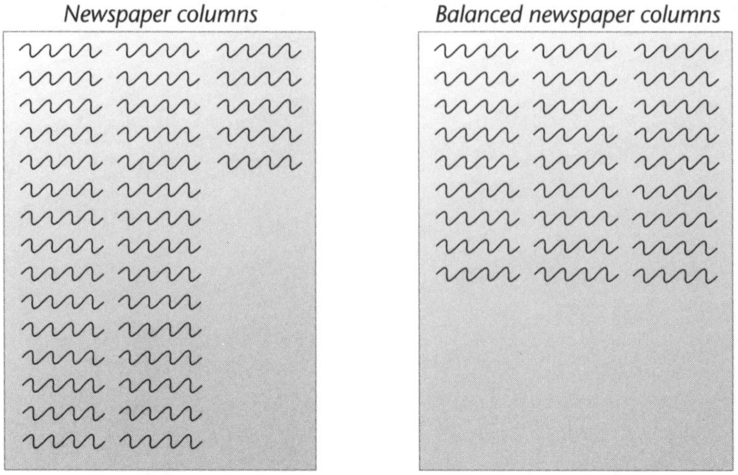

Newspaper columns

Balanced newspaper columns

FIGURE 4-3   Newspaper and balanced newspaper columns

column break is inserted in a balanced newspaper column, all of
the columns are adjusted so they are equal in length. Figure 4-3
shows an example of the difference between newspaper and
balanced newspaper columns.

**Is there a way to keep
words together so they are
not split when they
appear at the end of a line?**

You can keep words or numbers from
being separated by soft returns or
page breaks by using a hard, or *fixed*,
space instead of a regular space
between them. Insert a hard space by
pressing CTRL+SPACEBAR.

**My document will be printed double-sided and then
bound. Is there an easy way to adjust the margins to
allow for the space required to bind the document?**

Your problem is that since you are printing double-sided, the
space for binding needs to be added to the left side of
odd-numbered pages, and to the right side of even-numbered

pages. WordPerfect offers the Binding Options feature that adds the necessary space to the correct side of the pages.

Binding Options sets whether the document is printed on one or both sides of the document, which side of the page is to be bound, and the amount of space you wish to shift the text to allow for the binding. Note that if you specify a binding width amount after creating your document, the text needs to be reformatted for the new margins. It is best to specify binding options before you begin creating the document. Then, you can see how the document will look as you continue to add information to it.

To set the Binding Options:

1. Select Page from the Layout menu.

2. Select Binding, which opens the Binding Options dialog box.

3. Select the radio button in the Binding Width area of the dialog box for the side of the page that will be bound.

4. Enter the space needed for binding in the Amount text box.

5. If you are printing on both sides of the page, select an option from the Duplexing pop-up list. These options are:

   - *From Short Side* flips the pages top to bottom, so that the top of one page begins on the same edge of the paper as the end of the page on the other side. This option is used when the document is going to be bound at the top or bottom.

   - *From Long Side* flips the pages left to right, so that the top of one page begins on the same edge of the paper as the top of the page on the other side. This option is used when the document is going to be bound on the left or right.

6. Select OK to return to the document.

Can I create a graphic that appears "behind" the text in my document?

Yes, you can accomplish this using the Watermark feature. A watermark appears "behind" the normal document area. A watermark can display text or graphics with reduced shading so you can easily read the text in the regular document area. To create a watermark:

1. Select Watermark from the Layout menu.
2. Select the Watermark A radio button and Create.
3. Create your watermark, which can include both text and graphics.

   ■ Select Figure in the Watermark Feature Bar to select a graphic to insert.

   ■ Select File in the Watermark Feature Bar to select a file to insert.

   ■ Enter and format any text you want to insert into your watermark.

4. Select Close to close the Watermark Feature Bar and return to the document.

The watermark appears in the document area. When you type, the text appears on top of the watermark.

Is there some way to easily insert page numbers in the format "Page *X* of *Y*," where *X* is the current page and *Y* is the total number of pages for the document?

WordPerfect can easily create such a page numbering scheme, using the PAGEXOFY.WCM macro. This macro places a page number, using the format Page *X* of *Y*, in the location you specify. To use this macro:

1. Put the insertion point on the first page where you want this style of page number.
2. Select Macro from the Tools menu, then Play or press ALT+F10.
3. Type **PAGEXOFY.WCM** in the Name drop-down list.
4. Select Play. The macro displays the dialog box shown next.

Page X of Y Macro

Position: | Format
Top Left | Page X of Y

Select the page number position and format, then press OK.

☐ Print Document | OK | Cancel

5. Select where you want the page numbering to appear from the Position pop-up list.

6. Select the format of the page numbering scheme from the Format drop-down list.

7. Select OK.

If you want to print your document immediately, you can select the Print Document check box before selecting OK. The page numbering inserted with this macro is not automatically updated when you edit your document. If your pagination changes, you need to rerun this macro.

Can I change how much space appears between footnotes?

You can change the line spacing between footnotes. To do so:

1. Select Footnote from the Insert menu.

2. Select Options.

3. Type a new distance in the Space text box in the Spacing Between Notes area of the dialog box and select OK.

I created footnotes in my paper, then found out I was supposed to use endnotes. Is there an easy way to convert all 300 footnotes to endnotes?

WordPerfect comes with macros that will convert all footnotes to endnotes or vice versa. Run the FOOTEND macro to convert all your footnotes to endnotes. You can also run the ENDFOOT macro, which converts all endnotes to footnotes. To run these macros:

1. Select Macro from the Tools menu, then Play or press ALT+ F10.

2. Type **FOOTEND** or **ENDFOOT** in the Name text box and select Play.

Is there an easier way to create signature lines than using graphics lines?

Instead of creating signature lines by choosing Lines from the Graphics menu, then Horizontal, and specifying positions, you can create signature lines using underlines. To do this:

1. Put your insertion point where you want the line to begin.

2. Select Font from the Layout menu.

3. Select the Tabs check box from the Underline Options area of the dialog box.

4. Select the Underline check box in the Appearance area.

5. Select OK.

6. Press TAB to move the insertion point to where you want the signature line to end.

7. Press CTRL+U to turn off underlining.

Tech Tip: This method will work well if you print the document and then simply write on the line. However, if you try to type your name or other text on top of this line while in WordPerfect, you will want to use spaces instead of tabs, then press the INSERT key on your keyboard to turn on Typeover mode. Without the switch to spaces or the use of the INSERT key, when you type on top of this line, it will "insert" each character and cause the line to extend further and further to the right. If you select Status Bar from the View menu, you will see "Typeover" displayed on the Status Bar. By pressing the INSERT key again, you can toggle back to Insert mode.

Writing Tools

WordPerfect 6 for Windows provides three writing tools: Speller, Thesaurus, and Grammatik. The Document Info command is also useful as a writing tool even though WordPerfect classifies it as a special feature. Speller uses one or more dictionaries to insure that each word in a document is spelled correctly. You will find a few tips on getting the most from this essential tool in the Frustration Busters box that follows. You can use the Thesaurus when you want to find synonyms for words you have used repeatedly. Grammatik scans a document for errors in grammar, spelling, or document mechanics such as readability or sentence structure. Document Info provides some quick statistics about your document such as the number of words, sentences, and paragraphs as well as the average word and sentence length.

The Speller is an essential tool for creating professional-looking documents. To use it as effectively as possible, you need to familiarize yourself with the Spell-Hyphen utility included with WordPerfect 6. It packs a powerful punch if you want to add words to a dictionary quickly, transfer words from a supplementary dictionary to the main dictionary, or optimize the main dictionary after adding a number of words. To run the Spell-Hyphen utility, switch to the WPC20 directory, then type **SPELL** at the DOS prompt. Since the utility is not documented in the standard WordPerfect 6 documentation, a brief description of each of its options follows:

- **Change\Create Dictionary:** Allows you to change the dictionary selected or create a new dictionary.

- **Add Words to Dictionary:** Lets you add words to the main or common areas of a dictionary either from the keyboard or a file.

- **Delete Word(s) from Dictionary:** Lets you remove words from the selected dictionary.

- **Optimize Dictionary:** Lets you compress the main dictionary after adding a number of words to insure top performance.

- **Look Up Word or Hyphenation Points:** Provides a lookup feature to check the spelling or syllables in a word.

- **Phonetic Look Up:** Provides an optional lookup feature that searches by the sound of letters rather than actual spelling.

- **Display Common Word List:** Lets you look at words in the common word list that are checked first by the Speller.

■ **Check Location of a Word:** Lets you know if a word is in the common or main area of a dictionary or not found in either location.

■ **Convert 5.*x* Dictionary to 6.0:** Lets you use a dictionary created for WordPerfect 5.*x* in WordPerfect 6.

■ **Convert Supplementary Dictionary:** Provides an opportunity to write a supplementary dictionary to a file.

■ **Create Supplementary Dictionary:** Creates a new supplementary dictionary.

Speller, Thesaurus and Grammatik are not available on WordPerfect's Tools menu. What can I do?

Your writing tools are unavailable either because they were never installed, or because a setting was changed to disable them. To determine which situation exists:

1. Select Preferences from the File menu.

2. Select the Writing Tools icon by double-clicking it, or pressing ALT+W and ENTER.

   The Available Tool Items list box shows each of the installed writing tools preceded by a check box. If the check box is selected, the writing tool is available. If the check box is cleared, the writing tool will not appear in the Tools menu, though you will be able to start it using the Power Bar button.

3. Select the check boxes for the writing tools that you want to have available by clicking on them, or highlighting them and pressing SPACEBAR.

4. Select OK, then Close.

If a writing tool does not appear in the Available Tool Items list box, then it is not installed on your system. To install a missing writing tool, restart the installation program.

Tech Tip: Not only can you set which writing tools appear on the Tools menu, but you can also set the order in which they appear. To do this, highlight the writing tools you want to move in the Available Tool Items list box. Then select Move Up or Move Down to move that item up or down in the list. The items in the Tools menu appear in the same order as they appear in the Available Tool items list box.

Is there some way to find out how many words or paragraphs are in my document?

Yes, WordPerfect provides two ways to determine the number of words or paragraphs in your document. You can use Grammatik by choosing Grammatik from the Tools menu. Choose Statistics from the Options menu and select Start. A quicker approach is to select Document Info from the File menu. WordPerfect opens the Document Information dialog box, which displays several statistics about your document, as shown here. Although Document Info is a special feature rather than a writing tool, it provides the quickest answer.

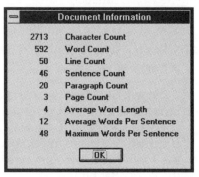

Document Information	
2713	Character Count
592	Word Count
50	Line Count
46	Sentence Count
20	Paragraph Count
3	Page Count
4	Average Word Length
12	Average Words Per Sentence
48	Maximum Words Per Sentence

OK

What is the difference between a main dictionary, a supplementary dictionary, and a document dictionary?

All three types of dictionaries—main, supplementary, and document—are used as resources while Speller checks your document for spelling errors. However, each dictionary serves a slightly different purpose. The order in which WordPerfect checks the dictionaries is document dictionary first, supplementary dictionary next, and main dictionary last.

Main dictionary Speller's main dictionary is its primary resource when checking for misspelled words in your document. Speller compares each word in your document that doesn't appear in the document or supplementary dictionary to this dictionary. If the word does not appear in this dictionary, Speller flags the word as a potential misspelling and notifies you.

Main dictionary files cannot be edited within WordPerfect because they use a special coding that requires less disk space. If you need to work with a main dictionary, use the Spell-Hyphen utility, described in the Frustration Busters box at the beginning of this chapter. This is important since these dictionary files are essentially just long lists of words. If they were not coded, they would be extremely large. The coding makes the files smaller and, consequently, easier and faster to search.

You can have more than one main dictionary file. Each main dictionary must be chained to the first or WordPerfect will not realize they are there. You can add dictionary files if you plan to work in a foreign language, or if you want to add a dictionary that contains professional, technical, or specialty words.

Supplementary Dictionary A supplementary dictionary is a special dictionary that you create. This dictionary contains only the words that you put in it. This allows you to add those words or names that aren't in WordPerfect's main dictionary, but which you use in many of the documents you create. You can add words to the dictionary when Speller flags them as incorrect in your document, or you can use Speller to edit this dictionary.

When you edit the dictionary, you can do more than add words indicating a correct spelling. You can also add words that you want Speller to automatically replace with other text. For example, you could have Speller automatically replace "Cramer, Cramer" with "Cramer, Cramer, Foster, Johnson and Severn, LPA" each time it encounters this phrase. You can also have Speller present you with several alternatives to words you add. For example, you could have Speller suggest using "female coworkers," "women," or "ladies" when it encounters the word "girls" in your business documents.

Document Dictionary A document dictionary is a type of supplementary dictionary. You can add words to a document dictionary or edit it, just as you do a normal supplementary dictionary. However, the document dictionary is not saved in its own file, nor can it be used with all documents you create. The document dictionary is saved as part of the current document. It is used only when you check the spelling of the current document.

I started Speller outside WordPerfect and tried checking the spelling in a document I created with another application. It won't work. Why?

The Speller is an independent application and can be started outside WordPerfect. However, it is designed to work closely with WordPerfect, and is not designed to work the same way with other applications. If you start Speller in WordPerfect, it can read WordPerfect documents and check their spelling. If you start Speller outside WordPerfect, it can only check the text you enter in the Word text box. You can copy text from your document to the Speller using the Clipboard, but the Word text box can only contain 64 characters, limiting the amount of text you can check at once. Its most practical use outside of WordPerfect is to allow you to check a word quickly if you are proofreading a document.

I created a supplementary dictionary in WordPerfect 5.2 for Windows. Can I use it with WordPerfect 6 for Windows?

You can use the entries in your WordPerfect 5.2 for Windows supplementary dictionary with WordPerfect 6 for Windows, but not directly. Instead, you need to add the entries in your WordPerfect 5.2 for Windows supplementary dictionary to the new WordPerfect 6 for Windows supplementary dictionary. You do not need to retype the words. To add the old dictionary's entries to the new dictionary:

1. While in WordPerfect 6 for Windows, open the WordPerfect 5.2 for Windows supplementary dictionary file, called WP{WP}US.SUP.

2. Select Speller from the Tools menu. You can also click the Speller button in the Power Bar or press CTRL+F1.

3. Select Start to run Speller.

4. Each time Speller flags a word in your dictionary as incorrect, select Add to add it to the WordPerfect 6 for Windows supplementary dictionary.

5. Select Close when you are finished checking this document.

The name of the default WordPerfect 6 for Windows supplementary dictionary is WPSPELUS.SUP.

Can I delete or edit words in my supplementary dictionary?

You can edit your WordPerfect supplementary dictionaries using the Speller. To do so, follow these steps:

1. Select Speller from the Tools menu to start Speller. You can also click the Speller button in the Power Bar or press CTRL+F1.

2. Select Supplementary from the Dictionaries menu, opening the Supplementary Dictionaries dialog box.

3. Highlight the supplementary dictionary you want to edit in the Dictionaries in Search Order list box. The default supplementary dictionary is WPSPELUS.SUP.

4. Select Edit.

5. Select Add when you want to add words to your supplementary dictionary.

Type the word to add to the dictionary in the Word text box, then select one of the Add Word/Phrase Options option buttons to indicate the way the word should be used.

- Skip tells Speller to ignore the word when it finds it in a document.

- Replacement tells Speller you want to replace this word with another word when it is found in a document. You must type the replacement word in the Replacement text box that appears.

■ Alternatives tells Speller to provide a selection of possible replacement words, and a message indicating what is wrong with the current word or phrase. Type each alternative word in the Alternative text box, then select Insert to add it to the List of Alternative Words list box. Type the message in the Comment text box.

When you are finished entering the word, and setting up how WordPerfect will respond when it encounters this word, select OK.

1. Select Delete to remove the word highlighted in the Key Words list box from the supplementary dictionary. Select Yes when prompted to confirm that you want to delete the word.

2. Select Edit to change the spelling or options of the word highlighted in the Key Words list box. You can change the spelling of the word, change how Speller will use the word, or change the replacement or alternative words. Select OK when you are finished editing the word.

3. Select Close twice to return to the Speller window.

Is there some way to check grammar in a part of my document instead of checking the entire document?

Yes, you can check the grammar of a section of your document when running Grammatik in WordPerfect. To specify how much of the document you want to check, start Grammatik, then select an option from the Check menu. You can select Sentence, Paragraph, Document, To End of Document, or Selected Text. When using the Selected Text option, you need to select the text before you start Grammatik, as shown in Figure 5-1.

Can I add technical and professional words to my main dictionary?

You cannot edit your main dictionary from within WordPerfect, but you can perform some maintenance activities with the Spell-Hyphen utility described earlier in the chapter. Also, you can

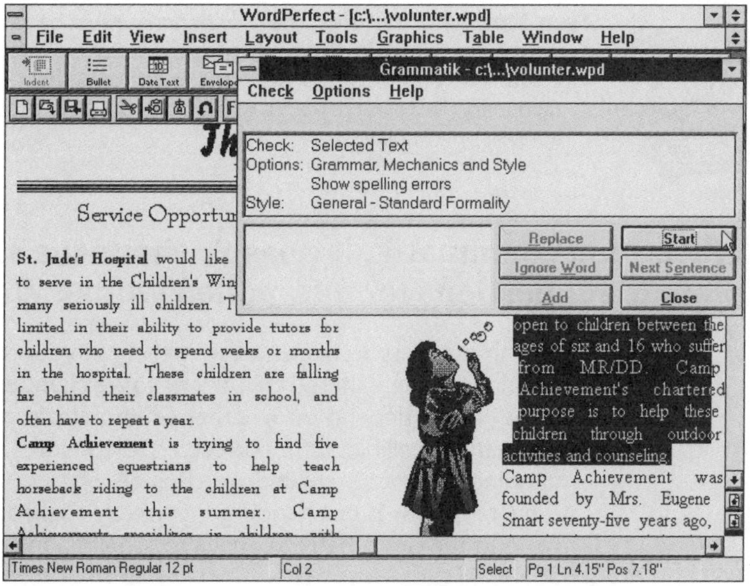

FIGURE 5-1 Checking grammar in selected text

purchase dictionaries that are created for specific professions or uses, such as dictionaries containing legal terminology. This dictionary must be set up as a WordPerfect main dictionary. You can *chain* this dictionary to your main dictionary. Speller will check this second dictionary the same way it checks your usual main dictionary. When you chain main dictionaries, you can think of them as all part of one main dictionary. Although they remain separate files, they function as one large file.

To chain a dictionary to your WordPerfect main dictionary:

1. Select Speller from the Tools menu. You can also click the Speller button in the Power Bar or press CTRL+F1.

2. Select Main from the Dictionaries menu.

3. Select Add.

4. Choose the dictionary file you want to link to your main dictionary.

5. Select OK, then Close.

Tech Tip: All WordPerfect main dictionaries must be stored in a coded format like the main dictionary supplied by WordPerfect. You cannot create a text file of words you want to add and chain it to the main dictionary. You can create a text file and add the words in it with the Spell-Hyphen utility.

When I run Grammatik, it doesn't check the spelling or provide suggestions for misspelled words. Why?

If Grammatik isn't checking the spelling in your document, a setting has been altered that needs to be changed back. The steps to take depend on whether Grammatik is not providing alternative spellings for incorrectly spelled words, or is not flagging incorrectly spelled words at all.

If Grammatik is not flagging incorrectly spelled words, you need to tell Grammatik to check the spelling in your document again. To do this:

1. Select Grammatik from the Tools menu. You can also click the Grammatik button in the Power Bar or press ALT+SHIFT +F1.

2. Select Show spelling errors from the Options menu.

3. Select Start to start checking the grammar in your document.

If Grammatik is flagging words as incorrect, but is not providing suggested spellings automatically, you need to change a different setting. To do so:

1. Select Grammatik from the Tools menu. You can also click the Grammatik button in the Power Bar or press ALT+SHIFT+F1.

2. Select Checking Options from the Options menu in the Grammatik window.

3. Select the Suggest spelling replacements check box, then select OK.

4. Select Start to start checking the grammar in your document.

When you start checking your document with Grammatik, it will provide suggestions about incorrectly spelled words.

I want to choose which grammar rules Grammatik enforces. Can I do this?

Yes, you can choose which grammar rules Grammatik enforces by selecting one of Grammatik's default writing styles, or by creating your own. Grammatik offers ten default writing styles: General, Advertising, Business Letter, Documentation, Fiction, Journalism, Memo, Proposal, Report, and Technical.

To create a writing style:

1. Select <u>G</u>rammatik from the <u>T</u>ools menu. You can also click the Grammatik button in the Power Bar or press ALT+SHIFT+F1.

2. Select <u>W</u>riting Styles from the <u>O</u>ptions menu.

3. Highlight the writing style in the <u>W</u>riting Style list box that is closest to the style you want to create, and select <u>E</u>dit.

Tech Note: If you just want to select a writing style, higlight it and select OK. Grammatik now opens the Writing Style Settings dialog box, shown in Figure 5-2. Select the grammar rules to be enforced by selecting or clearing their check boxes. Grammatik divides the grammar rules into three classes—<u>S</u>tyle, <u>G</u>rammar, and <u>M</u>echanical—as detailed in Table 5-1. Choose the appropriate option button to show the rules in that class. The text boxes at the bottom of this dialog box let you set the grammar rules to be applied.

4. Select <u>S</u>ave.

Your custom writing style is saved using the name shown in brackets in the upper-right corner of the Writing Styles dialog box. It appears in the <u>W</u>riting Styles list box, and can be selected like any other writing style.

Is there some way to check the spelling in only part of my document?

Yes, you can control the part of your document that Speller checks by changing a setting. The setting must be changed after opening Speller but before it actually starts checking your

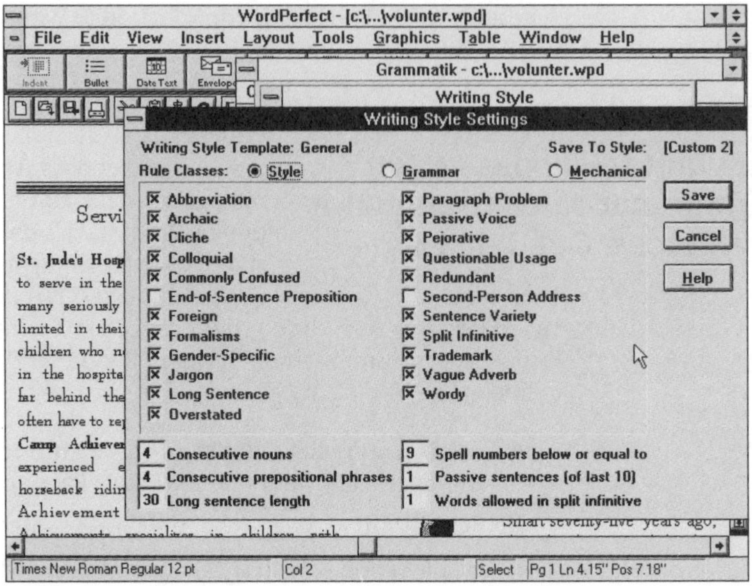

FIGURE 5-2   Grammatik's Writing Style Settings dialog box

document. To check part of a document, select an option from the Check menu after opening Speller. You can select Word, Sentence, Paragraph, Page, Document, To End of Document, or Number of Pages to set which part of your document will be checked when you start Speller. You can also choose the Selected Text option if you had selected some text before choosing the Speller. For example, in Figure 5-3, Speller will check only the selected paragraph.

The words I added to the supplementary dictionary while running Grammatik are still being flagged as incorrect when I use Speller. Why?

Speller is not recognizing the words you added to the supplementary dictionary in Grammatik because Grammatik and Speller use different supplementary dictionary files. When you

Style		
Abbreviation	Archaic	Cliche
Colloquial	Commonly Confused	End-of-Sentence Preposition
Foreign	Formalisms	Gender-Specific
Jargon	Long Sentence	Overstated
Paragraph Problem	Passive Voice	Pejorative
Questionable Usage	Redundant	Second-Person Address
Sentence Variety	Split Infinitive	Trademark
Vague Adverb	Wordy	
Grammar		
Adjective	Adverb	Article
Comma Splice or Fused Sentence	Comparative/Superlative	Conjunction
Double Negative	Homonym	Incomplete Sentence
Incorrect Verb Form	Infinitive	Noun Phrase
Object of Verb	Possessive Form	Preposition
Pronoun Case	Pronoun Number Agreement	Relative Pronoun
Run-on Sentence	Sequence of Tenses	Subject-Verb Agreement
Subordination	Tense Shift	
Mechanical		
Capitalization	Custom Rule Class 1	Custom Rule Class 2
Custom Rule Class 3	Doubled Word or Punctuation	Ellipsis
End-of-Sentence Punctuation	Number Style	Punctuation
Question Mark	Quotation Marks	Similar Words
Spelling	Split Words	Unbalanced (), {}, [], or "

TABLE 5-1   Grammatik's three rule classes contain 58 rule sets

add words to the supplementary dictionary in Grammatik, they are added only to Grammatik's supplementary dictionary file. Since Speller does not use this file, it continues to flag the words as incorrect.

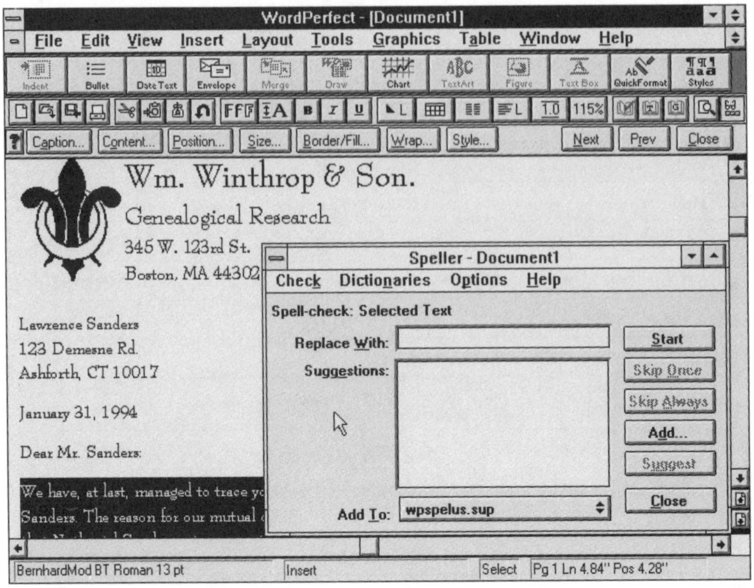

FIGURE 5-3   Speller checking only selected text

If you want Speller to stop flagging these words as incorrect, you need to add them to Speller's supplementary dictionary file. To add the words, run Speller with the file containing these words, and select Add when these words are flagged to add them to Speller's supplementary dictionary.

Tech Note: Grammatik's supplementary dictionary file is called GW51EN.USR. Speller's default supplementary dictionary file is WPSPELUS.SUP.

Can I set how strictly WordPerfect follows the writing style when checking grammar?

Yes, with Grammatik you can change how strictly it enforces various rules of grammar. Formal writing follows the rules of grammar more closely than other types of writing. You can choose from Informal, Standard, and Formal options to vary how strictly Grammatik enforces the rules. To change this setting:

1. Select <u>G</u>rammatik from the <u>T</u>ools menu. You can also click the Grammatik button in the Power Bar or press ALT+SHIFT+F1.

2. Select <u>W</u>riting Style from the <u>O</u>ptions menu.

3. Select the <u>S</u>tandard, <u>F</u>ormal, or <u>I</u>nformal option button to set the level of formality you want to use, then choose OK.

You will see a number of selections in the <u>W</u>riting Style list box, as well as the three option buttons under Formality Level. The options in the <u>W</u>riting Style list box set which rules of grammar are enforced when Grammatik checks your document, rather than how strictly those rules are enforced. For example, if you select Fiction in the <u>W</u>riting Style list box, Grammatik enforces fewer rules than if you select Proposal.

Can WordPerfect perform a statistical analysis of my documents?

Yes, the Statistics feature can supply a statistical analysis of the documents you create in WordPerfect. It provides word, sentence, and paragraph counts and a readability index that you can use to improve your writing. To see this statistical analysis:

1. Choose <u>G</u>rammatik from the <u>T</u>ools menu. You can also click the Grammatik button in the Power Bar or press ALT+SHIFT +F1.

2. Choose S<u>t</u>atistics from the <u>O</u>ptions menu.

3. Choose <u>S</u>tart.

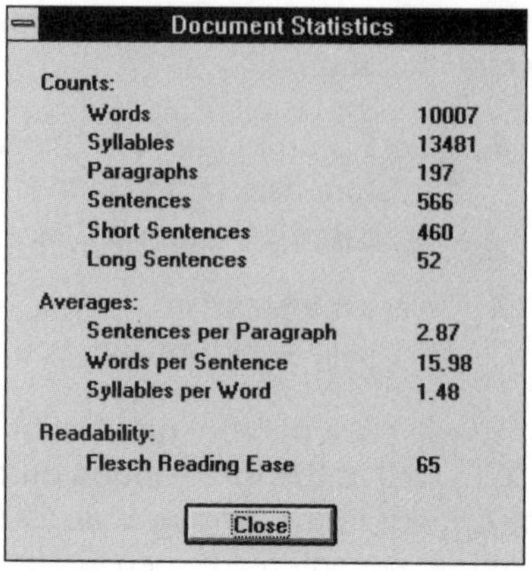

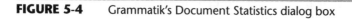

Document Statistics

Counts:
Words	10007
Syllables	13481
Paragraphs	197
Sentences	566
Short Sentences	460
Long Sentences	52

Averages:
Sentences per Paragraph	2.87
Words per Sentence	15.98
Syllables per Word	1.48

Readability:
Flesch Reading Ease	65

Close

FIGURE 5-4   Grammatik's Document Statistics dialog box

The Document Statistics dialog box appears, like the one shown in Figure 5-4.

Printing

In the past, printing problems often related to getting output that looked different from the image on the computer screen. Now, with WYSIWYG (What You See Is What You Get) features in WordPerfect 6, it is easy to see where boldface, underline, and other special features will appear since you are looking at a printing preview as you edit your document. However, new kinds of printing problems have replaced the old ones.

Today's print problems often relate to printer definitions, hardware, or the use of special features such as fonts and special paper sizes. The problems discussed in this chapter range from simple tasks such as creating a rush document, to more sophisticated options such as double-sided printing or collating multiple copies. If you encounter printing problems, you should look first at the list of easy fixes in the Frustration Busters box that follows.

When you encounter a problem printing your document in WordPerfect for Windows check the following simple fixes before looking for more complicated solutions.

- **Is the printer turned on?** This might sound stupid, but it's the first thing to check.

- **Does the printer have paper?** Like the answer above, this seems obvious until you are trying to solve a problem caused by an empty paper tray.

- **Is the printer's online button turned on?** Most printers have a button that turns the printer online and offline. Usually, this button has a light or some other indicator telling you that it is on. When the printer is offline, it cannot receive information from the computer.

- **Can the printer print from other applications?** Using the Notepad accessory is a quick way to test that the problem is not the settings Windows has for the printer. Open a text file in the Notepad accessory or type text in the accessory's window. Then select Print from the File menu. If it prints, Windows has the correct settings for the printer. You may even want to look at the settings through the Control Panel program.

- **Are you using a Windows printer driver or a WordPerfect printer driver?** If you are using a WordPerfect printer driver, the problem may be that its settings do not agree with how the computer is connected to the printer. Use WordPerfect's Select Printer command in the File menu to see which printer driver is selected and choose Setup to change the settings for that printer.

- **Are you printing on a network?** If so, the problem may relate to the network itself. In this case, you want to contact your network administrator and let that person resolve the difficulty.

I just purchased a new printer and received my new WordPerfect printer driver for it. How can I install the new driver?

To install the new printer driver in WordPerfect, follow these steps:

1. Select Run from the File menu in the Program Manager window.

2. Type **C:\WPWIN60\INSTALL.EXE** and select OK. Replace C:\WPWIN60 with the drive and path where the WordPerfect 6.0 for Windows installation program is located if it is not in C:\WPWIN60.

3. Select Options, then Printers from the WordPerfect Installation screen.

4. Type in the appropriate drive and directory where the printer driver is being installed from and to, and click OK. Be sure the disk containing the printer driver is in the drive specified.

   The appropriate file will be copied into the specified drive.

5. Start WordPerfect and choose Select Printer from the File menu, Click Add Printer and choose WordPerfect.

6. From the Add Printer dialog box, select the Additional Printers (*.ALL) radio button, then scroll through the list of installed printers and check the printer being installed. This process creates the .PRS file which is necessary for WordPerfect to collect information regarding fonts, paper sizes and types.

7. After selecting the printer to install, click OK, check that the PRS filename is correct, and click OK.

The printer is now installed and can be selected. Some editing may be necessary to ensure that the correct port is selected and the sheet feeder is set up correctly.

Tech Tip: To use the new printer in other applications, you must install the printer driver for Windows (or the appropriate DOS driver for that application). Installing the Windows printer driver is done through the Control Panel program. Once the printer driver is installed in Windows, you can print to your new printer from most Windows applications, including WordPerfect.

Tech Tip: To delete the old WordPerfect printer driver, choose Select Printer in the File menu. Select the printer with the WP symbol in the Printers list box and the Delete button. From the Delete Printer dialog box, you can select Delete the associated .PRS to remove this file from your hard disk. Select OK, and the Close button. If you select Delete while highlighting a Windows printer driver, WordPerfect opens the Control Panel's Printers dialog box that you can use to remove a printer driver.

Why can't I find a Print Preview feature?

WordPerfect 6.0 does not have a Print Preview feature. When you choose Page in the View menu, you are in full WYSIWYG mode. You will see all of the fonts, headers, footers, footnotes, page breaks, watermarks, rotated text, and label arrangements that appear when you print a document. This is the same as Print Preview except that you can still edit your text. Use the Zoom command in the View menu to see the whole page at once. Once you select this command, you can specify whether the document is displayed onscreen in its actual size or is shown in increased or decreased size as you select a Zoom percentage. Selecting Full Page sizes the document to show an entire page at once. You can also switch to the Page view and set the zoom percentage to show the full page by clicking the Page Zoom Full button in the Power Bar.

Clicking this button again returns you to the prior view and zoom percentage. Another option is to set the zoom percentage by dragging the mouse from the Zoom button in the Power Bar to the zoom percentage you want for the document.

Can I print my document summaries?

You can print the document summaries from the current document using either of these methods:

- Select Print from the File menu and the Document Summary radio button. When you select Print, WordPerfect prints the current document's document summary.

- Display the document summary by selecting Document Summary from the File menu. Select Options and Print Summary and WordPerfect will print the current document's document summary.

How can I cancel a print job that I have already sent to the printer?

The method you use to cancel a print job depends on how far the printing process has progressed. When you print your document, WordPerfect first prepares the document for printing. To cancel the print job at this point, select Print from the File menu, click Control, and click Cancel Print Job. If you cannot select Control from WordPerfect's Print dialog box, the print job has already gone to the printer or to an external print queue.

If the print job is in Windows' print queue, switch to the Print Manager application. Figure 6-1 shows a Print Manager window that lists all of the print jobs from all Windows applications as well as all of the printers your computer has installed in Windows. Highlight the print job, and select the Delete button.

If the print job is in the network print queue when you are printing on a network, the steps for canceling the print job are done using network commands. If you are not printing to a network printer and the print job is already being sent to the printer, you can cancel the information sent to the printer by simply resetting the printer.

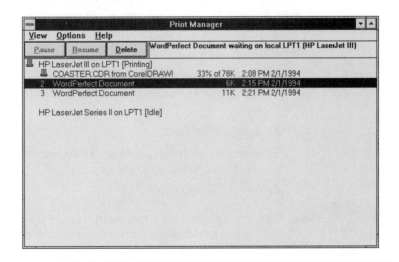

FIGURE 6-1   Print Manager window showing print jobs in the queue

How do I change the priority of a print request?

You can change the order in which your documents print using the Windows Print Manager. The Print Manager manages the printing of documents from all Windows applications. You can change the order of documents printed by changing the order of documents listed in the Print Manager.

To change the order of print jobs, switch to the Print Manager application window like the one in Figure 6-1. Highlight the document you need to increase in priority. Press CTRL+UP ARROW to move it up in the list. You cannot move the print job you want to rush above the job that Windows is currently printing. The current print job has a different icon from the other jobs.

How do I set the initial font for documents created for a specific printer?

A WordPerfect document remembers which printer you selected the last time you edited the document. This information remains in the document as you create and edit it. A document's initial font depends on which printer you choose to use. To set the initial font for documents created for a specific printer, follow these steps:

1. Choose Select Printer from the File menu and highlight the printer to assign an initial font from the Printers list box.

2. Select Initial Font.

3. Select the font face, style, and size just as if you are using the Font command in the Layout menu.

4. Select OK and Close.

Tech Tip: Changing the initial font for the current printer will not change the initial font for the current document. In order to change the initial font for the document, select Document from the Layout menu, then choose Initial Font. Select the font face, style, and size, then select the Set as Printer Initial Font check box and OK.

Why does the text in my document look different onscreen than when printed?

When you use printer fonts, your document may look different on paper from the way it appears on the screen. When you tell WordPerfect or another Windows applications to use a printer font, the application substitutes a different display font in the document on the screen. The reason for this is that the printer does not tell Windows how every font looks. If you want to be sure that the text looks the same on both your screen and the printed copy, use a TrueType font. These fonts are created by software and look the same onscreen as printed. You can tell which fonts are printer fonts and which ones are TrueType fonts by looking at the symbols next to the font names. In the illustration below, you can see WordPerfect marks printer fonts with a printer and TrueType fonts with two T's. Other typeface management software such as Adobe Typeface Manager can provide fonts that have the same appearance onscreen as when printed.

Times New Roman
Univers (WN)

Tech Tip: When you install additional TrueType fonts, they are installed for all Windows applications.

Windows also has screen fonts. These are the ones with the enlarged V's next to their names. Since these fonts are available only for the screen and not for both printer and screen, WordPerfect must substitute a TrueType or printer font for them when printing. You are better off avoiding these fonts.

How can I tell the difference between WordPerfect printer drivers and Windows printer drivers?

You select the printer you want for a document from the Select Printer dialog box. You can display this dialog box by choosing Select Printer from the File menu or by selecting Print from the File menu and choosing the Select button. In the Select Printer list box, WordPerfect printer drivers will have a WP icon next to them, while Windows printer drivers will have a Windows icon next to them as shown in the next illustration.

Printers:

HP LaserJet III on LPT1:
HP LaserJet III on LPT1:
HP LaserJet Series II on LPT1:
HP LaserJet Series II on LPT1:

Should I use a Windows printer driver or a WordPerfect printer driver?

WordPerfect for Windows can use printer drivers supplied either by WordPerfect or by Windows. Windows printer drivers are shared by all Windows applications.

Once you have installed the printer driver in Windows for a printer, you are ready to use it in any Windows application. WordPerfect printer drivers are used only by WordPerfect. The same printer drivers you use for WordPerfect 6.0 for DOS work for WordPerfect 6.0 for Windows. Also, WordPerfect has a separate utility called the Printer Definition utility that you can order to alter the settings in a WordPerfect printer driver. Thus, if you are using WordPerfect in both DOS and Windows, you can use a WordPerfect printer driver and know that you have the same printing features in both versions of WordPerfect. WordPerfect also has printer drivers for some printers that are not available in Windows.

If you decide to use a WordPerfect driver, you will need to install it before the printer driver appears in the list of printers to select. To install a WordPerfect printer driver, follow these steps:

1. Exit WordPerfect.

2. Start the WordPerfect for Windows installation program by double-clicking the WPWin 6.0 Installation icon in the Program Manager.

3. Select the Options button and then the Printers button in the installation program.

4. Put the first install disk into drive A and select OK when prompted to indicate where you want to install from and install to. If you put the WordPerfect Install disk in drive B, change the drive in the Install to text box before selecting OK.

5. Select the printers you want to use. Highlight the printer in the Printers list box and choose Select or double-click the printer you want to select. Some printers require a printer driver that you must order separately from WordPerfect.

6. Select OK when you have selected all the printers you will want to use. You may be prompted to replace the Install 1 disk with another disk to allow WordPerfect to install the printer driver files.

7. Select OK after the printer driver files are installed and you will leave the WordPerfect installation program. In WordPerfect, when you choose Select Printer from the File menu, the list of available printers will include the printers using WordPerfect printer drivers. These will have the WordPerfect logo.

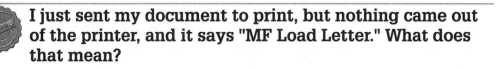

I just sent my document to print, but nothing came out of the printer, and it says "MF Load Letter." What does that mean?

When your printer displays a message such as "MF Load Letter," it is expecting you to manually feed a piece of paper to print the next page. You need to either insert a piece of paper, or press the Online or Continue button on the printer to resume printing using the default paper tray. You are seeing this information because WordPerfect's paper location is set to manual paper feed. To eliminate this problem, the paper location selection in WordPerfect needs to be set to Continuous or Default. To make this change, select Page from the Layout menu, and select Paper Size. Choose the paper size you are using from the Paper Definitions list box and select Edit. From the Edit Paper Size dialog box, select either Continuous or Default in the Location list box. Select OK, then Close to finish with the dialog boxes.

Tech Tip: WordPerfect for Windows uses its own paper size and paper location settings during printing, even when the Windows printer driver is selected. If you see the message "Feed Letter Paper" or "Feed Legal Paper," adjust the WordPerfect print settings to specify the paper size and orientation. Set the paper location selection in WordPerfect to Default. Change the paper location by selecting Page from the Layout menu, and then selecting Paper Size. Repeat these adjustments for each paper size to be printed from WordPerfect. Once you make these adjustments,

WordPerfect will remember the changes, and the Windows or WordPerfect printer driver will print without prompting you to feed paper.

Why do I have a WP Print Process icon or window when I print?

The WP Print Process icon or window indicates that WordPerfect is printing your document in the background. It appears when you print a document in WordPerfect and remains open until

you close it or leave WordPerfect. WP Print Process may appear as a window while you print a document or when you select Control from the Print dialog box. The WP Print Process icon and the window are shown here:

```
┌─────────────────────────────────────────────┐
│ ▬            WP Print Process             ▼ │
├─────────────────────────────────────────────┤
│ File   Window                                │
│                                              │
│ No print jobs waiting                        │
│                                              │
│                                              │
└─────────────────────────────────────────────┘
```

Does WordPerfect 6.0 for Windows support background printing?

WordPerfect 6.0 for Windows prints in the background automatically. Background printing will delay your computer for only a short period of time, while it creates a temporary file.

When you printed a document in WordPerfect 5.2 for Windows, you had to wait until the document completely finished printing before you could continue editing a document.

When I print a table, the table lines don't appear; only the text inside the table prints. What's wrong?

WordPerfect uses a printer's graphic capabilities to print lines in a table. If your printer does not support graphics, it will print only the text of the table, not the table lines. You will also want to choose Print from the File menu and check that the Do Not Print Graphics check box is cleared.

The lines WordPerfect prints around a table depends on different features including the lines added to the table. Choose Lines/Fill from the Table menu or select Lines/Fill from the

QuickMenu, and choose T̲able. If the default line style is set to
<None>, only the text within the table will print.

I am trying to print a document which includes both graphics and text, but only the text prints. What is wrong?

WordPerfect prints graphics and text at the print quality setting
chosen for the Print Q̲uality pop-up button in the Print dialog
box. When the Do Not Print G̲raphics check box is selected
under Document Settings, the document prints without any
graphics. Besides graphic box contents, WordPerfect will not
print enhanced text created with TextArt and other embedded
or linked objects that are drawn graphically if this box is checked.

How can I print selected pages, rather than printing the entire document?

To print several pages of a document,
select M̲ultiple Pages from the Print
dialog box. After you select P̲rint, type
in the Page(s) text box the range of
pages separated with a hyphen, a
comma, or both. For example, type **3**
for just page 3; or type **3,5,9** for page 3, page 5, and page 9;
type **3-10** for printing pages 3 through 10; and type **3-6,10** for
pages 3 through 6 as well as page 10. Selecting P̲rint again
prints the selected pages.

Tech Terror: When you
are typing the page
numbers you want to
print, they must be in
numerical order. For
example, WordPerfect will
accept 1, 5, 10 but not
10, 5, 1.

Tech Tip: WordPerfect 6.0 for Windows prints
multiple files in a different way than
WordPerfect 5.1 for DOS. In WordPerfect 5.1
for DOS, you can press F5 (List Files) and
select multiple files, then specify certain page
numbers to print from each file when you
select 4 (P̲rint). In WordPerfect for Windows,
you can select QuickFinder from the F̲ile
menu, choose F̲ind, and select multiple files
to print at once. However, you do not have the option to specify a
range of page numbers. The entire files are printed automatically.

I am creating a booklet but I am having problems getting the pages to print in the correct order. How do I print a booklet?

WordPerfect will handle many of the steps in creating a booklet including printing the pages so the booklet can be assembled correctly. To create a booklet, follow these steps:

- Select the page size by choosing Page from the Layout menu and then Paper Size. For example, if you are using standard 8 1/2 x 11-inch paper sideways, you would select the Letter Landscape paper definition.

- If you are using the same physical page for one or more pages in the booklet, you will want to subdivide the page. To do this, select Page from the Layout menu and Subdivide Page. Type the number of columns and rows on the page and select OK. To figure out the number of columns and rows on each subdivided page, take a piece of the paper you will use for printing and fold it vertically and horizontally so the folded paper is the size of one page in the booklet. Unfold the paper and count the number of columns and rows on each page.

- If you want a page in the booklet to be on the right side of the physical page, remember to select Page from the Layout menu and Force Page and Current Page Odd.

- Review the document to make sure that margins and page breaks are what you want. Often breaks that look good on a full page look unattractive on only half a page.

- Print the document as a booklet. Select Print from the File menu and Options. From the Print Output Options dialog box, select Booklet Printing and OK. When you select Print, WordPerfect prints the outside page of the booklet and works inward; then works its way out again. During the printing process, you may be prompted to reinsert previous pages.

As an example, suppose you have a booklet that when finished will have the following pages:

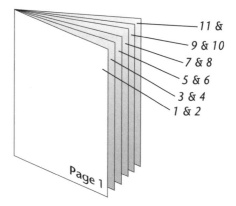

When you print this booklet, WordPerfect prints the pages in the following order:

- Page 1 on the right and page 12 on the left
- Page 3 on the right and page 10 on the left
- Page 5 on the right and page 8 on the left
- Page 6 on the left and page 7 on the right—this is the reverse side of the third piece of paper
- Page 4 on the left and page 9 on the right—this is the reverse side of the second piece of paper
- Page 2 on the left and page 11 on the right—this is the reverse side of the first piece of paper

WordPerfect determines what combination of document pages are printed on each piece of paper.

How can I use the fonts from my printer font cartridges in my WordPerfect documents?

WordPerfect can use the font cartridges installed on your printer but the printer driver must know they are installed before you can use them. Once the printer driver knows which font cartridges you have, you can select fonts from the cartridges when you select fonts for a document. The steps for telling the printer driver about font cartridges you have installed are different for Windows printer drivers and for WordPerfect printer drivers. To install a font cartridge for a WordPerfect printer driver, follow these steps:

1. Choose Select Printer from the File menu.
2. Highlight the WordPerfect printer driver (distinguished by a WP symbol), then choose Setup.
3. Choose the Cartridges/Fonts button.
4. Select Cartridges from the Font Source drop-down list box.
5. Double-click the cartridges you have to select them and place an asterisk (*) next to them.

   Do not choose Mark All because no printers are designed to handle all cartridges at once.
6. Choose OK twice to confirm your selections, then choose Update.
7. Select Close to leave the Select Printer dialog box.

To install a font cartridge for a Windows printer driver, follow these steps:

1. Open the Control Panel program by double-clicking its icon in the Main window of the Program Manager.
2. Select the Printers icon to open the Printers dialog box.
3. Highlight the printer that has the cartridges in the Installed Printers list box and select Setup.
4. Highlight the installed cartridges in the Cartridges list box. If you have more than one, select the subsequent ones by holding down the CTRL key while you click the other installed cartridges.
5. Select OK and Close to finish with the printer control options.
6. Press ALT+F4, select Exit from the Settings menu or double-click the control menu box to close the Control Panel.

After completing either set of steps, the fonts provided by the cartridges will appear in the list of fonts when a document is using the printer that has the installed font cartridge.

Why do I get the error message "Invalid Adobe Type Manager Version?"

WordPerfect is not compatible with versions of Adobe Type Manager earlier than 2.5. If the error "Invalid Adobe Type Manager Version" appears in WordPerfect 6.0 for Windows, contact Adobe Systems at (800) 83FONTS to get the updated version of Adobe Type Manager. Until you get the new and improved version of Adobe Type Manager, you should disable the old version by double-clicking on the ATM Control Panel and selecting Off. You will need to restart Windows after doing this.

Can I use the printer driver files from earlier versions of WordPerfect?

You cannot use printer driver files from earlier versions of WordPerfect. Use the WordPerfect 6.0 for Windows installation program to install the correct printer files to use with your printer. However, you can share printer files between WordPerfect 6.0 for DOS and WordPerfect 6.0 for Windows.

When I print a document to my laser printer, the pages end up in reverse order. If I am printing a long document it is very time consuming to rearrange the pages in correct order. Is there a way that WordPerfect can do this for me?

WordPerfect can print a document in reverse order so you don't have to reorder them. To print a document in reverse order, select Print from the File menu or click on the Printer icon. From the Print dialog box click the Options button. Then, in the Print Output Options dialog box, select the Print in Reverse Order check box. When your printer outputs pages in reverse order your final output on the printer will be collated in the proper order. You will need to change the print order for each document that you want printed in reverse order.

Can I print both landscape and portrait orientation on the same page?

You can print text that you want to appear sideways (landscape orientation) on a page that also has text in the regular, portrait orientation by putting the text to appear sideways in a graphics box. Follow these steps:

1. Select Custom Box from the Graphics menu then User from the Style Name list box and OK.

2. Select the Content button in the Graphics Box Feature Bar.

3. Select Text from the Content pop-up list.

4. Select either 90 Degrees if you want the bottom of the rotated text on the right side or 270 Degrees if you want the bottom of the rotated text on the left side.

5. Select Edit and type the text to appear sideways.

6. Select Close from the Graphics Box Feature Bar to finish editing the graphics box.

7. Make any other changes you want. For example, in the document in Figure 6-2, the sideways text is in a graphics box that has had its width set to Full by selecting Size in the Graphics Box Feature Bar and Full under Height.

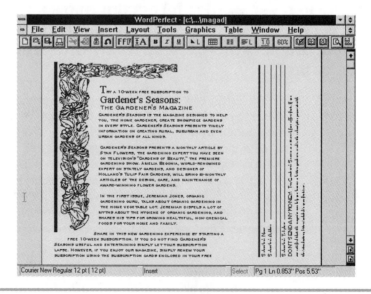

FIGURE 6-2   Document containing text using two print orientations

In Figure 6-2, the page size is set to landscape and the text on the right is placed in a graphics box that has the text rotated by 90 degrees.

Tech Tip: Some printers cannot print both orientations at once. Other printers will require that you use all graphics fonts rather than printer fonts for this to print correctly.

Why can't I edit or create a paper definition using a printer driver from the network?

When you create or edit a paper definition, that information is saved in the currently selected printer driver file. Since the directory where these .PRS files are located on the network is normally marked as read-only, you cannot create or edit the paper definitions. To make these changes, you need access rights to the directory where the .PRS files are located. At a minimum, you need read and write privileges. Your network administrator can help you with this.

Another method of changing the printer definition is to cop y the .PRS files to a local drive and use the local version of the printer driver. If you do this, you will then need to select Preferences from the File menu, select the File icon, select the Printers/Labels radio button and change the entry in the Default Directory text box to reflect this new directory. Selecting OK and Close finishes this change.

What is the difference between generating copies of printed documents from WordPerfect or from the printer?

The Generated By pop-up button in the Print dialog box sets the origin of multiple copies, generating them from WordPerfect or from the printer. WordPerfect creates multiple copies in one of two ways. It can print copies of entire documents one at a time or it can print multiple copies of each page. The second method requires that you set the number of copies you want through the printer, assuming your printer has this capability. The output generated with the first method prints one complete copy before beginning the next. The output generated by the second method prints all the copies of one page before starting on the next page, so you must collate the pages. The second method may be faster, depending on your printer. To set this option, select Print from the File menu, and, in the Copies area, select WordPerfect or Printer from the Generated By pop-up list.

When I print a document, one line of a paragraph prints alone at the top of the next page; on another page, one line of a paragraph prints alone at the bottom of the page. Is there anything that I can do to prevent this from happening?

These solitary lines are called *widows* and *orphans*. Orphans are the single line at the end of a page when the rest of the paragraph is on the next page. A widow line is the last line of a paragraph that appears by itself on the next page. These are illustrated in Figure 6-3. WordPerfect can prevent widows and orphans when printing a document. WordPerfect adjusts the placement of other lines in a document to prevent widows and orphans. For example, WordPerfect moves a line to the next page to prevent an orphan. To prevent a widow, WordPerfect moves the next to last line from the previous page to the current page so there are two lines from the paragraph on the page.

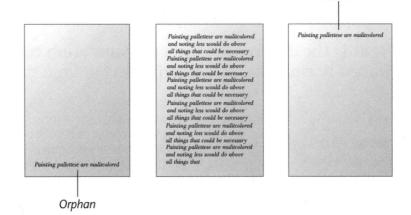

FIGURE 6-3   Widows and orphans in a document

To use the Widow/Orphan feature, place the insertion point anywhere on the page where you want to begin preventing widows or orphans. From the Layout menu, choose Page, then Keep Text Together. Finally, under Widow/Orphan, select the check box in front of Prevent the first and last lines of paragraphs from being separated across pages. Select OK. WordPerfect prevents widows and orphans from appearing on the page where you invoked the feature until the end of the document. When you want to allow widows and orphans again, repeat this command and clear the check box.

 My printer does not support duplex printing, but I want to print a document double-sided. Can I do this?

You can print a double-sided document even if the printer does not support duplex printing (printing on both sides of the pages at once). Perform the steps outlined below:

1. Select Print from the File menu and select Options.
2. Choose Odd from the Print Odd/Even Pages pop-up list, then click OK.
3. Choose Print from the Print dialog box to print the document.
4. When printing is completed, turn over the odd-numbered pages and reload them into the printer bin. If you are printing on continuous feed paper, keep an empty page before page 1, turn the pages around and feed the paper through the printer again with the printed side on the back.
5. Select Print from the File menu and select Options.
6. Change the Print Odd/Even Pages pop-up list to Even, then click OK.
7. Choose Print from the Print dialog box to print the document again.

The document will now appear with information on both sides of the pages.

Tech Tip: A neat trick for printing on two sides of the page using a laser printer is to remove the pages without rearranging them, leaving page one at the bottom of the stack. If the last page is an odd-numbered page, remove this page from the stack as you put the pages back into the laser printer's feeding tray with the printing face down. Also remember to keep track of which way the top of the page should face. When you print the even pages on a laser printer put page one at the bottom of the stack, select <u>O</u>ptions, Print in <u>R</u>everse Order, and OK. This little trick means you do not have to rearrange pages so page one is at the top, then page three, and so on.

Why doesn't my text from WP Chart or WP Draw print on my Hewlett-Packard DeskJet 1200C printer?

The Windows printer driver for a Hewlett-Packard DeskJet 1200C printer does not print text created in WP Chart or WP Draw. To print text from either of these features, select a WordPerfect printer driver. To select a WordPerfect printer driver, choose Se<u>l</u>ect Printer from the <u>F</u>ile menu, highlight HP DeskJet 1200C with the blue WP in the margin, and choose <u>S</u>elect. If the WordPerfect printer driver is not installed, you need to install it following the steps described under "Should I use a Windows printer driver or a WordPerfect print driver?" earlier in this chapter.

What does the error message "Invalid QCode Received by Printing Process" mean?

If this error message is received when printing a file from WordPerfect, follow these steps:

1. Select <u>O</u>pen in the <u>F</u>ile menu in WordPerfect.

2. Change directories to the WPC20 directory, and select the file SH_SH_.ENV.

3. Select <u>Y</u>es in response to the prompt to convert the file from ASCII DOS Text.

4. When the file opens on the screen, turn on Reveal Codes by pressing ALT+F3. There is an [HRt] code at the end of the one line that shows. Delete this code.

5. Select Close from the File menu, and answer Yes to save changes. Be sure to reselect ASCII Text (DOS) before clicking OK.

If users are on a network, the Network Administrator needs to make this change.

How can I prevent my printers from being updated each time I start WordPerfect 6.0 for Windows from the Network?

After WordPerfect 6.0 for Windows is installed to a server, be sure the network administrator runs the WPCNET Settings program. This program has an icon which is created on their workstation. This icon is similar to the NWPSETUP program from the previous version of WordPerfect. WPCNET Settings allows the administrator to specify certain default user setup information, including printer setup. Once a default printer setup is specified, printer information is no longer updated each time a user goes into WordPerfect. No actual updating is done to the printer itself; fonts are simply updated for the selected printer. Until the administrator runs WPCNET Settings, when you load WordPerfect from a workstation, all printers installed are updated, causing the loading of the program to be slowed considerably.

Why does my computer lock up when I select a Windows printer driver in WordPerfect?

If your system locks up after you choose Select Printer in the File menu and select a Windows printer driver from the Printers list box, check to see if Microsoft Works for Windows has been installed on your machine. Installing this program removes the last five characters of the printer port statement, LPT1:1, in your WIN.INI file. To reenter the five characters, go to the Windows Program Manager. From the File menu select Run and at the command line, type **SYSEDIT** and select OK. Click on the WIN.INI window. Scroll down the file until you reach the [Ports] section. Reenter the missing characters. Select Save from the File menu and then press ALT+F4.

Why do I get the message "Application error WPWINFIL.EXE has caused an error in WIN-OS2, General Protection Fault (GPF) in Module OS/2K286.EXE?"

This message occurs when you select a Windows printer driver under IBM OS/2 2.0 and there is no space in the OS2K286.EXE file. If you are using Novell NetWare, redirect the LPT*x* port to a NetWare print queue by using either the Novell NetWare Requester software or a Capture command. Redirect the WordPerfect printer drivers to the LPT1.OS2 port. This allows the OS/2 print spooler to manage the print job and deliver it to the proper port so that the network can then accept and route the print job to the print queue and printer.

Tables

7

WordPerfect's Table feature lets you create tabular lists of data without the bother of having to define tab settings. Once you define the number of rows or columns you want to appear in your table, a grid appears in your document to separate your entries. Tables offer useful formatting features that can affect the entries in individual cells or entire rows or columns. For instance, you can change column width or row height as well as insert or delete rows or columns. You can define the look of borders around the outside of a table or the lines that separate cell entries. Any of these appearance changes can be made before or after you enter data in your table.

As with other WordPerfect features, the creation of a table inserts hidden codes in your text. The Frustration Busters box that follows describes the codes you should be aware of when you are working with tables.

If you look at the Reveal Codes area of the window, you may be surprised to see how many codes are required for a table. In addition to a table definition code, [Tbl Def], there are codes representing each row in the table, [Row], and each column within a row, [Cell]. There is also a code that indicates the end of a table, [Tbl Off]. You cannot delete the [Row], [Cell], and [Tbl Off] codes. However, the [Tbl Def] code is not protected. Delete the [Tbl Def] code and you can delete the table structure alone or delete the table data as well. Deleting the table structure replaces the [Row] and [Cell] codes with [Tab] and [HPg] and deletes the [Tbl Off] code.

Can I change how the lines around cells in my table look?

Yes, you can add, remove, or change the style of lines around cells in your table. To change the line style, follow these steps:

1. Select the cells whose lines you want to change.

2. Select Lines/Fill from the Table menu or press SHIFT+F12.

3. Select the Current Cell or Selection radio button if you only want to change the lines for the selected cells. If you want to change how the lines look for the entire table, select the Table radio button.

4. Select the format for each line from the drop-down list for that line.

   a. If you selected the Current Cell or Selection radio button, you can select a line style from the Left, Right, Top, Bottom, Inside, and Outside drop-down lists.

   b. If you selected the Table radio button, you can select a line style from the Line Style and Border drop-down lists.

5. Select OK to close the Table Lines/Fill dialog box.

How can I select a tabular column in order to convert it to a table?

To select a tabular column, follow these steps:

1. Start selecting with the first character in the first row of the column. Extend your selection to the last character in the last row of the column, as shown here for selecting the contents of the second column:

Karen	Bridges	26
Katherine	Fergueson	28
Howard	Lash	27
Karl	Manzuk	25

2. Choose Select from the Edit menu.

3. Select Tabular Column.

WordPerfect will select only the entries in the column you want, as shown here:

Karen	Bridges	26
Katherine	Fergueson	28
Howard	Lash	27
Karl	Manzuk	25

I'm working on a table someone else created. The text in some of the cells is boldfaced. When I turn on Reveal Codes, I can't find the boldfacing code. Why?

The text is bold because of a table format, rather than because of a font formatting code. Here's how you remove the boldfacing from the table:

1. Select the cells from which you want to remove boldfacing.

2. Select F**o**rmat from the T**a**ble menu, or press CTRL+F12 to open the Format dialog box.

   The dialog box options that are available to you depend on which of the radio buttons is selected at the top of the dialog box—C**e**ll, Col**u**mn, R**o**w, or T**a**ble. Each radio button displays a different set of dialog box elements, since the features that can be set for each option are slightly different. If you select only a few cells, the C**e**ll radio button is selected and the dialog box looks like the one shown in Figure 7-1.

3. Clear the **B**old check box in the Appearance section. If there are other font formats you want to remove or apply, also clear or select those check boxes.

4. Select OK to return to your document, then repeat these steps as often as necessary to remove the boldfacing from all of the cells that use it.

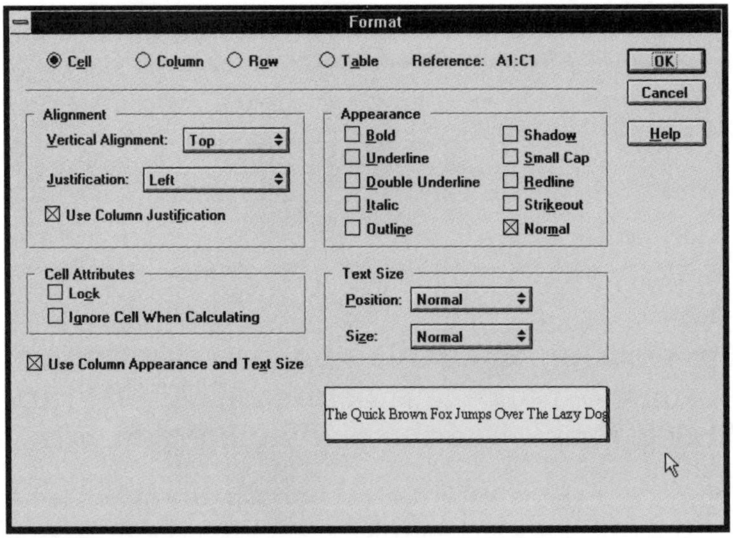

FIGURE 7-1   The Format dialog box for formatting table cells

I want to change the justification of text in my entire table. How do I do this?

The easiest way to change the justification of text in all cells of a table is by changing the table format. To do this:

1. Select the entire table.
2. Select Format from the Table menu.
3. Select the Cell radio button at the top of the dialog box.
4. Select a justification from the Justification pop-up list, then select OK.

My table extends across three pages. The first three rows of the table are repeated at the top of the second and third pages of the table. How can I stop them from repeating?

The first three rows are repeating on each page because they are marked as header rows. To confirm this, put the insertion point in any cell in one of these three rows and look at the Status Bar. If the row is marked as a header row, you will see an asterisk (*) next to the cell address. Only cells in header rows show asterisks next to their addresses in the Status Bar.

Here's how to make these header rows normal rows again:

1. Select all three rows.
2. Select Format from the Table menu or press CTRL+F12.

    The Format dialog box appears, with the Row radio button selected. The four radio buttons at the top of this dialog box set which dialog box elements appear. Your dialog box will look like the one shown in Figure 7-2.
3. Clear the Header Row check box in the lower-left corner of the Format dialog box.
4. Select OK to return to your document.

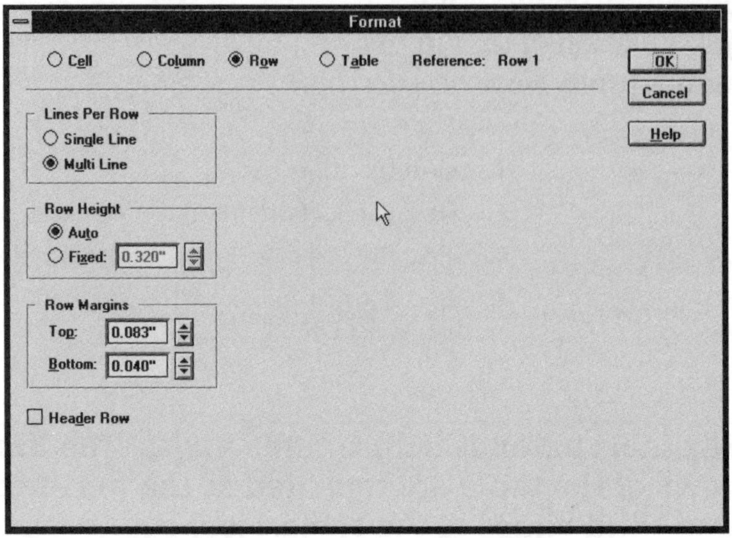

FIGURE 7-2   The Format dialog box for formatting rows in a table

How can I make sure that all text entered in a table will use the same font attributes?

Font attributes, such as bold and italic, can be applied to table cells so that all text entered in those table cells has those attributes. To apply the formatting, follow these steps:

1. Select the entire table, or simply the cells in the table you want to use this formatting.

2. Select Format from the Table menu.

3. Select the Cell radio button at the top of the dialog box.

4. You can now select the check boxes for font attributes in the Appearance area of the dialog box, or select position and size settings from the Text Style area. When you are finished, select OK to return to your document.

Is there any way to resize column widths without opening the Format dialog box?

Yes, you can resize columns with the mouse in one of two ways: using the table-sizing arrow or using the table-sizing markers in the Ruler Bar.

Here's how to change the width of a column by using the table-sizing arrow:

1. Position the mouse on the line between two columns. When your mouse is positioned correctly, the pointer becomes a two-headed arrow, like the one shown next. This is the table-sizing arrow:

2. Drag the line between columns to where you want it to be. To increase the width of the column, drag it away from the other side of the column. To decrease the width of the column, drag it towards the other side of the column.

When you drag the line between the columns, you see a dotted line that indicates where the column will extend to, as shown in Figure 7-3. This dotted line is called a table-sizing guide. When the Ruler Bar is displayed, you can use the table-sizing guide to see exactly where the line will end up. The table-sizing guide appears even when the Ruler Bar is not displayed.

To change the width of columns by using the table-sizing markers in the Ruler Bar, follow these steps:

1. Select <u>R</u>uler Bar from the <u>V</u>iew menu, or press ALT+SHIFT+F3. The Ruler Bar looks like this:

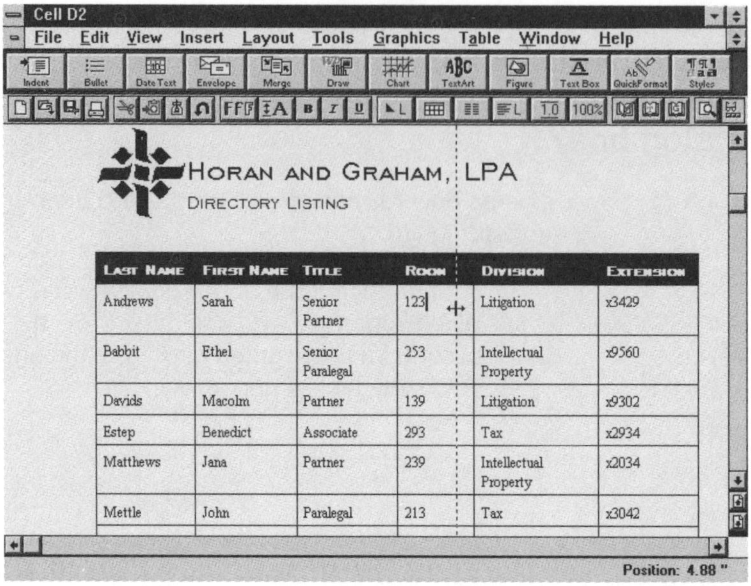

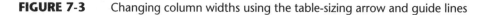

FIGURE 7-3   Changing column widths using the table-sizing arrow and guide lines

The upside-down triangles at the top of the Ruler Bar are table-sizing markers. These markers indicate the edge of columns.

2. Drag a table-sizing marker to move that side of the column, changing its width. For example, you could drag the table-sizing marker between the first and second columns to the left to make the first column narrower.

I set tabs for my table. When I press TAB, however, my insertion point moves to the next cell instead of the tab stop. How can I make the insertion point move to the next tab stop instead?

Pressing TAB in a table moves the insertion point to the next cell, and pressing SHIFT+TAB moves it to the previous cell. In order to insert a tab in a table, you need to insert a hard tab. Hard tabs move the insertion point to the next tab stop. However, the text does not use the alignment of that tab stop. Instead, you specify which type of alignment to use, depending on how you enter the tab:

- To enter a left tab, press CTRL+TAB.
- To enter a decimal tab, press ALT+SHIFT+F7.
- To enter a back tab, press CTRL+SHIFT+F7.

Tech Tip: You can also enter hard tabs by selecting Lines from the Layout menu, then Other Codes. Select the radio button for the type of hard tab you want to enter, then select OK.

Can I perform calculations using the data in my table?

You can enter formulas into WordPerfect tables that perform calculations using the data in the table or in floating cells. You can create formulas yourself using the operators, or you can use some of WordPerfect's predefined formulas, called *functions*.

WordPerfect offers two ways to enter formulas into a cell in a table: by using the Table Formula Feature Bar or by entering the formula in the cell itself. To enter a formula in a table using the Formula Bar, follow these steps:

1. Put your insertion point in the cell in which you want the formula.

2. Select Formula Bar from the Table menu, or right-click the table and select Formula Bar. The Formula Bar looks like this:

3. Click the Formula Edit text box next to the checkmark in the Formula Bar.

4. Enter the formula you want to calculate.

WordPerfect uses the standard mathematical and logical operators, as shown in Table 7-1. If you want to use one of WordPerfect's predefined functions, select the Functions button in the Formula Bar, select the function from the Functions list box, and select Insert.

Operator	Operation	Example
+	Addition	2+2=4
- (with no number after it)	Negation	-1+1=0
-	Subtraction	5-3=2
/	Division	10/2=5
*	Multiplication	3*3=9
%	Remainder	13/5=3
% (without a number after it)	Percent	13%=.13
	Power	2^3=8
! (without an equal sign after it)	Factorial	5!=120
=	Equal to	4=2+2
>	Greater than	4>3
<	Less than	3<4
<> or !=	Not equal to	4<>2
>=	Greater than or equal to	4>=4 4>=3
<=	Less than or equal to	4<=4 4<=5
& (AND)	Logical And	2+2=4&1+1=2 is true
! (NOT)	Logical Not	1+2!=4 is true
| (OR)	Logical Or	1+1=2|1+1=3 is true
^^ (XOR)	Logical Exclusive Or	1+1=2^^1+2=3 is false

TABLE 7-1   Mathematical and Logical Operators That WordPerfect 6 for Windows Supports

5. Select the checkmark button next to the Formula Edit text box to insert the formula into the current cell.

Tech Tip: WordPerfect's tables allow you to add formulas just as spreadsheets do. However, in spreadsheets you start a formula with + or a character indicating that you are entering a formula. If you do this when entering a formula in a WordPerfect table, the formula will not be calculated, since WordPerfect will take this to mean that you are entering text.

To enter formulas directly into the cell, follow these steps:

1. Select Cell Formula Entry from the Table menu. When this option is selected, a checkmark appears in front of it in the menu.

2. Put your insertion point in the cell in which you want to enter the formula.

3. Type the formula.

4. Press TAB or click another cell to move out of the cell. When the insertion point leaves the cell containing the formula, the formula's result is calculated and displayed.

WordPerfect uses the standard order of precedence, shown in Table 7-2. Of course, you can always change the order of the calculation by putting parentheses around the part of the formula you want to be calculated first.

To enter the predefined functions in a table, follow these steps:

1. Put your insertion point in the cell where you want the formula.

2. Select Formula Bar from the Table menu, or right-click the mouse in the table and select Formula Bar.

3. Select Functions in the Formula Bar.

1st	! (factorial), % (percent)
2nd	! (not), - (negation)
3rd	^ (power)
4th	*, /, % (remainder)
5th	+
6th	<, <+, >, >=
7th	=, <>, !=
8th	&
9th	^
10th		
11th	()
12th	,

TABLE 7-2 Order of Operator Precedence

4. Select the category of functions you want to see from the List drop-down list in the Table Functions dialog box. The Functions list box will show the available functions for the selected category.

5. Highlight the function you want to use, and select Insert. The function appears in the Formula Edit text box. The first argument keyword is selected.

6. Enter the appropriate data, or cell and range addresses to replace the keywords.

7. Click the checkmark to insert the formula into the cell. The cell displays the solution of the function.

I am creating a form using tables. There is some text that I don't want edited, such as the headings and instructions. Is there a way to prevent data in my table from being edited?

Yes, you can lock cells to prevent users from editing the data in those cells. To lock cells, follow these steps:

1. Put your insertion point in the cell you want to lock or select several cells to lock them all at once.

2. Select Format from the Table menu, or press CTRL+F12.

3. Select the Cell radio button if it is not selected.

4. Select the Lock check box in the Cell Attributes area.

5. Select OK to return to the document.

Is there some way to select my entire table without having to drag the mouse across it all?

Yes. WordPerfect has shortcuts for selecting the entire table, or a row or column, using the mouse.
To select the entire table:

1. Move the mouse toward the top or left side of a cell until the mouse pointer becomes an arrow.

2. Triple-click the mouse.

To select the entire row:

1. Move the mouse toward the left side of a cell in the row you want to select until the mouse pointer becomes an arrow pointing to the left.

2. Double-click the mouse.

To select the entire column:

1. Move the mouse toward the top of a cell in the column you want to select until the mouse pointer becomes an arrow pointing upward.

2. Double-click the mouse.

I want to insert a page break in the middle of text in a cell. Is this possible?

No, text within a cell cannot be split by a page break. Page breaks can only be inserted immediately before or after a row in a table, as shown in Figure 7-4. If you insert a page break in a cell by pressing CTRL+ENTER, the page break is inserted above that row, so that the entire row moves to the next page.

I'm trying to enter data in a table someone else created. No text appears when I type in one of the rows. Why does this happen, and what can I do to make text appear?

The row you cannot see data in may have a fixed row height. When a row has a fixed row height, it cannot expand to display all of its contents. Therefore, when you enter more data, it simply isn't being displayed. You need to change the row height to Auto, which does expand the row height to display the cells' contents. Here's how to change the row height:

1. Put your insertion point in a cell in the row in which the problem is occurring.

2. Select Format from the Table menu, or press CTRL+F12.

3. Select the R<u>o</u>w radio button at the top of the Format dialog box.

4. Select the Au<u>t</u>o radio button in the Row Height area, then select OK.

You should now be able to see all of the text that you've been adding to cells in this row.

You can't do this:

But you can do this:

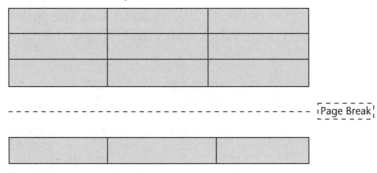

FIGURE 7-4 Possible and impossible page break insertions in a table

Tech Tip: A Hidden Text code will appear in Reveal Codes that holds all the extra text that didn't fit in the cell with the Fixed Row Height. When you set the Row Height to Auto, all that text will appear and the Hidden Text code will disappear.

Can I add rows to my table without using the menu?

Yes, you can easily add rows to a WordPerfect table without using the menu. To do so, move the insertion point to the last cell of the table and press TAB. The insertion point will move to the first cell in the new row at the end of the table. Continue pressing TAB in the last cell of the table until you have added all the rows you want.

I'm working with a table someone else created. The text in one column is right-justified, but I don't see the right-justification code when I turn on Reveal Codes. How can I change the justification?

The right-justification has been applied as a column format. To change the justification, you need to change the column format:

1. Put your insertion point in a cell in the column whose justification you want to change.

2. Select Format from the Table menu, or press CTRL+F12.

3. Select the Column radio button at the top of the Format dialog box.

4. Select the type of justification you want to use from the Justification drop-down list in the Alignment area, then select OK.

I tried right-aligning my table by selecting the entire page and choosing right-alignment. This didn't affect my table's position. How do I change the table's position on the page?

The justification you set for a document or a paragraph has no effect on the position of a table on the page. To change the justification for the table, follow these steps:

1. Put your insertion point in the table.

2. Select Format from the Table menu, or press CTRL+F12.

3. Select the Table radio button at the top of the Format dialog box if it is not selected.

4. Select the justification you want to use—Left, Right, Center, or Full—from the drop-down list under Table Position. You can also select From Left Edge, then enter a measurement in the text box after the pop-up button, in order to position the table at a specific distance from the left edge of the paper.

5. Select OK to return to the document and reposition the table.

The table's horizontal position on the page is now changed. This does not affect the table's vertical position on the page.

Can I have table gridlines as the default so that I don't have to turn them on each time?

Yes, by following these steps:

1. Select Preferences from the File menu.

2. Select the Display icon by double-clicking it, or highlighting it and pressing ENTER.

3. Select the Document radio button at the top of the dialog box if necessary.

4. Select the Table Gridlines check box in the Show area of the dialog box.

5. Select OK then Close to return to your document.

Can I insert additional rows in the middle of my table rather than at the end?

Yes, if you use the menus. Follow these steps to add rows:

1. Put your insertion point in a cell above or below where you want to add rows.

2. Select Insert from the Table menu, opening the Insert Columns/Rows dialog box.

3. Select the Rows radio button in the Insert area, then enter the number of rows you want to insert in the text box next to this radio button.

4. Select the Before or After radio button in the Placement area to determine whether the new rows are added before or after the current one.

5. Select OK to return to your document and insert the rows.

I want my table to extend to both margins, even when I delete a column. What can I do?

If you set the table's position to full, WordPerfect will automatically resize it so that it extends the full distance between the left and right margins. Here's how to do this:

1. Put your insertion point in the table.

2. Select Format from the Table menu or press CTRL+F12.

3. Select the Table radio button at the top of the Format dialog box.

4. Select Full from the drop-down list in the Table Position area of the dialog box.

5. Select OK to return to the document. From now on, when you add or delete columns, WordPerfect will automatically resize your table to make sure it still extends from the left to right margins.

I used Su_m from the T_able menu to insert a function that sums a column in my table. However, it's also adding the year that identifies the column into the final sum. How do I prevent this?

The easiest way to prevent WordPerfect from summing the column header in with the column entries is to tell it that you want the contents of that cell ignored in calculations. Here's how to do this:

1. Place the insertion point in the cell you don't want included in the calculations.
2. Select F_ormat from the T_able menu.
3. Select the C_ell radio button at the top of the Format dialog box, if it is not selected.
4. Select the I_gnore Cell When Calculating check box in the Cell Attributes area.
5. Select OK to return to the document.

Part of my table got pushed to the second page, even though I didn't insert a page break. Why is my table breaking off like that?

You probably have more text in the first row on the second page than can fit on the first page. Each table row must be entirely on the same page, because WordPerfect cannot put page breaks inside a row. Therefore, when a cell in a row has more text than can fit on the remaining page, WordPerfect inserts a soft page break to push that row and the remainder of the table to the next page.

If having your table split between two pages is a problem, you have two choices. You can either delete some of the text from your table so that it can fit on one page, or you can move the entire table to a new page. Inserting a page break before the table moves the table to the top of the next page. If the reason the table could not fit on one page was because there was too much text before the table on the page, this will allow the table to appear all on one page, because there is no preceding text.

Are there any keyboard shortcuts to quickly insert or delete a single row in a table?

Yes, WordPerfect does offers some keyboard shortcuts for working with individual table rows:

- To insert a row above the current one, press ALT+INS.
- To insert a row below the current one, press ALT+SHIFT+INS.
- To delete the entire current row, press ALT+DEL.

What can I insert in a table cell?

WordPerfect supports several types of entries in table cells, including:

- Text
- Numbers
- Formulas
- Alphanumeric characters
- Graphics

For example, Figure 7-5 shows a table that contains numbers, graphics, formulas, and text.

Can I insert WordPerfect characters in names when naming things in tables?

Yes, you can use WordPerfect characters when creating names for tables, floating cells, cells, ranges, columns, and rows. Use WordPerfect characters to add characters that are not available through your keyboard. These characters include letters from other alphabets and symbols. To create a name using WordPerfect characters, follow these steps:

1. Select the table, floating cell, cells, range, column, or row you want to name or rename.
2. Choose Names from the Table menu.
3. Select Create to name the object, or Edit to rename it.

```
┌─────────────────────────────────────────────────────────────┐
│  ═        WordPerfect - [c:\wpwin60\wpdocs\sum]         ▼ │▲│ │
│ ═ File  Edit  View  Insert  Layout  Tools  Graphics  Table  Window  Help      │▲│ │
│ [Indent][Bullet][Date Text][Envelope][Merge][Draw][Chart][TextArt][Figure][Text Box][QuickFormat][Styles] │
│ [][][][][][][]FFF[A][B][I][U][►L][▦][▦][▦L][1.0][115%][][][][][] │
│                                                               │
│  ┌──────────────────────────────────────────────────────┐   │
│  │                                                        │   │
│  │    🌸        ALL-SEASON              🌸               │   │
│  │             GARDEN SHOP                                │   │
│  │                                                        │   │
│  ├──────────┬─────────┬─────────┬─────────┬─────────────┤   │
│  │          │   Jan   │   Feb   │   Mar   │    1st Qtr   │   │
│  ├──────────┼─────────┼─────────┼─────────┼─────────────┤   │
│  │Sales - Garden │$98,765 │$120,987│$160,789│  $380,541  │   │
│  ├──────────┼─────────┼─────────┼─────────┼─────────────┤   │
│  │Sales - Plants │$45,321 │$58,765 │$98,754 │  $202,840  │   │
│  ├──────────┼─────────┼─────────┼─────────┼─────────────┤   │
│  │Sales - Tractors│$2,300 │$25,000 │$89,000 │  $116,300  │   │
│  ├──────────┼─────────┼─────────┼─────────┼─────────────┤   │
│  │          │$146,386 │$204,752 │$348,543│  $699,681  │   │
│  └──────────┴─────────┴─────────┴─────────┴─────────────┘   │
│                                                    I          │
│                                                               │
│ Arial Regular 12 pt           Insert        Select  Pg 1 Ln 4.21" Pos 1" │
└─────────────────────────────────────────────────────────────┘
```

FIGURE 7-5   A table containing different types of entries

4. Enter the name in the Enter Name Manually text box, pressing CTRL+W to open the WordPerfect Character dialog box. Use this dialog box as you normally do to insert the WordPerfect characters.

5. Make any other setting changes, then select OK twice to return to your document.

Is there some way to get WordPerfect to create a series of values in a table automatically, as my spreadsheet program can?

Yes. You can use the Data Fill feature to have WordPerfect create a series of numbers for an entire row or column based on a pattern. You create this pattern by entering values in at least two cells in the column or row that are part of the pattern you want to use.

For example, if you want to create a column of year numbers, you could enter 1992 in the first cell in the column, and 1993 in the next cell. After entering the values that start the pattern, you must select those cells, and all of the empty cells where you want WordPerfect to make entries extending the pattern, as shown in Figure 7-6.

Then select Data Fill in the Table menu or press CTRL+SHIFT+F12. WordPerfect will automatically extend the pattern created by the first entries to all of the empty cells that you selected.

You can use the Data Fill feature with values other than numbers. You can use days of the week, months, quarters, and Roman numerals. When you are using these alternate values, you can establish the pattern using only a single entry. For example, you can enter a single month and then use Data Fill as just described. WordPerfect will automatically extend the series to include every month. Figure 7-7 shows the result of entering a month in one cell and having WordPerfect add the rest of the months in the year automatically.

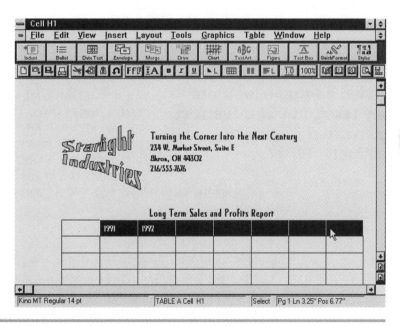

FIGURE 7-6   Selecting cells to use with the Data Fill feature

![Screenshot of WordPerfect table interface]

Title bar: Cell C3

Menu: File Edit View Insert Layout Tools Graphics Table Window Help

Formula bar: TABLE A.A2 X ✓

Toolbar: Sum | Functions... | Names... | View Error | Calculate | Data Fill | Copy Formula | Close

Monthly Sales Report For 1993

Month	Akron Division	San Diego Division	Yokohama Division
January			
February		⇧	
March			
April			
May			
June			
July			

Status bar: Kino MT Regular 14 pt   TABLE A Cell A8   Select   Pg 1 Ln 5.66" Pos 1.08"

FIGURE 7-7   A table after using Data Fill to add more month names

I tried adding a footnote to my table, but WordPerfect converted it into an endnote. Why?

WordPerfect does not allow footnotes in table header rows, and converts the footnote into an endnote when you save or close the footnote window. If you need to use a footnote, you will need to insert it in another row of the table, or make the table header row into a normal row, using these steps:

1. Select the table header rows.

2. Select Format from the Table menu or press CTRL+F12.

3. Clear the Header Row check box in the lower-left corner of the Format dialog box.

4. Select OK to return to your document.

What does it mean when I see ?? or ERR in a table cell?

When you see either ?? or ERR in a table cell, that cell contains a formula that WordPerfect cannot calculate. The ?? means that the formula in the cell is invalid. To correct this, you need to edit the formula so that it is correct. To edit the formula, follow these steps:

1. Move the insertion point to the cell displaying ??.
2. Select Formula Bar in the Table menu.
3. Click the Formula Edit text box to the right of the checkmark.
4. Edit the formula, then choose Close.

ERR means that the formula in the cell references a cell with an invalid formula. You need to edit the formula in the referenced cell in order to make it valid, as just described. The referenced cell displays ??, since its formula is invalid.

How can I find out what is wrong with a formula displaying ?? or ERR?

WordPerfect can provide a brief description of what is causing your formula to display these error messages. To see these messages, select the View Error button in the Table Formula Feature Bar. Select OK to close the message box.

Remember, you can display the Table Formula Feature Bar by selecting Formula Bar in the Table menu. Once you know the source of the error in your formula, you need to edit the formula to correct the error. See the question "Can I perform calculations using the data in my table?"

What is a floating cell and why would I use it?

Floating cells take the features of a table and extend them to normal text. You can insert formulas into floating cells. Since floating cells appear as part of normal text, this means you can include formulas in part of your normal text, instead of just as a part of a table. For example, in Figure 7-8, the pay rate and total pay in the last line are in floating cells.

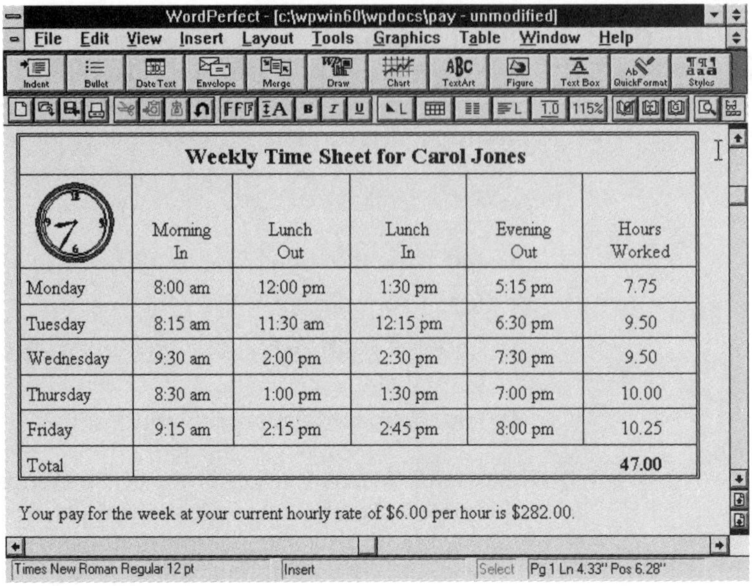

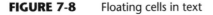

WordPerfect - [c:\wpwin60\wpdocs\pay - unmodified]
File Edit View Insert Layout Tools Graphics Table Window Help
Indent Bullet Date Text Envelope Merge Draw Chart TextArt Figure Text Box QuickFormat Styles
Weekly Time Sheet for Carol Jones
Morning In
Lunch Out
Lunch In
Evening Out
Hours Worked
Monday 8:00 am 12:00 pm 1:30 pm 5:15 pm 7.75
Tuesday 8:15 am 11:30 am 12:15 pm 6:30 pm 9.50
Wednesday 9:30 am 2:00 pm 2:30 pm 7:30 pm 9.50
Thursday 8:30 am 1:00 pm 1:30 pm 7:00 pm 10.00
Friday 9:15 am 2:15 pm 2:45 pm 8:00 pm 10.25
Total 47.00
Your pay for the week at your current hourly rate of $6.00 per hour is $282.00.
Times New Roman Regular 12 pt
Insert
Select
Pg 1 Ln 4.33" Pos 6.28"

FIGURE 7-8 Floating cells in text

You can insert anything in floating cells that you can in a table. To create a floating cell, follow these steps:

1. Put your insertion point where you want the floating cell to be.
2. Select Create from the Table menu.
3. Select the Floating Cell option button, and select OK.

You will not see any markings indicating the floating cell's boundaries unless you select Reveal Codes from the View menu. While you cannot use lines and borders to format the floating cell as you do tables, you can name the floating cell, or change the number type used to format any numbers inserted in the floating cell.

To name or edit the name of a floating cell, follow these steps:

1. Select Names from the Table menu.
2. Select the Table/Floating Cell list box; highlight the floating cell you want to name.

3. Select Edit.

4. Type the name in the Name list box, or edit the existing name.

5. Select OK, then Close to return to your document.

To change the number type of a floating cell, follow these steps:

1. Move your insertion point to the floating cell whose number type you want to change. You may want to Reveal Codes to make sure that the insertion point is between the floating cell codes.

2. Select Number Type from the Table menu or press ALT+F12.

3. Select the radio button for the number type you want to use from the Available Types area of the dialog box, then select OK to return to your document.

Is there a way to repeat the second row of my table at the top of every subsequent page?

Yes, you can format your second row as a Header Row by following these steps:

1. Position your cursor in the second row.

2. Select Format from the Table menu or press CTRL+F12.

3. Select the Row radio button.

4. Select the Header Row check box and OK.

Graphics

When used effectively, graphics and specially enhanced text can highlight important facts and add visual interest to everyday documents. WordPerfect allows you to create dazzling pages for any occasion by allowing you to incorporate clip art from WordPerfect and other sources, and by including two special programs: WordPerfect Draw, which lets you edit a graphic, and TextArt, which lets you create special effects with text.

WordPerfect provides three ways to anchor a graphics box. A *graphics box anchor* controls how a box moves with its surrounding text and where it is positioned as you edit your document. You can set the type of anchor by selecting Position from the Graphics Box Feature Bar or the graphics box's QuickMenu. The options under Box Placement in the Position dialog box set the anchor type for a graphics box. Figure 8-1 shows some of the position options for the different attachment types. You have the following choices:

- **Put Box on Current Page**—This anchor type keeps the box in the same position on the page. Position options are relative to the sides of the document's margin or page.

- **Put Box in Current Paragraph**—This anchor type keeps the box in the same relative position to the top of the current paragraph. The position options are set where the graphics box appears within the current paragraph.

- **Treat Box as Character**—This anchor type treats the box just like a character. When you have a graphics box anchored to a character, as that box's character position moves, so does the graphic image. A character-anchored graphics box has position options that move it relative to the character position of the graphics box.

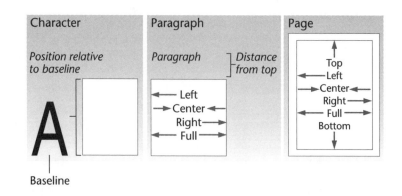

FIGURE 8-1   Different anchor and position options

What graphics formats does WordPerfect 6.0 for Windows support?

WordPerfect for Windows can import the following graphics file formats:

WordPerfect Graphics (.WPG)
Bitmaps (.BMP)
Computer Graphics Metafiles (.CGM)
Designer (.DRW)
AutoCAD (.DXF)
Encapsulated Postscript (.EPS)
HP Computer Graphics Language (.HPG)
PC Paintbrush (.PCX)
Lotus PIC (.PIC)
Macintosh Picture Format (.PIC)
Tagged Image Format (.TIF)
Windows Metafiles (.WMF)
Truevision Targa (.TGA)

You can also find out which graphic image formats WordPerfect supports with the Insert Image dialog box. To do this, select Figure from the Graphics menu. Scroll through the List Files of the Type drop-down list located at the bottom of the Insert Image box. This list includes the formats listed above as well as any others that were added since WordPerfect 6.0 for Windows was initially released.

Tech Tip: If you import a .CGM file from Freelance Graphics for Windows into WordPerfect for Windows and the spacing of the text condenses in the graphic, a solution is available if you have a copy of DrawPerfect. Copy the WP.DRS file from the DrawPerfect directory into the WordPerfect for Windows directory called WPC20. The WP.DRS file included with DrawPerfect is larger and can handle more detailed graphics.

How do I insert a graphic into my document?

To insert a graphic image into a document choose Figure from the Graphics menu, select the file and choose OK. WordPerfect adds the selected image to the document and displays the Graphics Box Feature Bar as shown here:

III 8-1

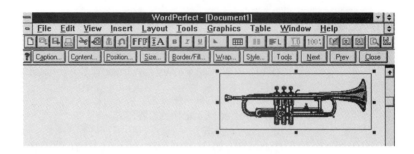

At this point, you can use the Graphics pull-down menu, the graphics box's QuickMenu, and the Graphics Box Feature Bar to change the appearance and placement of the image. Like other Feature Bars, you can select one of the buttons by pressing ALT+SHIFT and the underlined letter.

Can I see the graphic image before I add it to a document?

Previewing the graphic image you are about to add ensures that you select the correct graphic. You can open a Viewer that shows the image in a file when you are selecting the image to add. To add the Viewer, select the View button in the Insert Image dialog box. Figure 8-2 shows a Viewer displaying the contents of CHEETAH.WPG. Once you display the Viewer, you can continue to use the Insert Image dialog box to change which file you are

FIGURE 8-2   Viewer showing the contents of a graphics file

highlighting. The Viewer remains onscreen until you select the file you want or you close the Viewer using its Control menu box.

Tech Tip: If you accidentally select the wrong file to add, select the Content button in the Graphics Box Feature Bar and enter a new name in the Filename text box. You can click the list button to open another dialog box to select the file and, from this dialog box, select the View button to see the graphic image you are selecting.

I just opened a document with a graphic. How do I get the Graphics Box Feature Bar to appear?

When you open a document containing a graphics box, the Graphics Box Feature Bar will not appear unless you have already displayed it while using another document. If you want to display the Graphics Box Feature Bar, do one of the following:

- Right-click a graphics box to open its QuickMenu, then select Feature Bar.

- Select Edit Box from the Graphic menu.

- Press SHIFT+F11.

With the last two options, if you have one graphics box in the document, that box is selected and the Graphics Box Feature Bar appears. If you have more than one graphics box in the document, you must select which box to edit from the Box Find dialog box. When you select OK, the box is selected and the Graphics Box Feature Bar appears.

How do I choose a graphics box style?

The graphics box style is set by the command used to add the box. Graphics box styles are designed to hold certain types of contents, although nearly any style box can contain any type of entry. For example, a text box is set to contain text, and an equation box is set to contain an equation that you add with the Equation Editor. The Figure, Text, and Equation commands in the Graphics menu set the graphic image you are adding to the figure, text, and equation graphics box styles respectively. When you add TextArt, a chart, a drawing, or other OLE object, they use an OLE Box graphics box style, which is the one graphics box style you cannot modify. OLE Objects automatically use the OLE Object graphics box style when you add them to a WordPerfect document. You can also set the graphics box style yourself when you add a box, by selecting Custom Box in the Graphics menu, selecting the graphics box style from the Style Name list box, and OK. WordPerfect's initial graphics box styles and some of their settings are listed here:

Style Name	Initial Settings
Figure	Box Placement: Paragraph Content Type: Empty Height: Automatic Horizontal Position: Against the right margin Vertical Position: 0" from the top of the paragraph Width: 3.25" Lines and Shading: Thin line on all sides
Text	Box Placement: Paragraph Content Type: Text Height: Automatic Horizontal Position: Against the right margin Vertical Position: 0" from the top of the paragraph Width: 3.25" Lines and Shading: Thick line at the top and bottom
Equation	Box Placement: Paragraph Content Type: Equation Height: Automatic Horizontal Position: Full from the left margin to the right margin Vertical Position: 0" from the top of the paragraph Width: Full Lines and Shading: None
Table	Box Placement: Paragraph Content Type: Empty Height: Automatic Horizontal Position: Against the right margin Vertical Position: 0" from the top of the paragraph Width: 3.25" Lines and Shading: Thick line at the top and bottom

Style Name	Initial Settings
User	Box Placement: Paragraph Content Type: Empty Height: Automatic Horizontal Position: Against the right margin Vertical Position: 0" from the top of the paragraph Width: 3.25" Lines and Shading: None
Button	Box Placement: Character Content Type: Empty Height: Automatic Horizontal Position: Character Vertical Position: Baseline Width: 1" Lines and Shading: Enhanced like buttons in the Button Bar
Watermark	Box Placement: Page Content Type: Image Height: Full Horizontal Position: Full Vertical Position: Full Width: Full Lines and Shading: None
Inline Equation	Box Placement: Character Content Type: Equation Height: Automatic Horizontal Position: Character Vertical Position: Baseline Width: Automatic Lines and Shading: None
OLE Box	Box Placement: Paragraph Content Type: Empty Height: Automatic Horizontal Position: Against the right margin Vertical Position: 0" from the top of the paragraph Width: 3.25" Lines and Shading: Thin line on all sides

Tech Tip: You can set which graphics box styles appear in the Graphics menu. Select Graphics Styles from the Graphics menu, then select the Menu button. From the next dialog box, select the check boxes for the graphics box styles you want to appear in the Graphics menu. When you are done, select OK and Close. The graphics box styles selected by the check marks are in the top part of the Graphics menu.

How can I make a graphic image larger or smaller?

You can resize a graphic image using the keyboard or mouse. When you select a graphics box, its borders have small boxes called *handles* as shown here:

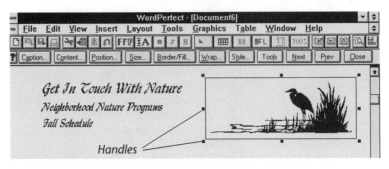

To resize a graphic image, use your mouse to drag one of these handles so the dotted outline is the size you want the graphics box to become. Dragging the handle towards the center of the image makes the graphic smaller and dragging the handle away from the center increases the size of the image. When you release the mouse, the box is resized to fit the dotted outline.

If you want to set the box to a specific height or width, select the Size button in the Graphics Box Feature Bar. You can select a radio button to set the size to fully use the area, be a predetermined height or width, or to be based on the size of the image. This is the only way to resize a graphics box without a mouse.

How can I make the graphics display on my screen faster so I can edit my document's text more efficiently?

Because graphics take some time to draw, the answer is not in getting the graphics to display faster, but rather in getting them not to display at all. To hide them from view, choose Graphics from the View menu and remove the check mark which indicates that WordPerfect is displaying the contents of graphics boxes. WordPerfect will print the graphics in your document even when they are hidden. Hiding graphics also hides OLE Objects that are presented graphically, such as TextArt.

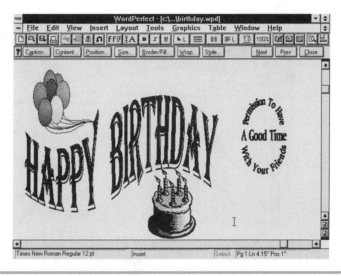

FIGURE 8-3   Document using text enhancements created with TextArt

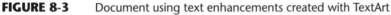

How can I add special effects to my text?

WordPerfect comes with a separate application called TextArt
which allows you to add special effects to your text. TextArt can
enhance the appearance of text up to 58 characters (including
spaces) on as many as three lines. With TextArt you can change the
shape, font, style, justification, rotation, width, height, and units of
text. You can also make the text all capital letters or add effects like
outlines, fills, and shadows. Figure 8-3 shows some of these effects.
To add text embellished with TextArt, follow these steps:

1. Select TextArt from the Graphics menu.

2. Type the text to embellish in the Enter Text box.

3. Select the embellishments you want for the text. Figure
    8-4 shows a TextArt screen and the options on this dialog
    box.

4. Choose Exit & Return to WordPerfect from the File menu
    when you are finished.

5. Choose Yes to return to your document with the TextArt
    image in your document.

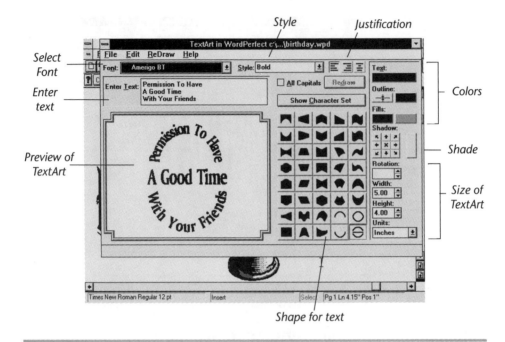

FIGURE 8-4   TextArt window for creating embellished text

Can I update my TextArt image within my WordPerfect document while still working in TextArt?

Yes, you can keep the image in your document up to date by selecting Update WordPerfect from the File menu. The version in your WordPerfect document will be updated while you remain in TextArt.

How do I change the text that I added with TextArt?

First, select the TextArt image that you want to edit, then choose Edit TextArt Object from the Edit menu. You can also double-click the image to edit it. Then you can use the TextArt window like the one in Figure 8-4 to change what appears in the document.

I have a choice to store an image in a document or by itself on disk. Why is this?

A graphic in a graphics box can be stored either in the document or in its own separate file. When a box uses an image stored on disk, the document containing the box does not have to retain a picture of the graphic when the document is saved; it simply points to the actual graphic file. You might choose to save the image on disk for the following reasons:

- You want the document file to be smaller. It will be smaller since it does not contain the image.

- You want the document to always use the updated version of the graphic. Every time you open a document using a graphic image from a disk file, WordPerfect retrieves the most recent copy of the image from the image disk file.

- The image files are always available and in a .WPG format.

To set a graphics box to use an image from disk, select the Content button from the Graphics Box Feature Bar or QuickMenu, then select Image on Disk from the Content pop-up list and OK. You need to select Yes when prompted if you want to delete the box's current contents. If the image is not from a .WPG file, you need to supply a filename to store the .WPG version of the image. If your graphics file is in another format, you should supply another filename for this prompt. If you use the same filename, WordPerfect replaces the graphic image with the image saved in a .WPG file format. Other programs cannot edit this graphic image.

How do I get a graphics box to use the newer version of the graphics file?

If the image used in a graphics box has changed, you need to tell WordPerfect to update the version of the graphics file included in the document. The steps for doing this are different when the image is saved on a disk versus saved within the document. You can tell where the image is stored by selecting Content from the Graphics Box Feature Bar or the box's QuickMenu. The image is saved within a document when the Content pop-up list is set to Image and the image is retrieved from a file when the Content pop-up list is set to Image on Disk. If the graphic image is saved within the document, select Content from the Graphics Box Feature Bar or the box's Quick Menu, make some change to the entry in the Filename text box, and select OK. If all of your files are on the same disk, you can change the text box entry without affecting where the file comes from by deleting the drive letter and colon at the beginning. After you select OK, you will need to select Yes to confirm that you want to delete the box's current contents to replace it with the updated file.

If the graphic image is saved in a separate file, you have two choices. You can close then reopen the document. WordPerfect updates the graphics boxes when you reopen the document. You can also open the image in WordPerfect Draw. To do this, select Content from the Graphics Box Feature Bar or the box's QuickMenu and select Edit, or select Edit Figure or Activate WP Graphic 2.1 Object from the graphics box's QuickMenu. When you open the image in WordPerfect Draw, it is the updated image which is also updated when you leave WordPerfect Draw to return to your document.

I have pieces of clip art that do not come with WordPerfect. Can I still use them in WordPerfect?

WordPerfect accepts many graphics file formats as well as its own, and you can use any clip art that is in one of WordPerfect's acceptable graphics file formats. (See the question "What graphics formats does WordPerfect 6.0 for Windows support?" earlier in this chapter for a list of the acceptable formats.) For example, the documents in this book include graphics from CorelDRAW, Presentation Task Force, and A. J. Graphics. You can order clip art for your documents from many vendors. Many clip art companies create specialized clip art, such as medical symbols or pictures of well-known individuals. Purchasing clip art from outside sources can save you time and money. With the more elaborate drawings, the cost of the clip art is usually less than the value of the time you would use to draw it yourself. If you have a scanner, you can scan images into a computer file and use those images as clip art.

Why am I unable to select a graphics figure with my mouse?

If you have selected the No Wrap radio button in the Wrap Text dialog box, you cannot select the graphics box by clicking it with the left mouse button. Instead, point to the figure and press the right mouse button, then choose Select Box from the QuickMenu. You can also select the graphics box using the Next and Prev buttons on the Graphics Box Feature Bar.

I don't like the changes I made to a graphic. Can I undo them?

When you make changes to a graphic, you can undo them in more than one way depending on the kind of change you want undone. If you want to undo the last change you made to a graphic in either WordPerfect or WordPerfect Draw, select Undo from the Edit menu or press CTRL+Z. If you want to remove all changes you have made to the graphics box settings, select Content from the Graphics box Feature Bar or the box's QuickMenu, then select Reset from the Box Content dialog box that appears. If you want to remove the changes you have made to the graphic with the Image Tools palette, click the Reset button on the Image Tools palette.

How can I create dropped capitals?

You have probably seen magazine articles that use large letters to begin sections of text. These large letters are called "dropped capitals." You can add the same feature to your documents using the DROPCAP.WCM macro. To run this macro, follow these steps:

1. Move the insertion point to the paragraph where you want to make the first letter a dropped capital.

2. Select Macro from the Tools menu, and select Play.

3. Type **DROPCAP.WCM** or select this macro from the list, and click Play.

4. Select No if you want the dropped capital to use the same font typeface and the larger font size displayed in a

dialog box or select Yes to choose a different font and size. If you select Yes, the Font dialog box opens for you to select the font typeface, style, and size. When you select OK, the macro creates the dropped capital with the font information you provided.

This macro removes the first letter of a paragraph and places it in a graphics box anchored to the paragraph. A paragraph with a dropped capital might look like this:

```
 ─                    WordPerfect - [c:\...\dbl_reed.wpd]              ▼ ‡
 ▬  File  Edit  View  Insert  Layout  Tools  Graphics  Table  Window  Help    ‡
    ▭ 🔲 🔲 🔲 ✂ 🔲 🔲 ∩ FFF ‡A B I U ▸L ▦ ▦ ▤L T0 115% 🔲 🔲 🔲 🔲 🔲

    D  ouble reed instruments create their sound by having two reeds that vibrate against each   ⬆
       other. These instruments create distinctive sounds that easily separate them from other
       instruments. Oboes, English horns, and bassoons are the double reed instruments that you
    see in an orchestra. Bagpipes also create their sound using double reeds. However, instead of
    blowing into the two reeds, you blow into a bag and use the air in the bag to blow air through the
    double reeds in the pipes.
```

How can I pull text from my document and display it somewhere else in a larger font so that it stands out?

Text that is taken from a document and repeated in a larger font elsewhere in the document is called a *pull-quote*. You may have seen this technique used in magazines, newspapers, and advertisements to add visual interest and to reinforce a particular point. To create a pull-quote in one of your documents, follow these steps:

1. Select the text for the pull-quote.

2. Copy the text for the quote to the Clipboard by selecting Copy from the Edit menu or clicking the Copy button in the Power Bar.

3. Select Text from the Graphics menu to create a text graphics box. You can easily use a different graphics box style for the pull-quote by selecting Custom Box instead

of <u>T</u>ext from the <u>G</u>raphics menu and selecting the graphics box style you want the pull-quote to use.

4. Paste the text from the Clipboard by selecting <u>P</u>aste from the <u>E</u>dit menu or click the Paste button in the Power Bar.

5. Make any other changes to the graphics box and its text. Possible changes include making the font size larger and positioning the graphics box on the page.

Figure 8-5 shows a document with a pull-quote. This pull-quote's text box is anchored to the page so it appears between the two columns of body text.

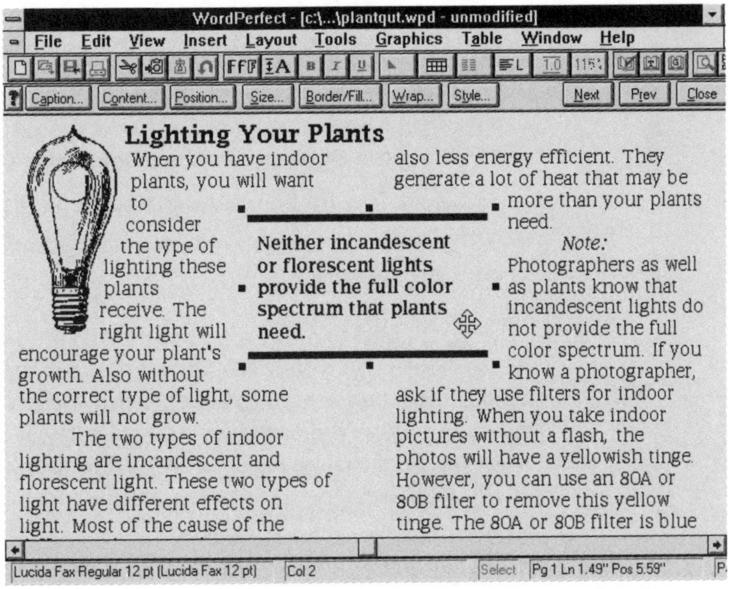

FIGURE 8-5   Pull-quote created by putting text into a graphics box

Can I create buttons in my document?

WordPerfect has a button graphics box style specifically for creating buttons in your document similar to the buttons you have in a dialog box. You can use these buttons when you are creating instructions and you want to indicate the button to press. A sample of a document using the button box graphics box style looks like this:

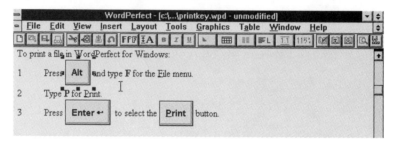

To create a button:

1. Select Custom Box from the Graphics menu.

2. Select Button from the Style Name list box and choose OK.

3. Select the Content Graphics Box feature bar.

4. Select Text in the Content drop-down list.

5. Choose Edit and type the text you want to appear on the button face.

The width and height for these buttons are set automatically. The BoxText system style has been changed to a larger font in the illustration above. To make entering the document quicker, once one button is created for a specific key, it is copied to every location where that key is used. If you frequently use buttons like this, you can develop a macro to handle most of the creation process for you.

How can I fit text to the contours of a graphic?

WordPerfect can wrap text to the shape of a graphic. To turn the wrapping on, select Wrap from the Graphics Box Feature Bar dialog box or the graphics box's QuickMenu. The Wrap Text dialog box has two sets of radio buttons. Using the radio buttons on the left, select the way you want the text wrapped. The example below uses a contour wrapping type. Using the radio buttons on the right, select the side of the graphic where you want text wrapped. The default of Largest Side lets WordPerfect decide based on the placement of the graphic, as the example below shows. When you select OK, WordPerfect changes the wrapping of text around a graphic to the settings you have chosen. If the graphic box had a border, setting WordPerfect to wrap around the graphic removes this border. You can set how closely WordPerfect wraps text around the graphic by changing the border spacing of the graphics box.

 ## How do I put a graphics box in a different location on the page?

A graphics box is positioned according to its anchor type since it is placed relative to the character, paragraph, or page it is anchored to. To move a box, select Position from the Graphics Box Feature Bar or the graphics box's QuickMenu. The options below Box Placement select the relative position. Select the position options depending on the anchor type chosen and select OK.

Tech Tip: You can also change the position of a graphics box by dragging it to a new location. This will not change its anchor type. However, if you drag it to a new character, paragraph, or page, you will change the character, paragraph, or page that the graphics box uses as an anchor.

How can I put text on top of a graphics box?

Most of the time when you add graphics to a file, you will want the document's text to flow around the text. However, there may be times when you want to overlay text and graphics. A watermark is an example of this. Watermarks are designs printed on a page and were originally intended to mimic watermarks created as part of the papermaking process. You have two options for printing text on top of graphics. You can set a graphics box so that text does not wrap around it, or you can create a second graphics box that contains the text you want to appear on top of the graphics image, and then place the box containing the text directly on top of the box containing the graphic.

The document in Figure 8-6 shows an example of text and graphics (from A. J. Graphics) combined. In this document, text does not wrap around the graphics box. To achieve this effect, select Wrap from the Graphics Box Feature Bar, the No Wrap radio button, and OK. In this document, the width of the graphics box is set to Full. Once you add a graphic to your document, you can use features such as line spacing, line height, and advance to move the text to where you want it to appear on top of the graphic. This text can be part of the main document, or, if the document includes other text that you do not want to place on top of the graphic, you can create a separate text box to contain the text to be overlaid. With this method, any changes made to the line spacing or line height of the overlaid text will not interfere with the remaining text in the document.

How can I change the distance between graphics in a graphics box and the wrapped text?

Graphics boxes usually have space between the contents of the box and any border, and also between the borders of the box and the text of the document. You can use more space to keep the contents of the box further away from the document's text, or less space to bring the text closer to the box. If the box does not use a border, the spacing is measured according to where a border would be if the graphics box used one.

FIGURE 8-6   Document containing overlapping graphics and text

To change the amount of space in the border, follow these steps:

1. Select the graphic image to change.

2. Select Border/Fill from the Graphics Box Feature Bar dialog box or the graphics box's QuickMenu.

3. Select the Customize Style button.

4. Select the spacing you want between the image and its border in the Inside Spacing text box or use its button to select a predefined space.

5. Select the spacing you want between the border and the surrounding text in the Outside Spacing text box or use its button to select a predefined space.

   You can return to letting WordPerfect set the spacing by selecting the Auto Spacing check box.

6. Select OK twice to return to the document and use the new spacing for the graphic.

Can I put graphics in a header?

You can place graphics in a document's header as well as in footers, endnotes, comments, and footnotes. As you work in these sections of your document, you can add graphics using the same commands and features that you use when you are in the main part of your document.

When I try to restore a deleted graphic, I get the message "Disk Full, Cannot Undelete Graphics." How do I restore my graphic?

When you are undeleting a graphic, WordPerfect writes a copy from the undelete buffer to a temporary file. If you receive the error message "Disk Full, Cannot Undelete Graphics," it means your disk does not have enough room to hold the temporary file.

Can I change the style of a graphics box I have already created?

WordPerfect lets you change the style that any graphics box uses. When you change the graphics box style for a box, you are switching it from one set of default settings to another. To change the style of a box, follow these steps:

1. Select the graphics box you want to change.
2. Select the Style button from the Graphics Box Feature Bar or the box's QuickMenu.
3. Select the graphics box style you want the box to use from the Style list box and select OK.

The graphics box will now use the default settings of the graphics box style you have selected. Changes you have made for the individual graphics box remain. WordPerfect handles renumbering graphics boxes for both the old graphics box style and the new.

WordPerfect keeps track of all graphics boxes you have in a document as well as which type each graphics box is. For example, if a document has two figure boxes and two table boxes, WordPerfect may remember the graphics boxes like this:

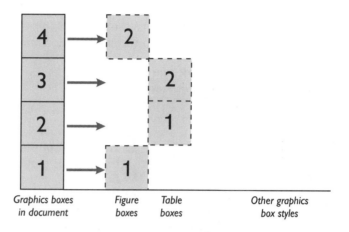

| Graphics boxes in document | Figure boxes | Table boxes | Other graphics box styles |

The number on the left is the number of the graphics box in the overall list of graphics boxes. The numbers in the other columns represent the graphics box number within its list according to style. This is the graphics box number used when you include the graphics box number in a caption. When you change the style a graphics box uses, you are moving the graphic from one column to another within the list.

How do I create my own graphics box styles?

In addition to the eight graphics box styles available in WordPerfect, you can create your own styles. To do this, follow these steps:

1. Select Graphics Styles from the Graphics menu.

2. Select Create from the Graphics Styles dialog box, and the Create Box Style dialog box like the one in Figure 8-7 appears.

3. Type the name for the graphics box style in the Style Name text box.

4. Change the settings for the graphics box style. Select buttons on the left side of the Create Box Style dialog box and use the dialog boxes that these buttons display to

change the graphics box settings. When you select OK to return to the Create Box Style dialog box, the dialog box will show a sample of the graphics box you are creating.

5. Select OK and Close to complete creating the graphics box style and return to your document.

The next time you select the style for a graphics box, you will see the style you have created in the list.

Can I change the way the graphics box styles look?

While each of the graphics box styles has settings that determine how the boxes look, you can change the styles so they appear as you want them to. The default settings for a graphics box type set the border, the space between the border and the box's contents, the space between the border and the surrounding document contents, the numbering of graphics

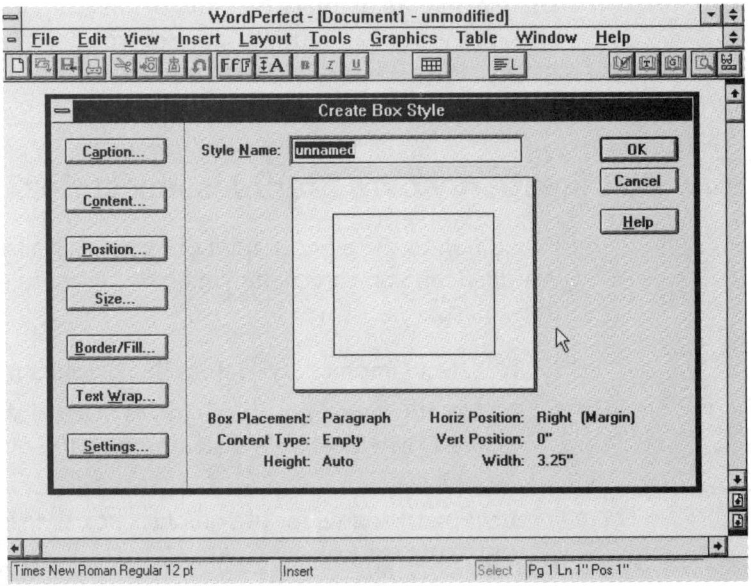

FIGURE 8-7   Create Box Style dialog box

boxes, the default figure caption, the caption position, and the shading level of graphics boxes. To change the settings:

1. Select <u>G</u>raphics Styles from the <u>G</u>raphics menu.

2. Highlight the type of graphics box you want to alter in the <u>S</u>tyles list box and select <u>E</u>dit.

3. Make changes to the graphics box settings. You make the changes by selecting buttons from the left side of the Edit Box Style dialog box. This dialog box looks just like the Create Box Style dialog box shown in Figure 8-7 except that you cannot change the style name.

4. Select OK and <u>C</u>lose to complete the graphics box settings.

The graphics boxes using that style from that point on will incorporate the changes. If you want the change to affect all documents, edit the template your documents use and modify the graphics box styles there.

When using the Chart Editor, how can I select all of my Worksheet cells?

The Chart Editor is accessed by selecting Cha<u>r</u>t from the <u>G</u>raphics menu or by clicking the Chart button on the Button Bar. Once in the Chart Editor within WordPerfect Draw, you can select all the worksheet cells by choosing <u>S</u>elect All from the <u>E</u>dit menu. The second way to select all cells in the Worksheet, which will include those without data, is to click in the upper-left cell in the Worksheet.

How do I enter my own data for a chart?

The Chart Editor in WordPerfect Draw has a worksheet that contains the data displayed by a chart in WordPerfect Draw. You can enter your own data into this worksheet thereby creating your own chart parameters. To add these entries, follow these steps:

1. Select Cha<u>r</u>t from the <u>G</u>raphics menu to start creating the chart.

The worksheet is the top section of the Chart Editor as shown in Figure 8-8. The text in the first column identifies each of the series in the chart's legend. The data for each series is what appears in each row. The chart uses the same color or pattern to identify each entry in a series. The entries in the top row label the axis in the chart. This worksheet is filled with cells where you make your entries. The worksheet appears because either <u>D</u>ata Only or Data <u>a</u>nd Chart is selected in the <u>V</u>iew menu. When you show both the chart and the worksheet, you can change the proportion that each uses in the WordPerfect Draw window by dragging the black bar that separates the two up or down.

2. Move from one cell to another and make the entries you want to appear in the chart as a legend, axis entry, or series value.

3. Make any other changes to the chart.

4. The Chart Editor has many commands that set the appearance of the chart you are creating. As you make changes with the commands, the chart is redrawn to show how it looks with the changes you have made.

5. Select E<u>x</u>it and Return from the <u>F</u>ile menu, then answer <u>Y</u>es when prompted for whether you want to save the changes to your WordPerfect document. You return to the WordPerfect document and your document has a chart containing the entries you modified or added.

Tech Tip: If you have the data for a chart in a WordPerfect table, select the data in the document, copy it to the Clipboard, start WordPerfect Draw, and paste the Clipboard entries onto the worksheet. If the data is in its own spreadsheet file, see the question "How can I add a chart of spreadsheet data to my WordPerfect document?" in Chapter 9 for a quick method of entering the data into WordPerfect Draw.

When I print graphics, only half the page prints or a memory error message appears. What can I do?

If a printed page has incomplete graphics, your printer might not have enough memory. When this occurs, you may encounter a page that cuts off part of the graphics, a printer

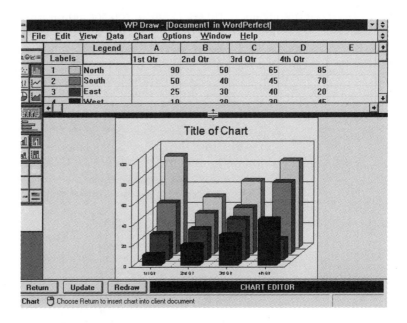

FIGURE 8-8   WordPerfect Draw window

memory overflow message, or a "printer out of memory" message from Windows. Try the following solutions:

- Reduce the size of the graphic images. For example, if a graphic occupies the whole page, resize it so it only uses half of the page.

- Change the document's fonts to printer fonts rather than those generated by software, such as TrueType fonts.

- Remove any watermarks.

- Try printing graphics and text separately.

- Reduce the resolution of the graphics.

 ## Can I invert a graphic image?

Inverting a graphic image does not reverse it, but turns it inside out by showing each color's opposite, or complementary, color. You can invert a graphic image in two ways. You can use the Image Tools palette, or you can edit the graphic in WordPerfect Draw. You should base your choice of method on how much of the image is to be inverted. Using the Image Tools palette inverts the entire graphic. Using WordPerfect Draw lets you select parts of the image to invert.

To invert a graphic using the Image Tools palette:

1. Select the graphic to invert.

2. Display the Image Tools palette by selecting the <u>T</u>ools button from the Graphics Box Feature Bar or by selecting <u>I</u>mage Tools in the graphics box's QuickMenu if the palette does not already appear. The Image Tools palette is shown here with the buttons labeled.

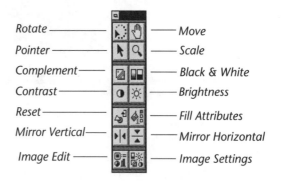

3. Click the Complement button in the Image Tools palette and all of the image is inverted.

To invert a graphic using WordPerfect Draw:

1. Select the graphic.

2. Start WordPerfect Draw by selecting Activate WP Graphic 2.1 <u>O</u>bject from the graphics box's QuickMenu, or by double-clicking the image.

3. Select the parts of the object that you want to invert. While the Select items button is on, you can select the parts of the image you want to change. To add another part of the graphic to the selections you have already made, hold down the CTRL key while you select objects.

4. Select <u>I</u>nvert from the <u>A</u>ttributes menu to reverse the colors of just the selected elements in the graphic image.

5. Select Exit and Return from the File menu to return to your document.

Can I move or rotate the graphic in a graphics box?

An image in a graphics box can be rotated, flipped, and moved within the box. You can rotate, flip, or move the image using either the Image Tools palette or WordPerfect Draw. Figure 8-9 shows four copies of the same graphic that are flipped, rotated, and moved. To rotate, flip, or move a graphic in a graphics box using the Image Tools palette, follow these steps:

1. Select the graphic to rotate, flip, or move.

2. Display the Image Tools palette by selecting the Tools button from the Graphics Box Feature Bar or by selecting Image Tools in the graphics box's QuickMenu if the palette does not already appear.

3. Rotate, flip, or move a graphic using these steps:

- To rotate a graphic, click the Rotate button on the Image Tools palette, then drag one of the extra sets of handles the graphic now has until the box outlining the graphic's shape is at the angle you want.

- To move a graphic within the graphics box, click the Move button on the Image Tools Palette, then drag the graphic from one location to another within the graphics box.

- To flip a graphic, click the Mirror Vertical button if you want the graphic flipped so what is on the left side is on the right. Click the Mirror Horizontal button if you want the graphic flipped so what is on the top is on the bottom.

To rotate, flip, or move a graphic using WordPerfect Draw:

1. Select the graphic.

2. Start WordPerfect Draw by selecting Activate WP Graphic 2.1 Object from the graphics box's QuickMenu, or by double-clicking the graphic image.

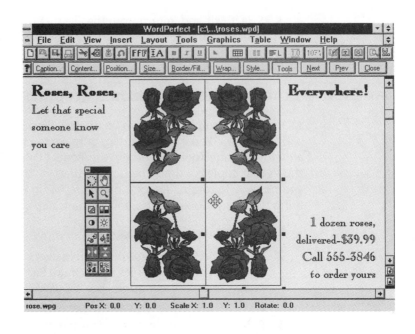

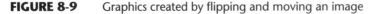

FIGURE 8-9   Graphics created by flipping and moving an image

3. Select the parts of the object that you want to rotate, flip, or move. While the Select items button is selected, you can select the parts of the graphic image you want to change. To add another part of the graphic to the selection of graphic parts you have already chosen, hold down the CTRL key while you select objects.

4. Rotate, flip, or move a graphic using these steps:

   ■ To rotate a graphic, select Rotate from the Edit menu. Drag one of the extra sets of handles the graphic now has until the box outlining the graphic's shape is at the angle you want.

   ■ To move a graphic within the graphics box, drag the selected parts of the graphic to a new location.

   ■ To flip a graphic, select Flip Left/Right or Flip Top/Bottom from the Arrange menu. Selecting Flip Left/Right flips the selected graphic items the way the Mirror Vertical button in the Image Tools palette flips the entire graphic. Selecting Flip Top/Bottom flips the selected graphic items the way the Mirror Horizontal button in the Image Tools palette flips the entire graphic.

5. Select Exit and Return from the File menu to return to your document.

Tech Tip: Usually after moving or rotating the graphic, you will need to resize the graphics box. Remember that you can resize a box by dragging one of its four corners to a new position.

How can I make color graphics look better when I print in black and white?

WordPerfect has several settings that specify how a graphic appears in a box. You can adjust these settings to make color pictures look better when printed. These settings can be done for the entire graphic using the Image Tools palette or items within the graphic using WordPerfect Draw.

1. Select the graphic to modify.

2. Display the Image Tools palette by selecting the Tools button from the Graphics Box Feature Bar or by selecting Image Tools in the graphics box's QuickMenu if the palette does not already appear.

3. Make the changes to the graphic using these features:

- Convert an image to black and white by clicking the Black & White button in the Image Tools palette. From the box this button displays, select the Black & White check box. If you want to change the threshold shade of gray, select this button again and click the shade of gray you want to use for the threshold. The threshold is the shade of gray that WordPerfect uses to determine which shades of gray or colors convert to black and which ones convert to white.

- Make an image brighter by clicking the Brightness button on the Image Tools Palette, then click the button representing the brightness setting you want to use.

■ Enhance the differences between light and dark areas in the image by clicking the Contrast button on the Image Tools palette, then click the button representing the contrast setting you want to use.

To change the brightness or contrast using WordPerfect Draw:

1. Select the graphic.

2. Start WordPerfect Draw by selecting Edit Figure or Activate WP Graphic 2.1 Object from the graphics box's QuickMenu, or by double-clicking the graphic image.

3. Select Adjust Image from the File menu.

4. Enter new numbers in the Brightness and Contrast text boxes and select OK.

5. Select Exit and Return from the File menu to return to your document.

Tech Tip: Just because your printer cannot print colors doesn't mean that you cannot print a color picture. Very often, when you print a color picture on a printer with only one color, the different colors will appear as varying shades of gray. Try printing the picture without converting it to black and white and then again after converting it to see which one you like better.

 ## I added an image to a graphics box and it continues to contain an OLE object. Why?

When a graphics box contains an image that is not a .WPG image saved on disk, and you alter the image with WordPerfect Draw, WordPerfect Draw changes the image into a WordPerfect Draw OLE Object. WordPerfect Draw is a separate application designed to work with images and with OLE objects that you have embedded into your WordPerfect documents. Nothing is wrong with your image. The only change you will notice is that when you display the Box Content dialog box, it will contain OLE Object in the Content pop-up list.

Tech Terror: Changing the .WPG image in WordPerfect Draw alters the .WPG file, not just the image in the document. You can tell that WordPerfect will change the original .WPG file because the title bar in WordPerfect Draw will contain the .WPG filename in place of the WordPerfect document name. If you do not want the original image altered, do not set the contents to Image on Disk.

I'm a programmer interested in creating some WordPerfect graphics files (.WPG); where can I obtain code information?

Specifications on the graphics file formats that WordPerfect uses can be obtained by purchasing the WordPerfect Developer's Toolkit from WordPerfect Corporation.

Can I scan an image into WordPerfect Draw?

WordPerfect Draw can accept an image from a scanning device if it is TWAIN-compatible. TWAIN is a set of scanner protocols that many paint programs support for bringing scanned images into the program. To check if your installed scanner is TWAIN-compatible, switch to WordPerfect Draw and select Image Source Setup from the File menu; if this option is grayed out, your scanner is not TWAIN-compatible. If Image Source Setup is available, select this command, then select your scanner from the list and follow the screen prompts or refer to your scanner's manual for help.

Can I capture a screen the way I can in WordPerfect for DOS?

You can capture a picture of a Windows screen stored in the Windows Clipboard, then put the screen capture in a WordPerfect document. To capture a Windows screen and put it into a WordPerfect document, follow these steps:

1. Set up the screen to capture.
2. Press the PRINT SCREEN key.

3. Switch to WordPerfect and open the WordPerfect document where you want to insert the screen capture.

4. Select <u>P</u>aste from the <u>E</u>dit menu.

At this point, WordPerfect creates a figure graphics box containing the bitmap picture of the screen's contents when you pressed PRINT SCREEN. Figure 8-10 shows a Windows screen pasted into a WordPerfect document. You can use WordPerfect Draw and the Image Tools palette to change the size and section of the screen that you see in the figure graphics box.

What is the difference between vector graphics and bitmap graphics?

A graphic image can be saved in a vector or bitmap format. Bitmap images are the type of images created with the Paintbrush application, where colors may be applied to any area of the drawing surface. Bitmap images remember an image by the dots of each color that make up the image. For example, when

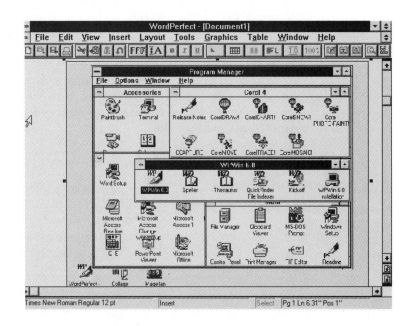

FIGURE 8-10   Windows screen pasted into a WordPerfect document

you draw a line, the program remembers the line by a series of dots that make up the line. Vector graphics, on the other hand, record the lines and endpoints of shapes used in the image. For example, instead of remembering every point on a line, a vector format remembers the end points of the line and the line's features, such as colors and styles. Vector graphics make certain types of editing easier, such as changing the line style, changing its size, or moving the line without moving anything below it. Vector graphics look smoother than bitmap graphics, especially when enlarged. Vector files usually also have the advantage of being smaller than bitmap files. WordPerfect's .WPG graphics file format saves images as vectors.

A third way graphic images are stored is using a Metafile format, such as .WMF or .CGM files. Metafiles store both vector and bitmap data used to create an image.

Sharing Data

WordPerfect has several features that make it easy for you to work with data from other applications. WordPerfect can incorporate and manipulate data stored in formats used by most popular word processors, spreadsheets, and databases. Importing data from these other applications makes WordPerfect a real time-saver—you can build your documents using the data you have rather than typing everything from scratch. Some of the different terms for using outside data with WordPerfect are described in the following Frustration Busters box.

As you start sharing data between applications, you may encounter new terms that you are unfamiliar with. Here is a short list of terms that you are likely to run into:

- **DDE (Dynamic Data Exchange)**—A data-sharing method that allows you to link and transfer data from other Windows applications that support DDE to your WordPerfect document.

- **OLE (Object Linking and Embedding)**—A data-sharing method that lets you embed data from another application into a file, and allows you to edit the data in the application that it came from.

- **Importing**—A method of copying data into WordPerfect. Once the data has been imported, you can use WordPerfect features to change its appearance. Since imported data is a copy of the original, changing the imported version has no effect on the original and vice versa.

- **Linking**—A method of bringing data stored in another file into WordPerfect and retaining a link to the original file. Any change in the original file will be reflected in the WordPerfect file because the link will update the WordPerfect file.

- **Clipboard**—A Windows feature that stores data and lets you copy it from one location to another even if the receiving application is not the same as the one in which you created the data. The Clipboard can store data in more than one format. WordPerfect's Paste Special command in the Edit menu lets you select the format you want to use to paste Clipboard data into a WordPerfect document.

171

Chapter 9 *Sharing Data*

What are General Protection Faults? How can I avoid them?

A General Protection Fault is a Windows 3.1 error that you may encounter occasionally. General Protection Faults occur when a Windows application writes information to a place in memory that "belongs" to another program, causing any data in that space to become corrupted. In most cases, you can select the Ignore button to clear the error message and save your file. Once you save your data, exit Windows and reboot your system to reset the memory. Sometimes, you will only have the option to Close. When you select Close, the application closes and you lose any work done since you last saved your document. If you have not yet saved this document, it may be lost entirely. (If you have the Timed Backup feature enabled, then you may have a chance to recover the unsaved document.) In this case, you will also need to exit Windows and reboot your computer.

If General Protection Faults become a problem, you should try the following to help eliminate them:

- Close other applications open in Windows before starting WordPerfect. You may not have sufficient memory available to perform the operation that resulted in the General Protection Fault.

- If you use a screen saver program such as After Dark, disable it while you use WordPerfect.

- If you use a file compression utility such as STACKER or DOS 6's DoubleSpace, check that your permanent swap file is on a host or uncompressed drive.

- Exit any running terminate-and-stay-resident (TSR) programs.

- If the General Protection Fault occurs when you use the Windows printer driver, try the WordPerfect printer driver, or vice versa. If you can print successfully, the Windows printer driver file is corrupted. Delete it and install a new copy.

- Try performing the same operation that caused the error with a different document. General Protection Faults caused only by a specific document indicate a corrupted document. You can try to save the data in your document by copying and pasting it into a new document, essentially creating a new copy. Choose Select from the Edit menu and All, then Copy from the Edit menu, New from the File menu, and finally Paste from the Edit menu. Save this document with a new name and try to perform the operation that causes the General Protection Fault in the new document.

■ If you are working with a file that was created on another computer, make sure your computer has all of the fonts or graphics the document uses.

■ Make sure your system has enough memory.

■ General Protection Faults can occur when you try to retrieve a document created with an older version of WordPerfect and no printer driver is selected in WordPerfect 6.0 for Windows. Select a printer driver, then retrieve the document.

 ## What text formats are supported by WordPerfect 6.0 for Windows?

The text formats that you can import into WordPerfect 6.0 for Windows are:

■ WordPerfect for DOS 4.2, 5.0, and 5.1

■ WordPerfect for Windows 5.*x*

■ WordPerfect Macintosh 2.0, 2.1, 3.0

■ WordStar 3.3 to 6.0

■ WordStar 2000 1.0 to 3.0

■ OfficeWriter 6.*x*

■ MultiMate 3.3 to 4.0

■ Microsoft Word 4.0, 5.0, and 5.5

■ Microsoft Word for Windows 1.0, 1.1, and 2.0

■ Lotus Ami Pro 1.2, 2.0, and 3.0

■ IBM DisplayWrite 4.0, 4.2, and 5.0

■ IBM DCA/FFT

■ IBM DCA/RFT

- Kermit (7-Bit Transfer)
- Navy DIF Standard
- Rich Text Format (RTF)
- Windows Write
- ASCII Delimited Text (DOS)
- ASCII (DOS)
- ANSI Delimited Text (Windows)
- ANSI (Windows)

How do I convert a file created in earlier versions of WordPerfect to WordPerfect 6.0?

To convert a file created in an earlier version of WordPerfect, open the file in WordPerfect 6.0 by selecting Open under the File menu. When you later save the file, select Save As from the File menu to enter a new filename and verify that WordPerfect 6.0 is selected in the Format drop-down list. WordPerfect will prompt you to confirm that you want to replace the original file. If you resave the file with the same name by selecting Save from the File menu, WordPerfect will prompt you with an option to save the file in its original format, WordPerfect 6.0 format, or Other.

I am using WordPerfect 6.0 for Windows; however, my secretary uses WordPerfect 6.0 for DOS. Can we read each other's files?

WordPerfect 6.0 for DOS and 6.0 for Windows files are completely compatible. You can simply save the files in one program and open them in the other; no conversion is necessary.

A caution: You may want to use only the fonts that both you and your secretary have in common. If one person uses fonts that the other does not, WordPerfect makes a font substitution. In other words, WordPerfect will replace the unknown font with one it does know. This will not hurt your document, but it will cause the printed version to look different from what you saw onscreen. You may both want to use WordPerfect's rather than

Windows' printer drivers to ensure you are sharing the same printer features.

Tech Tip: You can use the TrueType fonts installed in Windows in WordPerfect 6.0 for DOS. You need to install these fonts in WordPerfect for DOS using the Install Fonts utility.

When I open an Ami Pro 2.0 file I see the message "Unknown File Format." How do I open my file?

The error message "Unknown File Format" when opening an Ami Pro 2.0 file in WordPerfect indicates that the file is password protected in Ami Pro. Open the file again in Ami Pro, turn off password protection, save the file again, and then open it in WordPerfect.

How do I share documents between Professional Write and WordPerfect for Windows?

WordPerfect for Windows does not have a conversion filter for Professional Write files. You can save a WordPerfect for Windows file in an IBM DCA/RFT or a WordPerfect 5.1 for DOS format, both of which Professional Write can read. You can also save Professional Write files in either format to create files that you can open in WordPerfect.

Can I convert documents from other applications into WordPerfect?

You can open a document stored in one of the formats that WordPerfect supports by using the same <u>O</u>pen command in the <u>F</u>ile menu that you use to open WordPerfect documents. To open a document from another application in WordPerfect for Windows:

1. Select <u>O</u>pen from the <u>F</u>ile menu.
2. Change to the correct directory and drive where the file is located.

3. Highlight the filename and select OK. The Convert File Format dialog box appears, as shown here:

4. Select the file's format from the Convert File Format From drop-down list box.

5. Select OK to convert the file and open it in a WordPerfect document window.

Tech Tip: When you save the document with Save As in the File menu, the Format drop-down list is set to WordPerfect 6.0. You need to select another format if you do not want the data saved in a WordPerfect format. When you save the document with Save in the File menu or close the document window and respond Yes when asked if you want to save the document, you will see a dialog box like the one in the following illustration. From here, you can select whether you want to save the data as a WordPerfect document, in its original or a different format. Selecting Other and OK will open the Save As dialog box; you can then use the Format drop-down list to select the format of the saved file.

How do I insert a file into my current document?

To insert a file into the current document, choose File from the Insert menu, select the filename, and choose Insert. This command places the contents of the file in your current document at the position of the insertion point.

When I open my WordPerfect 5.1 document in WordPerfect 6.0 for Windows, the font looks different. What happened and what can I do?

When you open a document in WordPerfect that was formatted with a font that is not available with the currently selected printer, WordPerfect makes a font substitution. When you look at the codes in your document, you will see that the codes reference fonts not available from the list of fonts you can use within WordPerfect for Windows. You can leave these font codes in and when you return to WordPerfect 5.1, the text will appear in the same fonts it used originally. You can also delete these codes and reformat the text to use a different font. A third option is to change the font WordPerfect uses for font substitution. You can edit the document's Font Map to specify which fonts WordPerfect will use when the originally selected font is not available. To change the substitute font:

1. Open the document that you plan on working on with a different printer.

2. Select Font from the Layout menu.

3. Select the Font Map button and select the Document radio button.

4. Select the font within the document from the Font drop-down list.

   If the document uses the font in more than one size, you can select which size you want to change from the Size drop-down list.

5. In the Printer Font section, select a typeface, style, and size from the Face, Style, and Size drop-down lists that you want WordPerfect to use when the document font is not available. To return to the font substitutions originally used by WordPerfect, select the Automatic Selection check box.

6. Select OK and Cancel to return to the document using the new document font mapping.

Why can't WordPerfect open my Microsoft Word 6.0 for Windows document?

WordPerfect cannot *directly* open Microsoft Word 6.0 for Windows documents. However, if you go back to Word for Windows and save your document in WordPerfect 5.1/5.2 or Word for Windows 2.0 format, WordPerfect will be able to import it just fine. WordPerfect 6.0 for Windows currently does not have a filter to convert a file to or from Word 6.0 for Windows.

What file formats for spreadsheets does WordPerfect for Windows support?

WordPerfect supports the following file formats for spreadsheets:

- PlanPerfect 3.0-5.1 (.PLN)
- Lotus 1-2-3 1A (.WKS), 2.01, 2.3, 2.4 (.WK1), 3.0, and 3.1(.WK3)
- Excel 2.1, 3.0, 4.0 (.XLS)
- Quattro Pro 3.0, 4.0 (.WQ1)
- Quattro Pro for Windows 1.0 (.WB1)
- Spreadsheet DIF

Tech Tip: If a Lotus 1-2-3 spreadsheet was formatted with the Allways add-on product, the formatting will not carry over when you import the file. Use WordPerfect's formatting features to change the spreadsheet data's appearance.

How do I import a spreadsheet into WordPerfect?

To import a spreadsheet into WordPerfect, perform the following steps:

1. Place the insertion point in the document where you want to import the spreadsheet.
2. Choose Spreadsheet/Database in the Insert menu.
3. Choose Import to place a copy of the spreadsheet into your document.

4. Select <u>S</u>preadsheet from the Data <u>T</u>ype pop-up list.

5. Select <u>T</u>able, Te<u>x</u>t, or <u>M</u>erge Data File from the <u>I</u>mport As pop-up list to specify how the information will be formatted in WordPerfect. <u>T</u>able creates a WordPerfect table with the same number of columns and rows as the original spreadsheet data. Te<u>x</u>t imports the data with the columns of data separated by tabs. <u>M</u>erge Data File sets up a data file for merging using each column as a field and each row as a record.

6. Type the filename of the spreadsheet file to import in the <u>F</u>ilename text box.

7. Select the range from the <u>N</u>amed Ranges list box if you want to specify a range from the spreadsheet. You can also manually enter the range in the <u>R</u>ange text box.

8. Choose OK to insert the information into your document.

When a spreadsheet is imported, the imported data is a separate copy from the original spreadsheet data. If changes are made in WordPerfect to the document, this has no effect on the original spreadsheet, and changes made to the original spreadsheet will not be reflected in the WordPerfect document. Figure 9-1 shows a spreadsheet imported into WordPerfect as a table and the Excel spreadsheet where the data originated.

I've imported a large spreadsheet and all the data didn't come in. How do I get the rest of my data into WordPerfect?

You can only import up to 64 columns of a spreadsheet. Any spreadsheet you try to import with more than that number is truncated after the 64th column. To solve this problem, either divide your spreadsheet into sections and import each section separately, or import the first 64 columns, then the 65th through 128th columns, and so on until the entire spreadsheet is imported.

How can I add a chart of spreadsheet data to my WordPerfect document?

WordPerfect can create a graph from your imported spreadsheet data. Assuming WordPerfect can import your spreadsheet data, follow these steps to create a chart based on that data:

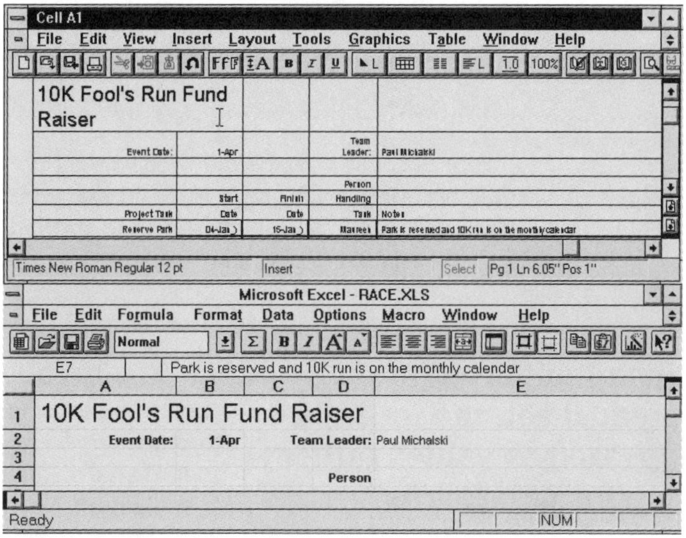

FIGURE 9-1   Excel spreadsheet imported into a WordPerfect document

1. Select Cha<u>r</u>t from the <u>G</u>raphics menu in WordPerfect.

    WordPerfect opens the Charting Editor in WordPerfect Draw. This window is shown in Figure 9-2.

2. Select <u>I</u>mport from the <u>F</u>ile menu or press F4.

3. Select the spreadsheet data file containing the data you want in the graph.

4. Select the I<u>m</u>port button.

5. Select the range you wish to import from the Import Spreadsheets dialog box, then select OK.

    The spreadsheet data now displays in the table portion of the charting screen.

6. Select <u>G</u>allery from the <u>C</u>hart menu.

7. Double-click the desired chart style.

    You can change the basic chart type by selecting Chart <u>T</u>ypes, clicking the one you want, and selecting <u>C</u>hart Styles.

8. Select <u>T</u>itles from the <u>O</u>ptions menu.

9. Enter appropriate titles in the text boxes.

10. Select OK.

11. Select any other charting options.

12. Select Exit from the File menu or click the Return button in the bottom of the Chart Editor window.

13. Select Yes to save the chart and add it to your document.

Your graph is now in your WordPerfect document. You can drag and drop your graph to position it where you want in the document. You can modify the chart further by double-clicking it in the WordPerfect document.

When I imported a spreadsheet, the formulas appeared as values rather than formulas. Why?

If WordPerfect for Windows does not support a particular spreadsheet formula, it will import only the value that the formula returns, not the formula itself. To determine before importing a spreadsheet which formulas cannot be imported, you may want to compare the list of functions and operators in the WordPerfect manual with one in the manual

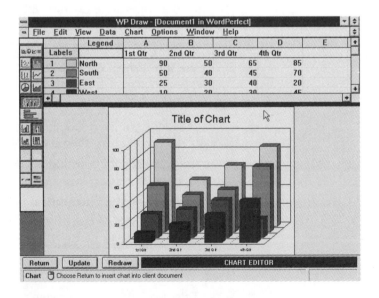

FIGURE 9-2   Chart Editor in WordPerfect Draw

for the spreadsheet program you are using. The functions or formulas WordPerfect does not support will vary by spreadsheet.

I imported a protected spreadsheet. The cells with entries remained locked, but I can enter data in the blank cells. Why?

Blank cells are imported unlocked even if they are protected in the spreadsheet. If you want to keep the entire spreadsheet protected, you can put a space in the blank cells before importing. After you import the spreadsheet, you can select the table, then lock the cells with the F<u>o</u>rmat command in the T<u>a</u>ble menu.

What is the difference between linking a file and importing a file?

When you link a file to your WordPerfect document, the information in your WordPerfect document remains connected to that original spreadsheet or database file. It is easy to update the spreadsheet or database information within WordPerfect to keep it current.

When you import a file into your WordPerfect document, you actually make a copy of the information and insert it into the document. The information exists as a separate copy from the original spreadsheet or database file. Any changes you make afterwards to the spreadsheet or database file do not affect the copy of the data within WordPerfect.

When I paste and link my WordPerfect data in other applications I have fewer options than when I paste and link other applications' data into WordPerfect. Why is this?

When you try to paste data from WordPerfect into another application via the Clipboard, you are only presented with a few format options, as shown here:

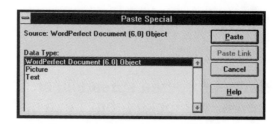

Currently, WordPerfect can act as an OLE client or server, but only as a DDE client. Therefore, you have fewer formats for pasting and linking WordPerfect data from the Clipboard into other applications.

How do I link a spreadsheet to my WordPerfect document?

Linking a spreadsheet ensures your WordPerfect document uses the most up-to-date version of your data. To link a spreadsheet to a WordPerfect document, follow these steps.

1. Move the insertion point to where you want to link the spreadsheet information.

2. Choose Spreadsheet/Database from the Insert menu.

3. Choose Create Link.

4. Select Spreadsheet from the Data Type pop-up list.

5. Select Table, Text, or Merge Data File from the Link As pop-up list for how you want the linked data to appear in your document. Table creates a WordPerfect table with the same number of columns and rows as the original spreadsheet data. Text imports the data with the columns of data separated by tabs. Merge Data File sets up a data file for merging using each column as a field and each row as a record.

6. Type the name of the spreadsheet file you want to link in the Filename text box.

7. If you are linking to a specific range from the spreadsheet, select the range from the Named Ranges list box, or manually type in the range in the Range text box.

8. Choose OK to insert the information into the document.

When a spreadsheet is linked to the WordPerfect document, the information in WordPerfect remains connected to the original file. When you update the data in the WordPerfect document, the data in the original spreadsheet file is also updated and vice-versa. Linking this way helps save you work, since you do not need to make such changes twice.

Tech Tip: If you change the formatting of a table containing data from a linked spreadsheet, and then update the link, all the formatting changes made after the initial link are lost. When the link is updated, the data is brought back in its original format.

Why does my document have icons where I have put spreadsheet or database data?

WordPerfect marks the beginning and ending points of data that is linked to a spreadsheet or database file with icons. These icons tell you that the data between them will change. They appear only onscreen, not on the printed document. If you do not want to see them, select Spreadsheet/Database from the Insert menu and Options, clear the Show Link Icons check box, and select OK. The icons are illustrated here, on the left side of the screen:

CUST_NAME	CUST_NUM	ADDRESS	CITY	ZIP
Palamo Construction	341562	3209 Payne Avenue	Lakewood	44107
J & P Roofers	234836	3413 Euclid Avenue	Cleveland	44101
Sam McKintyre	168452	11549 East 256 St	Cleveland	44123
Camelot Builders	563791	2306 SOM Center Rd	Eastlake	44095

My computer locked up while importing a Lotus spreadsheet. Why?

When importing a spreadsheet or a database, make sure the Data Type, Import As, Filename, and Range (Fields for databases) settings in the Import Data dialog box are correct. If any of these options is set incorrectly, the computer may lock up.

I want to use some database data in WordPerfect for Windows. What are the supported database formats?

WordPerfect supports the following database formats:

- Clipper (.DBF)
- Fox Pro 1.0, 2.0 (.DBF)
- DataPerfect 2.2, 2.3 (.STR)
- dBASE III, IV (.DBF)
- Paradox 3.5, 4.0 (.DB)
- SQL Databases including DB2, Informix, Netware SQL 2.11 or higher, Oracle, SQL Base Server 4.0 or higher, SQL Server, Sybase, and XDB 2.41 or higher

Databases are linked or imported just like spreadsheets. The only difference is that you select the database format from the Data Type pop-up list in the Import Data or Create Data Link dialog box. When you select the data type, the Named Ranges list box and the Range text box change to the Fields list box. This list box is where you select the database fields you want to import or include in the link. Depending on the database format chosen, you may have other dialog box options. For example, when you import or create a link to a dBASE database, you also have a Query button to query the database and limit the group of records you want returned. Figure 9-3 shows a database imported into a WordPerfect document as a data file for merging. The database is saved in a dBASE format and displayed using Access, which can work with files of other databases.

Tech Tip: If not all the database fields you select are imported or appear in the linked data, the page may not be wide enough to hold all your data. Change the page size or which fields you include. You can import or link the database multiple times in a document and select different fields each time.

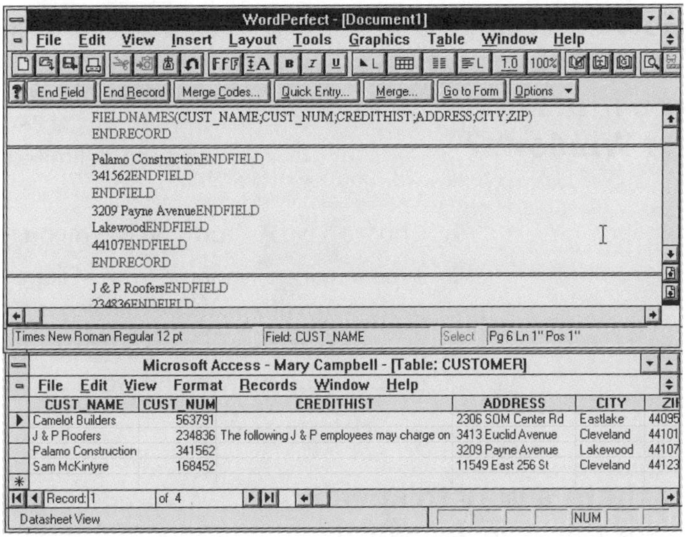

FIGURE 9-3   Database added to a WordPerfect document

Can I put my 1-2-3 for Windows data and graphs into a WordPerfect document using the Clipboard?

When you want to bring 1-2-3 for Windows spreadsheet data or charts into a WordPerfect document, you can use the Clipboard rather than the commands in the Insert menu. First, copy the graph by selecting it in 1-2-3 and choosing Copy in 1-2-3's Edit menu. Then, switch to WordPerfect, and select Paste from the Edit menu.

You cannot link a Lotus 1-2-3 for Windows spreadsheet to a WordPerfect document unless you save the 1-2-3 spreadsheet in a .WK3 format. Once you save a file in this format, you can link the spreadsheet using the Clipboard. After selecting the spreadsheet data you want linked in a WordPerfect document, choose Copy from the 1-2-3 Edit menu, then switch to WordPerfect. Choose Paste Special from the Edit menu and Paste Link. The Paste Link option is grayed unless the Lotus spreadsheet has been saved at least once.

How can I save my WordPerfect data file to use it in Microsoft Access for Windows?

WordPerfect 6.0 for Windows can directly save data files in a comma-delimited format that you can import into Access. To create the comma-delimited file:

1. Choose Save As from the File menu.

2. Type a unique filename in the Filename text box, preferably with a .TXT extension.

3. Select ASCII Delimited Text (DOS) in the Format drop-down list, then choose OK.

Is there a way to specify how WordPerfect will import my documents from other formats?

WordPerfect 6.0 for Windows has an Import Preferences feature that customizes importing ASCII-delimited text files, WordPerfect 4.2, DCA, and DisplayWrite files. To change import preferences for these types of files, select Preferences from the File menu and the Import icon. From the Import Preferences dialog box, you can select how fields and records are separated, the characters that enclose character field entries, the characters to strip from character field entries, and how Windows Metafiles are stored within a WordPerfect document. By selecting Options, you can set other options specifically for importing DCA/DisplayWrite and WordPerfect 4.2 documents. When you have finished setting the import options, select OK and Close to return to your documents.

Can I link a Freelance slide into a WordPerfect document?

To create a dynamic data exchange (DDE) link from a slide in Lotus Freelance Graphics for Windows 2.0 into WordPerfect, save the source file in Freelance and select Page Sorter from the View menu. Select the slide to be linked and choose Copy from the Edit menu. In WordPerfect, select Paste Special from the Edit menu, choose FLWPresentation Object in the Data Type list box, and select Paste Link.

Coaster Name	Operational	Estimated Cost	Track	Height	Speed	Features
Scream Machine	10/5/95	$7,800,000	5780	168	70	All wood coaster with steep drops and many curves. Each train holds 28 passengers
Blue Arrow	8/21/94	$4,000,000	5200	205	73	Steep 60 degree first hill drop on this steel tubular track coaster with fiberglass cars each holding 36 passengers
Astro Transport	5/22/94	$7,500,000	2000	68	50	Special effects are the highlight of this space age transport

(WordPerfect - [Document1] window shown above, Microsoft Access - Mary Campbell - [Table: Project Data] window shown below)

Coaster Name	Operational	Estimated Cost	Track	Height	Speed	Features
Scream Machine	10/5/95	$7,800,000	5780	168	70	All wood coaster with steep drops and many
Blue Arrow	8/21/94	$4,000,000	5200	205	73	Steep 60 degree first hill drop on this steel tu
Astro Transport	5/22/94	$7,500,000	2000	68	50	Special effects are the highlight of this spac
Red Dragon	4/16/95	$4,500,000	2950	78	42	Each suspended train holds 28 passengers.
Taurus	6/1/96	$4,500,000	4200	135	65	All wood coaster with 30 passenger trains th
Corker	7/5/95	$2,500,000	1980	100	50	Triple loop coaster provides an upside thrill a
Wild One	9/16/94	$3,900,000	1895	100	50	The four passenger trains can move quickly
White Lightnin	2/15/93	$2,800,000	2600	68	50	Sharp spiral turns and splashing water make
The Runaway	3/28/92	$3,215,000	2675	120	46	Twenty four passengers experience negativ

FIGURE 9-4 Access data transferred to WordPerfect using the Clipboard

---

I want to bring in data from a Windows application that WordPerfect does not support. Can I do this with the Clipboard?

The Clipboard can handle copying data from one application to another even when the applications do not recognize each other's files. You can copy data from several applications that WordPerfect does not support and paste it into a WordPerfect document. The appearance of the pasted data depends on how WordPerfect places the Clipboard data into the document. Figure 9-4 shows Access data that is copied to the Clipboard, then pasted into WordPerfect.

I received the error message "Draw server could not be loaded." What does this mean?

This error message either means that the path pointing to WP Draw's executable file is wrong or the Draw part of the program is corrupted. To check the path to the WP Draw executable file, follow these steps:

1. Check the location of your WPDRWIN.EXE file. You can use WordPerfect, the Windows File Manager, or any other convenient application to do this.

2. Select <u>R</u>un from the <u>F</u>ile menu in the Program Manager, type **REGEDIT /V** in the <u>C</u>ommand Line text box, and select OK. This starts the Registration Info Editor program that manages your registration database. The registration database is where Windows stores information about the applications that it uses for printing, opening files, and sharing data between applications.

3. Select <u>F</u>ind Key from the <u>S</u>earch menu, type **WPChart21**, and select <u>F</u>ind Next. You now see the section for WPChart21.

4. Move down to the line that says "server=*path*" like the line highlighted below. Make sure the path is the legitimate location of the Draw executable file.

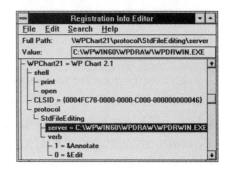

5. Modify the entry in the Value text box if necessary or leave it alone if it is correct.

6. Select E<u>x</u>it from the <u>F</u>ile menu, press ALT+F4, or double-click the Control menu box to leave the Registration Info Editor program.

If the path is correct, the Draw executable file is damaged. Do a custom install and reinstall only the Draw program.

I pasted WordPerfect data that I copied to the Clipboard into another application. Why do I see a WordPerfect icon instead of my data?

The WordPerfect icon, shown below, represents the WordPerfect data that you embedded in the other application by pasting it from the Clipboard. You can double-click the icon to edit the embedded data with WordPerfect.

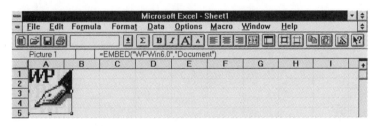

Merges

WordPerfect's merge feature is a very powerful tool which can greatly enhance your productivity. At its most basic level, merging combines the text in one document with the data stored in another document to create multiple, individualized documents. The power of merging can be seen in the form letters you have received as advertisements or announcements. Merging makes it possible to quickly create documents to communicate with hundreds or thousands of people.

WordPerfect's advanced programming commands take the merge features beyond the simple act of combining two files. You can use these features to create documents based on a variety of conditions, add text from the keyboard during a merge, or assemble a finished document from several sources. A careful study of advanced merge techniques pays off in greatly increased productivity.

FRUSTRATION BUSTERS!

The greatest cause of frustration in performing merges is a lack of careful preparation. Merging is a powerful productivity tool, but only if you plan how to use it. Before you begin a merge, you should design your data file to contain all the information you need for current and future projects. If you focus only on today's need for mailing labels, for example, your data file will not have the entries you need to create form letters tomorrow. To get the most mileage from a data file, follow these simple rules.

- Before creating a data file, consider what information may be useful to you, now and in the future.

- Break this information down into the smallest reasonable components to create the greatest flexibility; for example, break addresses into the street address, city, state, and ZIP code.

- Take the time to ask other people what future uses they may have for this data file.

When you create your data files, whether intended for simple or complex merges, carefully consider how the data needs to be merged. For instance, will you have entries for all of the fields you plan to use in all of the records? If not, what will you do for records that do not have entries for particular fields?

If you plan your data file and form file to account for all possible events, you are much more likely to have a successful merge that creates consistent and expected results. When you initially develop your data files, expect to spend time adding and rearranging fields, and altering how your data file is set up. Planning your merge needs will reduce time-consuming editing later.

What is a data file and how do I create it?

A data file contains the variable data that will be merged into the form file to create the final merge document. For example, if your form file is a form letter to send to each of your customers, the data file should contain your customers' names and addresses. To create a data file in WordPerfect:

1. Choose Me_rge from the _Tools menu, or press SHIFT+F9.

2. Choose _Data to create a data file.

3. After choosing _Data, the Create Data File dialog box appears. By default, you create a text data file in which each unit of data appears on one line and is separated from other data by merge codes, as shown in Figure 10-1. If you want to create a table data file with the data arranged in a table, as shown in Figure 10-2, select the _Place Records in a Table check box before choosing _Data. There is no particular advantage to the merge process if you use a table data file, as opposed to a text data file. However, you may want to create a table data file since it is much easier to work with,

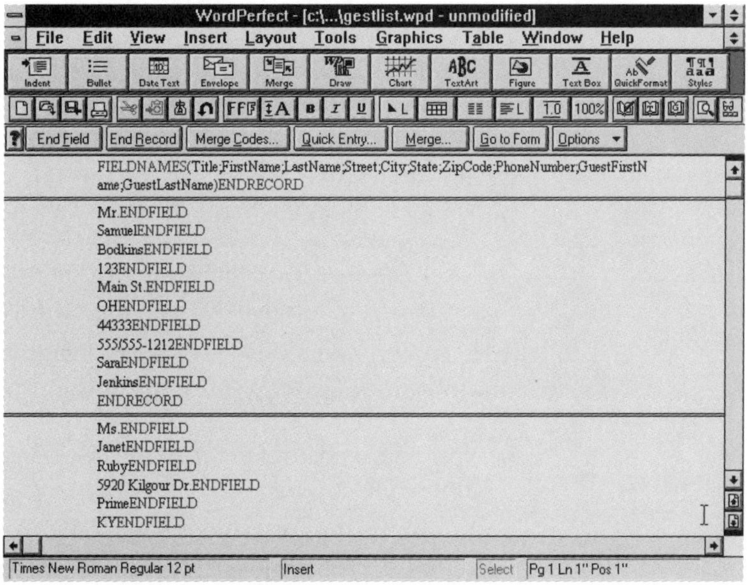

FIGURE 10-1   Data file for merging as a text data file

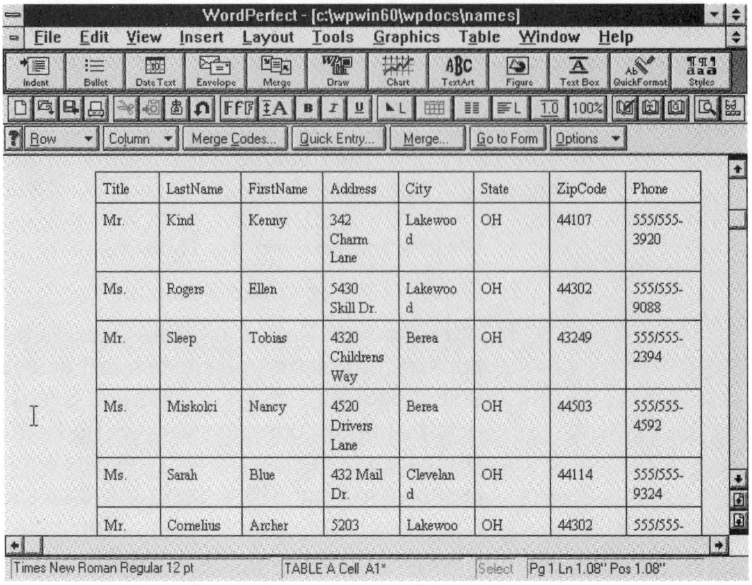

Title	LastName	FirstName	Address	City	State	ZipCode	Phone
Mr.	Kind	Kenny	342 Charm Lane	Lakewoo d	OH	44107	555/555-3920
Ms.	Rogers	Ellen	5430 Skill Dr.	Lakewoo d	OH	44302	555/555-9088
Mr.	Sleep	Tobias	4320 Childrens Way	Berea	OH	43249	555/555-2394
Ms.	Miskolci	Nancy	4520 Drivers Lane	Berea	OH	44503	555/555-4592
Ms.	Sarah	Blue	432 Mail Dr.	Clevelan d	OH	44114	555/555-9324
Mr.	Cornelius	Archer	5203	Lakewoo	OH	44302	555/555-

FIGURE 10-2 Data file for merging in a table

does not have all the end field and end record codes, and is easier to convert between other applications.

4. Add a name for each field you want in the data file by entering the name in the Name a Field text box and selecting Add. The names are added to the Field Name List list box.
5. You can edit the contents of the Field Name List list box by highlighting the name in the list box and selecting:
   - *Replace*, to give the field a new name
   - *Delete*, to remove the field from the list box
   - *Move Up*, to move the field higher in the list
   - *Move Down*, to move the field lower in the list
6. After adding names for all of the fields and editing them, choose OK.

   Another option besides naming fields is to select OK from the Create Data File dialog box without any fields in the Field Name List list box. WordPerfect displays the

Number of Fields dialog box, which then asks you to input the number of fields for each record. Once you select OK, you continue with the Quick Data Entry dialog box. However, instead of field names, you have numbers to identify each field.

7. The Quick Data Entry dialog box for this data file appears, as shown in Figure 10-3. This dialog box contains a text box for each field in the data file. Enter the data for each record using this dialog box. To do so:

a. Type the data for the first field of the first record in the appropriate text box.

b. Select Ne<u>x</u>t Field or press ENTER.

c. Continue this until you have filled in all of the fields for the first record. If you need to move back to a field, select Pre<u>v</u>ious Field.

d. When all of the data for the first record has been entered, select New <u>R</u>ecord or press ENTER. Pressing

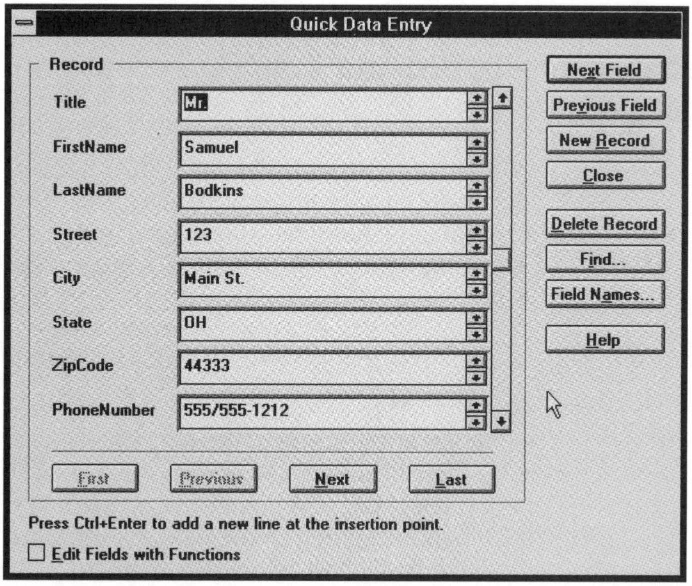

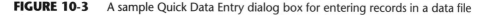

FIGURE 10-3   A sample Quick Data Entry dialog box for entering records in a data file

ENTER moves you to the next record when you are on the last field.

   e. Continue using the previous steps for entering records.

   f. After entering several records, you can use the First, Previous, Next, or Last button to move between the records. You can also delete the record that appears in the Quick Data Entry dialog box by selecting Delete Record.

   g. If you want to change a field name, or add or delete a field, select Field Names, make your changes, and select OK.

8. After adding all of your records and making any changes, select Close.

9. When prompted, select Yes to save this data file. You must provide a filename, just as you normally do when saving a file.

When you later open the file, you can return to the Quick Data Entry dialog box by selecting Quick Entry in the Merge Feature Bar.

What is a form file and how do I create one for a mail merge?

A form file contains the text that does not vary when you merge documents. For example, if you are creating a form letter to send to clients, the form file contains the text that is the same for all clients, such as the paragraph announcing the sale. To create a form file:

1. Select Merge from the Tools menu or press SHIFT+F9.

2. Select Form.

3. Enter the name of the data file you want to use with this form file in the Associate with a Data File text box and select OK. If you have not yet created the data file that you are going to use with this form file, select the None radio button before selecting OK.

4. Enter and format your form file just as you would any other document.

5. Position the insertion point at the first location where you want data from your data file merged into the form file. Select Insert Field from the Merge Feauture Bar, select the field from the Field Names list box, and select Insert. Insert all the fields you want merged and select Close.

When you insert a field name, the field code displays in this form file, as shown in Figure 10-4. When you merge this form file with the data file, these field codes are replaced by the data in the data file.

6. Save the form file by selecting Save from the File menu, providing a filename, and selecting OK.

Form files and data files are treated as two separate files. You can use a data file with more than one form file, and you can do the same with the form file. For example, one form file can be used with multiple data files to print mailing labels. You can also use the same data file for both a form letter and the mailing labels that you use to mail the letters.

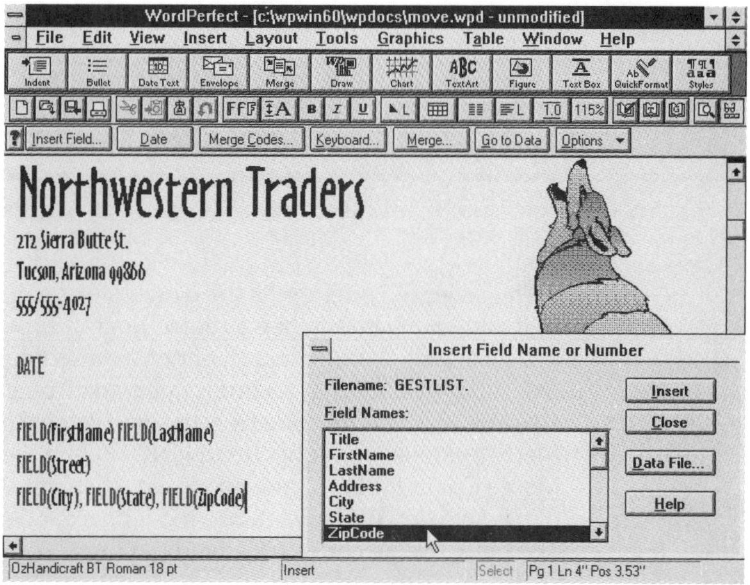

FIGURE 10-4   Adding merge codes to a form file

How many records can I put in a data file?

WordPerfect lets you add up to 65,535 records in a single data file. However, you may not be able to store this many records in one data file if your computer does not have sufficient memory to load the entire data file at once. If memory becomes a limitation, you can break your records into more than one data file, and perform merges using each of the data files you create.

Tech Tip: You can have up to 255 named fields in a text data file or up to 64 columns in a table data file.

Some of the names in my merge documents have blank spaces, because some of my records do not have entries in the middle initial field. Can I prevent the extra spaces, but still use middle initials when I have them?

Yes, you can prevent these extra spaces in names without middle initials and still use the middle initials of names that do have them. To eliminate the blank space when a data field is empty and the form has other field names on the same line, use the IFNOTBLANK merge code in the form file.

For example, when some of the records have no entry for the MI field, enter:

```
FIELD(fname)  CODES(IFNOTBLANK(mi)INSERT(FIELD(mi))ENDIF)  FIELD(lname)
```

This series of codes omits the extra blank space between the First and Last Names when a record does not have a middle initial because WordPerfect does not try inserting that field unless the field for that record is not blank. You can insert the ISNOTBLANK merge code by selecting Merge Codes from the Merge Feature Bar, highlighting ISNOTBLANK(field) in the Merge Codes list box, selecting Insert, then entering the name of the field you don't want inserted if blank and selecting OK. The other merge codes are added the same way.

Merge Code	Result
BEEP	Makes your computer beep
CHAR	Prompts the user for a single character response
COMMENT	Lets you insert text that is not included in the merged document
DISPLAYSTOP	Stops the display of further text after a KEYBOARD code
KEYBOARD	Pauses a performing macro to let the user enter information at the keyboard that will appear in that location in the form file
LOOK	Checks if a key has been pressed and assigns that key to a variable

TABLE 10-1   Some merge commands commonly used in keyboard merges

Why would I use a keyboard merge?

Keyboard merges allow some or all of the information inserted in the merge document to be entered at the keyboard while the merge is being performed. You can create keyboard merges by entering merge codes that call for entry at the keyboard. Some commands often used with keyboard merges are shown in Table 10-1.

You can use keyboard merges when you are merging small numbers of documents and do not expect to save the data for future use. For example, if you are working for a chemical company, you may have to respond to local residents' requests for environmental information but not need to keep their names and addresses. A keyboard merge lets you quickly create letters without having to save the data to a file. Keyboard merges are also useful for filling out onscreen forms. For example, if you answer telephones, you may run a keyboard merge in which each merge document is the response to one phone call.

What is the easiest way to edit a data file?

The easiest way to edit a data file, which contains the fields and records used in a merge, is to use the Quick Data Entry dialog box.

1. Retrieve or create a data file.

2. Choose Quick Entry from the Merge Feature Bar.

   Use the Quick Data Entry dialog box to add, edit, or delete records, data, or fields as described in the answer to the question "What is a data file and how do I create it?" earlier in this chapter.

3. Save the file by choosing Save from the File menu.

How do I create a form file for labels?

Creating a form file formatted with labels provides you with a lot of power for many different tasks. For example, you can merge a mailing label form file with your client data file to quickly print labels for mailing letters to all of your clients. You can also format a document to create name tags for people attending your meeting, or to create master business cards for new employees, such as the ones shown in Figure 10-5. To create a form file for labels:

1. Select Labels from the Layout menu.

2. Highlight the appropriate label size from the Labels list box and choose Select. You can restrict the labels displayed in this list box to laser or tractor-fed formats by selecting the Laser or Tractor-Fed radio buttons in the Display area of the dialog box.

   You can select Edit to edit the label size currently selected or select Create to manually create a label size by providing the label's specifications.

3. Select Merge from the Tools menu or press SHIFT+F9.

4. Select Form.

5. Select the Use File in Active Window radio button and select OK.

6. Enter the name of the data file you plan to use with these labels and select OK.

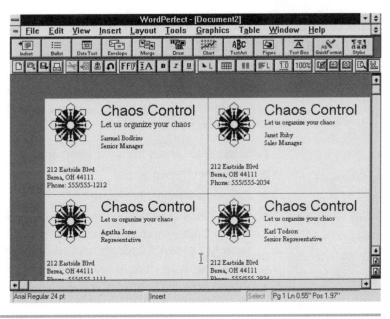

FIGURE 10-5   Master business cards created by a merge

7. Create the form file. To insert the field names, select Insert Field from the Merge Feature Bar. Select the field from the Field Names list box and select Insert. Repeat this step until all fields have been inserted on the label, then select Close. Enter any text that does not change from record to record the same way you enter text in any other WordPerfect document.

8. Select Merge from the Merge Feature Bar after creating the form file, then the Merge button.

9. Select where you want the merged document to go from the Output File pop-up list. Your choices are <Current Document>, <New Document>, <Printer>, or Select File.

10. If you merge to a document or file, you will later need to print the labels as you would normally, by selecting Print from the File menu. Printing to a document or file lets you look at the document so you can see that the labels are merged exactly as you wish. If you merge the labels to the printer and you print a lot of them, you may end up wasting paper if the merge isn't exactly what you want.

I used to be able to see my merge codes, but now I can't. What happened?

You've changed a setting that controls whether or not merge codes are displayed. You can change this setting in two ways, by using the File menu or the Merge Feature Bar. To change this setting using the File menu:

1. Select Preferences from the File menu.
2. Select the Display icon.
3. Select the Merge radio button.
4. Select either the Display Merge Codes or the Display Merge Codes As Markers radio button. If you select the latter, your merge codes display as diamonds.
5. Select OK, then Close to return to the document. You should now see your merge codes again.

To display the merge codes again using the Merge Feature Bar:

1. Select Options from the Merge Feature Bar.
2. Select Display Codes or Display as Markers.

Can I get rid of the blank lines in my merge documents that appear when some records do not have data for all the fields used in the form file?

You can avoid including blank lines like the ones shown in Figure 10-6 in your final merge document. These appear because some records do not include entries in all of the fields that appear in the form file. In Figure 10-6 these blank lines appear because some records do not include a company name. However, you can prevent blank lines by changing a merge option. To do so:

1. Select Merge from the Merge Feature Bar while in the form or data file, then select Merge.
2. Select Options in the Perform Merge dialog box.
3. Select Remove Blank Line from the If Empty Field in Data File pop-up list.
4. Select OK twice to perform the merge.

WordPerfect - [c:\marketng\mrglette.wpd - unmodified]

File Edit View Insert Layout Tools Graphics Table Window Help

Indent Bullet Date Text Envelope Merge Draw Chart TextArt Figure Text Box QuickFormat Styles

parker & parker

212 W. 134th
Cleveland, OH 44302

February 16, 1994

Lewis Sinclair

3424 Blake St.
New York City, New York, 11011

Dear Mr. Sinclair:

Times New Roman Regular 12 pt   Insert   Select   Pg 1 Ln 1" Pos 2.52"

FIGURE 10-6   A merge document with blank lines indicating empty fields

Tech Tip: Another way to prevent these blank lines is to include a
question mark in the field name that appears in the form file. For
example, the code FIELD(MidInit?) will not print blank lines for records
that have no middle initial recorded.

Can I select which records to merge if I don't want to merge the entire data file?

WordPerfect lets you choose which records you want to merge
with the form file. You can mark the records you want to
include, or specify the conditions the records must meet before
they can be merged.

To specify conditions records must meet:

1. Create your data and form files.

2. Select Merge from the Merge Feature Bar from the data
or form file, then Merge.

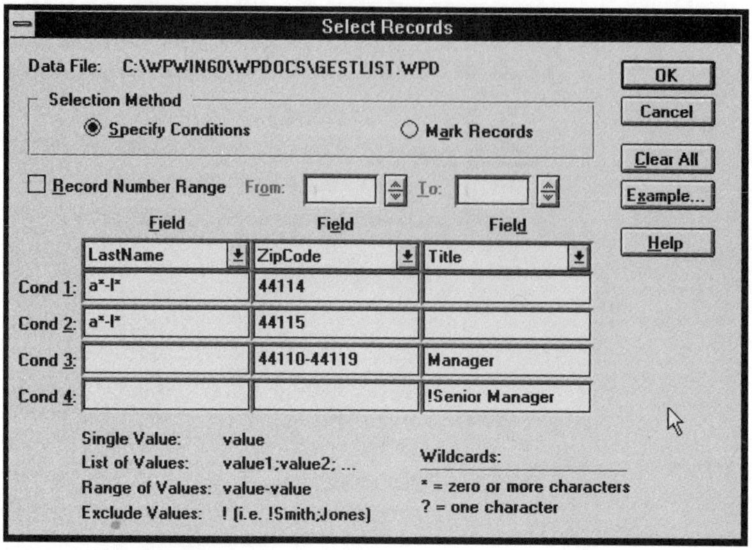

FIGURE 10-7   The Select Records dialog box

3. Choose Select Records.

4. Select the Specify Conditions radio button in the Selection Method area of the dialog box.

5. If you want to limit which records can be selected by their position in the data file, select the Record Number Range check box, then enter the first record number you want to use in the From text box and the last one in the To text box.

6. Select the fields you are going to use to create your conditions in the three Field drop-down lists shown in Figure 10-7. These are the three fields you want to test to match the conditions you specify.

7. Specify your conditions in the Cond 1, 2, 3, and 4 text boxes under the field drop-down list boxes. The conditions you enter in these fields are tested against the fields listed above them. For a record to be merged, it must meet all of the entries for one condition.

For conditions, you can enter a single value, a list of values, or a range of values. You can also enter values to exclude. If you enter a single value, or a list or range of values, the records must contain one of the values entered. If you enter an exclude value, the records must not contain that value.

8. After specifying the conditions you want met, select OK twice to start the merge.

You can also mark which records you want to include in the merge. To do so:

1. Create your data and form files.

2. Select Merge from the Merge Feature Bar from the data or form file, then Merge.

3. Choose Select Records.

4. Select the Mark Records radio button in the Selection Method area of the dialog box.

5. The Record List list box displays all of your records, each preceded by a check box. Each record with a selected check box will be merged. You can select or clear a check box by clicking it or by highlighting the record and pressing SPACEBAR.

   ■ You can set which records are shown in the Record List list box by entering the first and last record numbers in the Display Records From and To text boxes.

   ■ Change which field is shown first in the Record List list box by selecting it from the First Field to Display drop-down list.

   ■ After changing the Display Record From and To text boxes or the First Field to Display drop-down list, select Update Record List to change the display in the Record List list box.

6. Select Mark all Records or Unmark all Records to select or clear all of the records in the Record List list box.

7. To perform the merge, select OK twice when you have selected all of the records you want to merge.

Can I stop WordPerfect from inserting a page break between each record in the merge document?

You can prevent WordPerfect from putting each record's merge document on its own page. You may want to avoid page breaks when, for example, you are doing the merge to assemble a catalog from a data file which lists many different products and information about them. You can also perform a merge without page breaks to assemble telephone directories for members of your group or employees of your company, like the directory shown in Figure 10-8. To do so:

1. Select <u>M</u>erge from the Merge Feature Bar while in the form or data file, then select <u>M</u>erge.

2. Select <u>O</u>ptions in the Perform Merge dialog box.

3. Clear the <u>S</u>eparate Each Merged Document With a Page Break check box.

```
┌──────────────────────────────────────────────────────────────┐
│  ─                  WordPerfect - [Document2]          ▼ │▲│▼ │
│  ─  File  Edit  View  Insert  Layout  Tools  Graphics  Table  Window  Help  ▲│▼ │
│  [toolbar icons: Indent Bullet Date Text Envelope Merge Draw Chart TextArt Figure Text Box QuickFormat Styles] │
│  [toolbar icons row 2]  115%                                   │
│                                                                │
│                   Johnson Industries              I            │
│                     Directory Listing                          │
│   Bass, Mark  - - - - - - - - - - - - - - - - - - - - - 342-9502 │
│   Bethel, Greg - - - - - - - - - - - - - - - - - - - - -530-3940 │
│   Bielan, George- - - - - - - - - - - - - - - - - - - - 694-2934 │
│   Bonner, Carlton - - - - - - - - - - - - - - - - - - - 454-2049 │
│   Forslund, Cynthia - - - - - - - - - - - - - - - - - - 454-0694 │
│   Horning, Patricia- - - - - - - - - - - - - - - - - - - 342-5940 │
│   Jefferson, Lynette - - - - - - - - - - - - - - - - - - 454-2093 │
│   Jolley, Ginger - - - - - - - - - - - - - - - - - - - - 530-2043 │
│   Knudson, Carolyn - - - - - - - - - - - - - - - - - - - 342-4902 │
│   Luginbuhl, William  - - - - - - - - - - - - - - - - - 630-3940 │
│   Mack, Barbara - - - - - - - - - - - - - - - - - - - - 454-0932 │
│   Purdy, Richard - - - - - - - - - - - - - - - - - - - - 694-3942 │
│   Purdy, Paul - - - - - - - - - - - - - - - - - - - - - 342-5390 │
│  Times New Roman Regular 18 pt      Insert    Select  Pg 1 Ln 1.39" Pos 3.57" │
└──────────────────────────────────────────────────────────────┘
```

FIGURE 10-8   Merging without page breaks lets you create complete documents

4. Select OK twice to perform the merge.

Can I stop a merge while it is happening?

Yes, you can a stop a merge that is in progress in two ways.

- Press ESC.
- Press CTRL+BREAK.

Both my form and data files have passwords. Will this affect my merged document?

The passwords on your form file will have an effect if you are merging to another file. If you are merging to a file instead of to a window or the printer, that output file will use the same password as your form file.

Some of my client records don't have a contact name. How can I use a generic greeting for these records, but insert the contact's name for other records?

You can simply remove a blank line created by an empty field by changing an option while preparing to merge. However, if you want to substitute other text rather than just remove the blank line, you will need to use some of WordPerfect's programming codes.

For example, Figure 10-9 shows a letter written by WID Waste Disposal to various prospective clients. The company does not have contact names for all of them. Therefore, if the field for the contact's last name is blank, the letter is addressed "Attention Waste Manager." If this field is not blank, WordPerfect proceeds to the next command, which inserts a greeting to the contact, using his or her name.

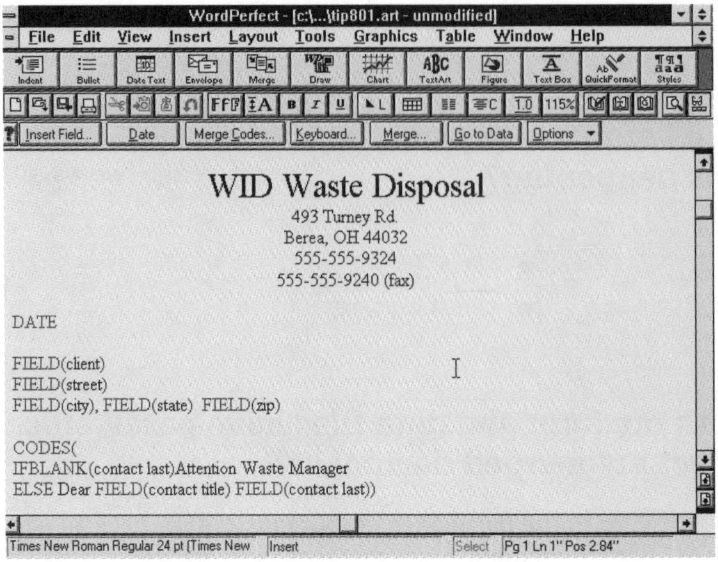

WordPerfect - [c:\...\tip801.art - unmodified]
File Edit View Insert Layout Tools Graphics Table Window Help
Indent Bullet Date Text Envelope Merge Draw Chart TextArt Figure Text Box QuickFormat Styles
Insert Field... Date Merge Codes... Keyboard... Merge... Go to Data Options
WID Waste Disposal
493 Turney Rd.
Berea, OH 44032
555-555-9324
555-555-9240 (fax)
DATE
FIELD(client)
FIELD(street)
FIELD(city), FIELD(state) FIELD(zip)
CODES(
IFBLANK(contact last)Attention Waste Manager
ELSE Dear FIELD(contact title) FIELD(contact last))
Times New Roman Regular 24 pt (Times New
Insert
Select
Pg 1 Ln 1" Pos 2.84"

FIGURE 10-9 Using merge programming codes to substitute text for blank lines

I am performing a merge using a form and data file created with an earlier version of WordPerfect. The merge is very slow. Can I speed it up?

Yes. When WordPerfect 6.0 performs a merge using data or form files created in an earlier version of the program, the files are converted to WordPerfect 6.0 format during the merge. Then, when the merged document is saved, it is saved in the new format. You can speed up the merge by converting the files to WordPerfect 6.0 format before you merge them.

To save files in WordPerfect 6.0 format, perform the following steps:

1. Retrieve the file by selecting Open from the File menu.
2. Select Save As from the File menu.
3. Enter a filename in the Filename text box.
4. Select WordPerfect 6.0 from the Format drop-down list.
5. Choose OK.

The file is now saved in WordPerfect 6.0 format. After converting both your form and data files to WordPerfect 6.0 format, try the merge again. This time, it should go much faster.

I am creating a text data file. Is there a limit to how much information I can enter in one field?

Yes. WordPerfect 6.0 for Windows lets you enter between 1 and 9,000 characters in one field.

How do I restart a keyboard merge after typing an entry?

When you set up a keyboard merge, use an INPUT command where you want input when the merge is run. When WordPerfect encounters an INPUT merge command during the merge, WordPerfect pauses the merge until you indicate you are ready to resume it. To continue the merge after entering the data, select Continue from the Merge Feature Bar.

When I perform a merge using a data file containing graphics, the merge is very slow. Can I speed it up?

You can speed up merges that include graphics by using the Image on Disk option instead of actually inserting the image file into the data file. This option means that the image is actually stored in its original file instead of your data file. This speeds up the merge process because instead of merging the large data file, WordPerfect simply needs to merge the note that indicates where the file needs to get the image from. You can choose to insert the graphic as an image on disk when you first insert the graphic, or by editing the graphics box. When you add the graphic, select the Image on Disk check box. To change to using the image on disk after you have added the graphic, select the Content button on the Graphics Box Feature Bar, select Image on Disk from the Content pop-up list, and select OK.

There's an error in my merge. Can WordPerfect help me find what is causing it?

WordPerfect can help you isolate the merge codes that are causing your merge error. The program does this by *stepping* through the merge, which means executing one code at a time, then waiting for your signal to go to the next step. This helps you find the error because you will see precisely when the problem develops in the merge, so you know exactly which merge codes are causing it.

To make WordPerfect step through a merge, enter the STEPON code at the beginning of the form file. You can insert this code by selecting Merge Codes from the Merge Feature Bar, STEPON in the Merge Codes list box, and Insert. After encountering a STEPON code, WordPerfect will execute the merge one code at a time and wait for you to press a key before going to the next step. All codes and text will display on the screen, as that part of the file is read and performed. If you know the problem is occurring in a particular section of the document, you can insert a STEPON code at the beginning of the section and a STEPOFF code at the end of the section. When WordPerfect encounters the STEPOFF code, it starts performing the merge normally. The STEPOFF code is inserted by selecting Merge Codes from the Merge Feature Bar, STEPOFF in the Merge Codes list box, and Insert.

Macros and Templates

Macros and templates are wonderful productivity tools that allow you to handle repetitive tasks with ease and efficiency. If you've had difficulties with macros or have heard of problems other people have encountered, take heart! The questions and answers in this chapter will help you reach success whether you are creating your first macro or your fiftieth one. The Frustration Busters box describes ways to avoid some of the most common problems with macros.

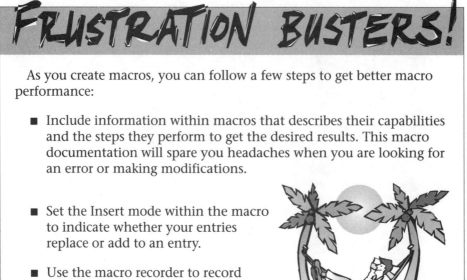

FRUSTRATION BUSTERS!

As you create macros, you can follow a few steps to get better macro performance:

- Include information within macros that describes their capabilities and the steps they perform to get the desired results. This macro documentation will spare you headaches when you are looking for an error or making modifications.

- Set the Insert mode within the macro to indicate whether your entries replace or add to an entry.

- Use the macro recorder to record menu commands rather than typing them yourself and possibly making typing mistakes.

What is the default template that WordPerfect for Windows uses?

The default template is the STANDARD.WPT template, and all new documents are based on it. This template contains settings for styles, menus, button bars, power bars, formatting codes, and other features within WordPerfect. STANDARD.WPT is the default template because it is selected as part of WordPerfect's default preferences. To change the template WordPerfect uses as the default, select Preferences from the File menu and select File. Select the Templates radio button and type the name of the file to use as the default template in the Default File text box. While you are in this dialog box, you can also select the directory for the template files and their default extension.

Are there predefined templates within WordPerfect 6.0 for Windows?

WordPerfect has predefined templates called ExpressDocs, which can guide you through the steps for creating memos, faxes, or other documents. These templates also provide customized styles, menus, button bars, power bars, formatting codes, and other features expressly designed to help you create that specific type of document. To access one of these templates, choose Template from the File menu, then select one of the templates in the Document Template To Use list box, then click OK. All of the templates listed are ExpressDocs except for Standard and the templates that you or someone connected to your system has created.

To:	Dianne Moore
Fax:	(212) 555-5555
From:	Mary Campbell
Date:	February 25, 1994
Pages:	5 page(5) including this page.

fax

From the desk of...

Mary Campbell
President
Campbell & Associates
413 Timberidge Trail
Gates Mills, OH 44040

(216) 555-5555
Fax: (216) 555-5555

FIGURE 11-1 Document created using an ExpressDoc template

WordPerfect includes a booklet showing samples of the different documents you can create with ExpressDocs, among them invoices, resumes, fax cover sheets, and calendars. Figure 11-1 shows a sample document created with an ExpressDoc. In this document, the company information is part of the personal information your template saves to share with all ExpressDocs. The fax recipient and phone number can be typed or selected from one of the address book entries stored along with the personal information. The picture that was put in afterwards by adding a graphics box comes from Presentation Task Force.

Frequently, an ExpressDoc includes personal information. To make creating these ExpressDocs easier, WordPerfect will prompt you the first time you use an ExpressDoc for personal information that all subsequent ExpressDocs will use. This information is stored as part of the abbreviations in the default template.

How do I get my own personal information to be entered automatically for templates in a network version of WordPerfect 6.0?

Several of the ExpressDocs templates automatically use personal information that you provided when prompted by the Autofill macro the first time you opened an ExpressDocs template. That information is used to create documents using ExpressDocs so that you do not need to fill in that personal information each time you use an ExpressDocs template. If you are on a network and you want to have your own personal information for templates that use Autofill, you need to have your own personal default template file. To create this:

1. Select Preferences from the File menu.

2. Select File, then the Templates radio button.

3. Type the drive and directory for your personal directory in the Default Directory text box; for example, **C:\WPDOCS** or **C:\WINDOWS**.

4. Type a template filename in the Default File text box, such as **JOE.WPT** or **STANDARD.WPT**.

5. Click OK.

Enter Your Personal Information	
Name:	Mary Campbell
Title:	President
Company:	Campbell & Associates
Address:	P.O. Box 38573
City, State Zip:	Gates Mills, OH 44040
Telephone:	(216)555-5555
Fax:	(216)555-5555

OK   Cancel

FIGURE 11-2   Dialog box for entering personal information

6. Select <u>Y</u>es if WordPerfect pops up a dialog that says "Template file c:\wpdocs\joe.wpt does not exist. Do you want to create the default Template file?"

7. Select <u>C</u>lose to exit the Preferences dialog window.

The next time you open an ExpressDocs template, it will ask you to enter your personal information, as shown in Figure 11-2. WordPerfect saves this personal information in your default template file (not the network's), which in this case is C:\WPDOCS\JOE.WPT. Styles, macros, and abbreviations are not copied over from the current template to the new one.

You may also copy an existing template from the network directory to your personal directory and use that as your personal default template. However, the template will include any of the personal information contained in the network's version of that template.

Tech Tip: You can change the personal information (whether or not you are on a network) by using a template that uses the personal information and clicking the Personal Info button. Changing the personal information this way preserves the styles, macros, and templates associated with the standard template.

How do I convert my WordPerfect 5.1 for DOS macros to WordPerfect 6.0 for Windows?

WordPerfect 6.0 for Windows comes with a Macro Conversion utility called MCVWIN.EXE which converts WordPerfect 5.1 for DOS macros. MCVWIN.EXE is a utility that runs in Windows independent of WordPerfect 6.0 for Windows. To run this conversion utility, switch to the Windows Program Manager and choose Run from the File menu. Type **C:\WPC20\MCVWIN** in the Command Line text box (be sure to replace C:\WPC20\ with the directory containing MCVWIN.EXE if you have this file in another location) and click OK. The Macro Conversion utility opens and displays a window like the one in Figure 11-3. In the Macro(s) to Convert text box, type the path and name of any macros you wish to convert. You can use wildcard characters. For example, if you want to convert all your WordPerfect 5.1 for DOS macros and they are all located in a directory called C:\WP51\MACROS, you can type **C:\WP51\MACROS*.WPM**. Also, in the text box labeled Output File or Directory, you must type the new filename and path to the directory where you wish to save the converted macros, as in **C:\WPWIN60*.***. Then select Convert, and the Macro Conversion Utility will complete the job. Select Cancel after you have converted your macros to exit this utility.

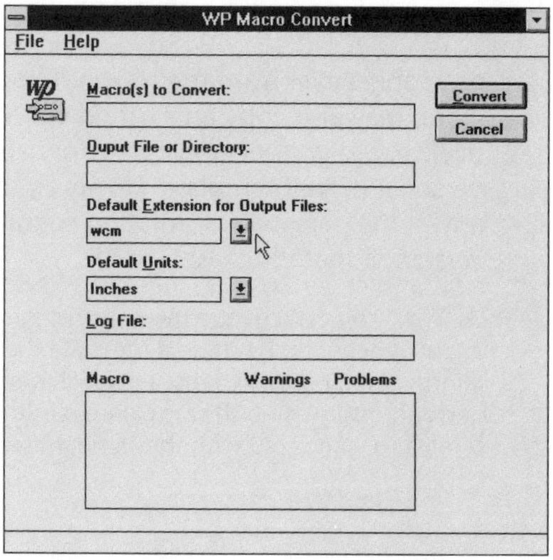

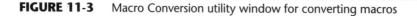

FIGURE 11-3   Macro Conversion utility window for converting macros

Some macros do not completely convert and require some editing on your part. If this is the case, MCVWIN.EXE will list the macros with problems. You may want to provide a filename in the Log File text box to store a list of the errors found in a file. WordPerfect 6.0 for Windows will not convert or run the following WordPerfect 5.1 for DOS macro commands: {INPUT}, {LOOK}, {MENU OFF}, {MENU ON}, {ORIGINAL KEY}, {PAUSE KEY}, {RESTART}, {SHELL ASSIGN}, {SHELL MACRO}, {SHELL VARIABLE}, {STATUS PROMPT}, {STEP OFF}, {STEP ON}

Tech Tip: You can also run WordPerfect 6.0 for DOS and 5.*x* for Windows macros directly from WordPerfect 6.0 for Windows. If a WordPerfect 5.*x* for Windows macro cannot run in WordPerfect 6.0 for Windows, you will see a detailed error message describing what must change. Usually, the problem is the inclusion of one of the following commands that WordPerfect 6.0 for Windows does not support: CommentCreate, DateFormat, Font, KeyboardSelect, OverStrikeCreate, OverStrikeEdit, PaperSizeAdd, PaperSizeDelete, PrintMultiplePages, Sort, TableSplit, TabSet, and ToCMark.

Tech Tip: Programming commands that return a value have changed from WordPerfect 5.*x* for Windows to WordPerfect 6.0 for Windows. In WordPerfect 5.*x* for Windows, several programming commands included a Variable parameter where the return value was placed. In WordPerfect 6.0 for Windows, these commands do not require a Variable parameter. Rather, they are designed to be included in expressions. For example, in WordPerfect 5.2, a macro might contain EXISTS(*TestValue,TestResult*) where *TestValue* is the variable to test and *TestResult* stores the result of the EXISTS command. In WordPerfect 6.0, this macro would insert EXISTS(*TestValue*) where you wanted to use *TestResult*.

Is it possible for me to save a frequently used document layout as a template?

To save a document as a template, save the file with the WPT extension, as in *NAME*.WPT. Also, save this file in your default template directory. To check the default template directory: Select Preferences in the File menu. Select the file. Choose the Template radio button and note the entry in the Default Directory text box.

You can avoid saving your edited document over your template by setting the template file's attributes to read-only, following these steps:

1. Make sure the template is not currently in use or open.

2. Select Open from the File menu and highlight the file. You may need to change the directory to match the correct location of your templates.

3. Select the File Options pop-up button and select Change Attributes.

4. Check the Read-Only check box in the Change File Attributes dialog box and select OK.

5. Select Cancel to leave the Open File dialog box without opening a file.

Now every time this template file is opened, a message will be displayed saying that this file is read-only, and that you can make changes to it but will have to save it to a different name.

How do I add descriptions to the templates I create?

At the bottom of the Template dialog box, you will see a description of the highlighted template. This description is taken from the Descriptive Name text box of the document summary of the template. You can add descriptions to your own templates by following either option listed below:

■   Open the template. Select Document Summary from the File menu, type an entry in the Descriptive Name text box, and select OK. Then save and close the template.

■   Select Template from the File menu. Select the template from the Document Template in Use list box, and select Edit Template from the Options pop-up menu. Select Description in the Template Feature Bar. Type or edit the description in the Description text box and select OK. Then select Exit Template from the Template Feature Bar.

How do I assign a macro to my button bar?

To add a button that will run a macro to a button bar, follow these steps:

1. Select Preferences from the File menu and Button Bar.

2. Select the button bar name you would like to change from the Available Button Bars list box, and select Edit.

3. Select Play a Macro from the Button Bar Editor dialog box and choose Add Macro.

4. Enter the macro filename in the Name text box. You can click the list box on the end to select the macro file.

5. Choose Select and Yes to save the path for the macro's filename.

6. Select OK, then Close.

7. Select Close to exit the Preferences dialog box.

Just like other buttons in a button bar, you can change the text and picture that appear on the button.

What macros does WordPerfect provide?

WordPerfect ships with 31 macros. These macros and a brief description of what they do are listed in Table 11-1.

Macro Name	Results
ABBREV.WCM	Adds, changes, and deletes abbreviations stored in the default template
ADRSBOOK.WCM	Adds, changes, and deletes addresses in the address book stored in the default template
ADRS2MRG.WCM	Creates a merge data file containing the address book stored in the default template
ALLFONTS.WCM	Lists all fonts and shows a sample for each font available with the currently selected printer
AUTOFILL.WCM	Automates supplying personal information that ExpressDocs use
CAPITAL.WCM	Capitalizes the first letter of the current word
CLIPBRD.WCM	Opens the Windows Clipboard Viewer
CLOSEALL.WCM	Closes all open documents and prompts you to select whether you want to save any that you have modified

TABLE 11-1   Macros shipped with WordPerfect

Macro Name	Results
CTRLSFTF.WCM	Prompts for FROM and TO values for the equation editor
DROPCAP.WCM	Makes the first letter in the current paragraph a large drop capital
ENDFOOT.WCM	Converts endnotes in the document or selected text into footnotes
EXPNDALL.WCM	Expands every abbreviation in the current document
FILESTMP.WCM	Adds the filename and path of the current document to a header or footer
FONTDN.WCM	Decreases the font size of the selected text by two points
FONTUP.WCM	Increases the font size of the selected text by two points
FOOTEND.WCM	Converts footnotes in the document or selected text into endnotes
GOTODOS.WCM	Opens a DOS prompt application window
LINENUM.WCM	Moves the insertion point to a specified line and character in the current document
PAGEXOFY.WCM	Adds the page number in the format "Page *x* of *y* pages" at one of several predefined locations
PARABRK.WCM	Separates paragraphs with graphical characters
PGBORDER.WCM	Adds a background graphic page border to the current page
PROMPTS.WCM	Creates and edits the prompts displayed by templates such as ExpressDoc
READCLP.WCM	Reads the text stored in the Clipboard, assuming you have ProVoice or Monologue installed
READFILE.WCM	Reads a text file or plays a sound file, assuming you have ProVoice or Monologue installed
READSEL.WCM	Reads the selected text, assuming you have ProVoice or Monologue installed
REVERSE.WCM	Switches the color of the selected text and its background
SAVEALL.WCM	Saves all open documents and prompts you to select whether you want to save any that you have modified
SQCONFIG.WCM	Opens a dialog box to configure the Smart Quotes utility
SQTOGGLE.WCM	Turns the Smart Quotes utility on and off
TRANSPOS.WCM	Transposes the two characters before the insertion point
WATERMRK.WCM	Creates a watermark using the contents of a text or graphics file that you select

TABLE 11-1   Macros shipped with WordPerfect (continued)

Tech Tip: Use these sample macros to help you create the macros you want. For example, you can look at the WATERMRK macro to see the commands it uses to display dialog boxes, process dialog box entries, and add the watermark.

How do I edit my macro?

WordPerfect macros are stored as documents; this allows you to use the program to edit them. Rather than use the Open command in the File menu to open these documents, select Macros from the Tools menu and Edit. Type the name of the macro in the Name text box or click the File Name box at the end of the text box to open another dialog box for selecting the macro to edit. When you select OK, the macro is opened for editing like the one shown below. You can also see the Macro Edit Feature Bar that you can use to save, close, and compile your macro.

```
WordPerfect - [c:\...\testing.wcm - unmodified]
File  Edit  View  Insert  Layout  Tools  Graphics  Table  Window  Help

Command Inserter...    Save & Compile    Save As...    Close

Local(CompanyName;ContactName)
DialogDefine("MyDialog";50;50;173;85;1+2;"Company Information")
DialogAddText("MyDialog";1002;5;5;100;25;1;"Company Name:")
DialogAddEditBox("MyDialog";1003;60;4;100;13;1;CompanyName;25)
DialogAddText("MyDialog";1004;5;23;100;25;1;"Contact Name:")
DialogAddEditBox("MyDialog";1005;60;22;100;13;1;ContactName;25)
DialogDisplay("MyDialog";1)
// More Macro commands here
DialogDestroy("MyDialog")
```

How can I change the date for my MEMO2 template?

The MEMO2 template which ships with WordPerfect 6.0 for Windows uses date text rather than a date code in the date line of the memo heading. Therefore, when you use the MEMO2 template, the date always reads "September 16, 1993," which is the text that was entered in the template originally. To edit the template and insert a date code which will automatically update to reflect the current date, follow these steps:

1. Select Template from the File menu and choose the MEMO2 template from the list.

2. Click the Options pop-up button and select Edit Template.

3. Select the table cell containing the date.

4. Select Format from the Table menu. Under Cell Attributes, clear the Lock check box to remove the cell lock, and select OK.

5. Delete the date in the table cell, then select Date from the Insert menu, and Date Code.

6. Select Format from the Table menu and select the Lock check box to relock the cell.

7. Click the Exit Template button in the Template Feature Bar and select Yes to save the changes to the template.

Can I use a mouse to record a macro?

Since WordPerfect records the results of what you are doing when you record a macro rather than how you go about it, you can use either the keyboard or mouse in this process. For example, when you use the Open command in the File menu, WordPerfect records the FileOpen macro command whether you used the keyboard or mouse to select the command. Recording the results also means that you can select commands with arrow keys or by typing underlined letters to record the same result. This process is different from those used by macro recorders such as WordPerfect 5.1's, which recorded only your keystrokes so you had to make sure you started the macro from the same location every time.

Is there a macro I can use to apply a border to my document?

WordPerfect 6.0 for Windows ships with a macro named PGBORDER.WCM, which will apply the selected border to the page. To run this macro, follow these steps:

1. Move the insertion point to the beginning of the page where the border will be applied.

2. Select Macro from the Tools menu, and select Play.

3. Type **PGBORDER.WCM** or select this macro from the list, and click Play.

Where is the macro documentation for WordPerfect 6.0 for Windows?

WordPerfect 6.0 for Windows comes with online macro documentation rather than a printed manual. To access macro information, select <u>M</u>acros from the <u>H</u>elp menu.

Tech Tip: You can print any of the help screens by clicking the <u>P</u>rint button in the Help window or by selecting <u>P</u>rint Topic in the <u>F</u>ile menu.

Does WordPerfect have a shortcut for entering macro commands?

Macros can include many commands, so rather than remembering the correct syntax, you can insert a command using the Macro Command Inserter. When you are looking at the macro's commands, you can move the insertion point to where you want the command added. Then, click the C<u>o</u>mmand Inserter button in the Macro Edit Feature Bar or press ALT+SHIFT+O. From the dialog box displayed, like the one shown below, you can create the command you want to add to the macro. From <u>C</u>ommands, select the command to add to the macro. When you do this, the <u>P</u>arameters list box displays the parameters the selected command uses. For some of the parameters, when the command uses predefined choices for the parameter, the <u>M</u>embers list box lists the possible choices. For many of the parameters, you can type the parameter entry into the C<u>o</u>mmand Edit text box for the command you are building. When the command is finished, you can select <u>I</u>nsert and WordPerfect adds the command you have built at the insertion point's location. You can continue building more commands to add to the current location in the macro file. When you are finished, select <u>C</u>lose to close the Macro Command Inserter dialog box.

WordPerfect Macro Command Inserter			
Commands (98)	**Parameters (4)**	**Members (1)**	**Type**
//	ProductPrefix	Default!	Program-US
AppActivate	ApplicationName		
AppExecute	Default		
AppExecuteExt	Language		
Application			
Returns:	**Type:** Enumeration	**Value:**	**Edit**
Description: Specify an application that is used in the macro			**Insert**
Command Edit			
Application()			**Close**

Can I save a macro in a template?

You can save a macro in a template rather than saving it as a separate file. Saving it in a template ensures that the macro will always be available when using the template; if the location of the macro file changes, the template still has the macro to run. Also, if you distribute the template, the macro will be available because it is stored in the template. To create a macro and store it as part of the template rather than as a separate file:

1. Select Template from the File menu. Select the template to store the macro from the Document Template to Use list box, and choose Edit Templates from the Options pop-up button.

2. Select Create Object from the Template Feature bar by clicking it or by pressing ALT+SHIFT+C. Then select Macro.

3. From the Record Macro dialog box, type the name of the macro in the Name list box and select Record.

4. Record the macro.

5. Select Macro from the Tools menu and select Record to stop recording the macro. You can also press CTRL+F10.

6. Select the Exit Template button, and select Yes when prompted to save the changes to the template file.

When you select Macro from the Tools menu and then Edit, you can select one of the listed macros from the Macros In Template list box.

How can I make a macro wait while the user makes an entry?

To make a macro pause for user input, first record the macro that will type the entries where you want the user to make an entry. Then edit the macro and enter the line **PauseKey (Key:0)** where you want the user to make an entry. When you play this macro, WordPerfect waits at this point for user input and continues only when ENTER is pressed.

Is there a macro I can use to close, save, or close and save all open documents?

WordPerfect 6.0 for Windows ships with two macros for this purpose. The macro CLOSEALL.WCM closes all open documents. As the documents are closed, the user is prompted to save documents if necessary. The macro SAVEALL.WCM saves all open documents. Users are prompted for a filename if one has not been assigned yet.

To use either of these macros, follow these steps:

Tech Tip: There is no macro command to exit WordPerfect.

1. Select <u>M</u>acro from the <u>T</u>ools menu, and select <u>P</u>lay.

2. Type **CLOSEALL.WCM** or **SAVEALL.WCM** or select either one from the list, and select <u>P</u>lay.

Can I see the dialog boxes a macro uses as it runs?

When you are recording a macro, you can alert WordPerfect to display particular dialog boxes when the macro is run. Do this by clicking the check box in the upper-right corner of the dialog box while recording the macro. As you display dialog boxes, you will notice that the title bar now includes a check box as shown here:

You can also edit a macro and enter a line that forces the dialog box to remain open during execution. For example, if you want a macro to open the Open File dialog box and remain open so you can choose a file, you would add the line **FileOpenDlg()** to the macro to keep the box open for input.

The following is a very simple macro that changes to the WordPerfect directory and opens the Open File dialog box:

```
Application (WP; "WPWP"; Default; "WPWPUS.WCD")
FileChangeDir ("C:\WPWIN60")
FileOpenDlg()
```

How do I assign macros to button bars when I want to share my button bar with others?

You assign a macro to your button bar differently to make sharing the button bar easier. When assigning the macro to the button bar, select the Location button, then select either the Current Template or Default Template radio button. This actually embeds the code for the macro into the button bar. When you choose the File on Disk radio button, WordPerfect adds the macro button to the button bar with the path to the macro file. The button bar is assigned to the selected template, which can be used in a network environment or copied to another computer running WordPerfect locally.

I am writing a macro, and I want my user-defined dialog box to show an ampersand (&) in it. How can I do this?

This is easy. Just put two ampersands together within the character expression. For example, "City && State" in a character expression appears as "City & State" in the dialog box.

Is there a macro I can use to increase or decrease the font size of selected text?

WordPerfect 6.0 for Windows includes two macros which can increase or decrease the font size of selected text. The macro FONTDN.WCM decreases the font size of selected text by two points. For example, text formatted as 12 point decreases to 10 point. The macro FONTUP.WCM increases the font size of selected text by two points. For example, text formatted as 12 point increases to 14 point.

To use either of these macros, follow these steps:

1. Select the text whose font size you wish to change.

2. Select Macro from the Tools menu, and select Play.

3. Type **FONTDN.WCM** or **FONTUP.WCM** or select either one from the list, and select <u>P</u>lay.

How do I create my own dialog boxes?

WordPerfect 6.0 for Windows uses dialog boxes to display and receive information from the macro's user. These dialog boxes are created by following four steps:

1. Define and name the dialog box you are creating with the DialogDefine command. This command names the dialog box, sets its size and position, and sets which command buttons appear on it. An example of this command is

```
DialogDefine("MyDialog";50;50;173;85;1+2;"Company Information")
```

This example creates a dialog box named MyDialog. This dialog box displays "Company Information" in its title bar. You can also use a number, say 100, in place of text. Its upper-left corner is 50 units from the top of the application window and 50 from the left. Dialog boxes use dialog units to measure distances. A vertical dialog unit is 1/8th the character height and a horizontal unit is 1/4th the character width.

2. Define the controls that appear in the dialog box. A control is any item that appears in the dialog box. You do not need to define buttons such as OK and Cancel since they are provided through the DialogDefine command. Each control is defined separately. This includes the text that appears next to controls such as the text that identifies text boxes and list boxes. The dialog box elements and the macro commands that add them are listed in Table 11-2.

Control	Macro Command
Check box	DialogAddCheckBox
Color wheel	DialogAddColorWheel
Drop-down list	DialogAddComboBox
Counter (text box that accepts only numbers and has arrows you can click to increase or decrease its value)	DialogAddCounter
Text box	DialogAddEditBox
File Name box (a text box with a file folder icon that you can select to choose the filename to place in the box)	DialogAddFileNameBox
Frame (placed around another control or group of controls)	DialogAddFrame
Group box that encloses related controls	DialogAddGroupBox
Horizontal line	DialogAddHLine
Hot spot that you can click to make the dialog box disappear	DialogAddHotSpot
Icon stored in a .DLL file	DialogAddIcon
List box	DialogAddListBox
Item in a list displayed by a list box, a drop-down list, or a pop-up list	DialogAddListItem
Pop-up button	DialogAddPopUpButton
Push button (other than OK, Help, and Cancel)	DialogAddPushButton
Radio button	DialogAddRadioButton
Scroll bar	DialogAddScrollBar
Text	DialogAddText
Viewer (Mini-window that display the contents of a file)	DialogAddViewer
Vertical line	DialogAddVLine

TABLE 11-2   Macro commands that create dialog box controls

After each of the commands are parentheses and the arguments that define how the control appears and what the control contains. For most of the commands shown in Table 11-2, the first argument identifies which dialog box contains the control.

3. Display the dialog box using the DialogDisplay command. You can have several commands between the commands that define the dialog box and the DialogDisplay command that displays it. The DialogDisplay command is placed where you want the dialog box displayed when the macro is run.

4. Remove the dialog box from WordPerfect's memory with the DialogDestroy command. You must delete a dialog box if you want another dialog box to use the same name.

When you combine the steps, your macro may contain the following commands:

```
Local(CompanyName;ContactName)
DialogDefine("MyDialog";50;50;173;85;1+2;"Company Information")
DialogAddText("MyDialog";1002;5;5;100;25;1;"Company Name:")
DialogAddEditBox("MyDialog";1003;60;4;100;13;1;CompanyName;25)
DialogAddText("MyDialog";1004;5;23;100;25;1;"Contact Name:")
DialogAddEditBox("MyDialog";1005;60;22;100;13;1;ContactName;25)
DialogDisplay("MyDialog";1)
// More Macro commands here
DialogDestroy("MyDialog")
```

When you play a macro performing these commands, the dialog box looks like this:

Company Information	
Company Name:	
Contact Name:	
	OK Cancel

Tech Tip: If you want an underlined letter to select the adjoining control, make sure that the command that displays the text with the underlined letter comes immediately before the command that displays the control you want selected with the underlined letter.

Customization

Many features of WordPerfect can be tailored to your preference, making it easier for you to work with your documents. You can customize such features as the tools that appear onscreen by default, the options for saving documents, and the units of measurement for defining margins or graphic box positions. The flexibility of the program makes it easy for you to use the features that enhance your productivity, and to remove the ones you do not use very often.

WordPerfect has so many features that you can get lost trying to find the one you want to change. Most customization options are found by selecting P<u>r</u>eferences from the <u>F</u>ile menu. Then you must select the appropriate icon or command from the <u>P</u>references menu to change the feature. The following table lists the icons and the changes you can make with them.

Icon	Features
<u>D</u>isplay	Sets various display related settings, including the default screen elements, the unit of measure, default view and zoom, Ruler Bar options, the symbols displayed by the Show ¶ feature, how Reveal Codes appears, and how merge codes appear.
<u>E</u>nvironment	Sets a variety of options including when your computer will beep, what your user information shows, when WordPerfect hyphenates words in your document, whether the last open files display in your <u>F</u>ile menu, whether WordPerfect saves your arrangement of windows when you close WordPerfect, whether closing a document inserts a QuickMark, and whether hypertext is active.
<u>F</u>ile	Sets the default directories for documents, backups, templates, spreadsheets, databases, printer drivers, label definitions, hyphenation dictionaries, graphics, and macros, as well as the default extension for WordPerfect documents, and the original and timed backup options.
<u>S</u>ummary	Sets the default Document Summary search options, whether WordPerfect uses Descriptive Names, and whether you are prompted on saves and exits to create document summaries.
<u>B</u>utton Bar	Sets which Button Bar appears by default, sets display defaults including the Button Bar's location and font, and lets you edit, create, or delete Button Bars, or copy them between templates.
P<u>o</u>wer Bar	Adds, moves, or deletes items on the Power Bar.
S<u>t</u>atus Bar	Adds, moves, deletes, or resizes items on the Status Bar.

Icon	Features
Keyboard	Selects a keyboard layout or edits, creates, deletes, or copies a keyboard layout.
Menu Bar	Selects a menu bar to use or edits, creates, deletes, or copies a menu bar.
Writing Tools	Selects which of the writing tools are available and the order in which they appear in the Tools menu.
Print	Sets the ratio for relative font sizes and print defaults such as how many copies of a document are printed, whether WordPerfect or the printer generates them, and specifies quality settings for printing text and graphics. You can also define a palette of colors for printing, if you have a color printer.
Import	Defines field and record delimiters, specifies characters to contain text data and to strip from imported documents, and specifies whether to convert Windows Metafiles.

I want the Ruler Bar to appear at all times. Can I do this?

Yes, you can set WordPerfect so that the Ruler Bar appears by default. To do this:

1. Select Preferences from the File menu.
2. Select the Display icon.
3. Select the Ruler Bar radio button.
4. Select the Show Ruler Bar on New and Current Documents check box.
5. Select OK and Close to return to your document.

The ruler will appear for the current document and all documents you subsequently create.

When I start WordPerfect, my documents are too small to read. Can I make them bigger?

Yes, you can change the default zoom used to display your documents. The zoom percentage sets the size by which the document is magnified or reduced. To change the zoom percentage:

1. Select Preferences from the File menu.
2. Select the Display icon.
3. Select the View/Zoom radio button.
4. Select the radio button for the default zoom percentage you want from the Default Zoom area of the dialog box. Selecting 100% displays your document at the same size it will print.
5. Select OK and Close to return to your document.

The text in my Button Bar buttons is too large. Can I make it smaller?

Normally WordPerfect uses the Helvetica font to display text in the Button Bar and other bars. However, Windows 3.1 doesn't include Helvetica as Windows 3.0 did. Therefore, in Windows 3.1 WordPerfect substitutes MS Sans Serif for Helvetica. Although the two fonts are quite similar, MS Sans Serif characters are generally less condensed than Helvetica. If your computer is not making the correct font substitution, you may not like the substitution font that WordPerfect uses. To specify a substitution font for Helvetica:

1. Open the WIN.INI file which is located in your \WINDOWS directory.
2. Move to the section containing the header [FONTS].
3. Enter the following statement if it is not already there:

```
MS Sans Serif 8,10,12,14,18,24 (VGA res)=SSERIFE.FON
```

4. Move to the section containing the header [FONT SUBSTITUTION].

5. Enter the following statement if it is not already there:

```
Helv=MS Sans Serif
```

6. Save the WIN.INI file. Be careful not to change its format from ANSI Text (Windows).

7. Leave WordPerfect and Windows, then restart Windows. Changes to the WIN.INI file take effect only by restarting Windows.

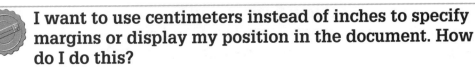

I want to use centimeters instead of inches to specify margins or display my position in the document. How do I do this?

You can change the units of measure that WordPerfect uses in the dialog boxes and in the Status Bar or Ruler. To do so:

1. Select Preferences from the File menu.

2. Select the Display icon.

3. Select the Document radio button at the top of the dialog box.

Tech Tip: The only difference between Inches (") and Inches (i) is the indicator that appears after the measurement: " or i. Otherwise, these choices are identical.

4. Select the units you want to use when entering measurements in dialog boxes from the Units of Measure pop-up list. Your choices include Inches ("), Inches (i), Centimeters (c), Millimeters (m), Points (p), or 1200ths of an inch(w).

5. Select the type of measurement you want to use in the Status Bar and Ruler Bar, from the Status/Ruler Bar Display pop-up list. Your choices are the same as in the Units of Measure pop-up list.

6. Select OK, then Close to return to your document. The new system of measurement is in effect.

For example, if you select <u>C</u>entimeters in the Status/Ruler Bar Displa<u>y</u> pop-up list, your Ruler Bar would look like this:

Tech Tip: Even though you set the measuring system by following the steps above, you can continue to use other systems of measurement. To use another measuring system, type the character that appears in parentheses in step 4 above after the number. For example, to enter a measurement of 2 centimeters in a dialog box, type **2c**. When you move to a different part of the dialog box, WordPerfect converts the distance you entered to use the current measurement system.

I frequently use the <u>S</u>how ¶ command on the <u>V</u>iew menu to show my spaces, tabs, etc. Can I set WordPerfect so this feature is on automatically?

Yes, you can set WordPerfect to automatically show symbols for spaces, tabs, and hard returns as shown in Figure 12-1. To do so:

1. Select P<u>r</u>eferences from the <u>F</u>ile menu.
2. Select the <u>D</u>isplay icon.
3. Select the <u>S</u>how ¶ radio button.
4. Select the Sho<u>w</u> Symbols on New and Current Documents check box.
5. Select OK and <u>C</u>lose to return to the document.

In Reveal Codes, I can't see the details of a code until I highlight it. Can I change this?

Yes, you can change Reveal Codes so that all the codes show their full detail even if you are not highlighting them. To change this setting:

1. Select P<u>r</u>eferences from the <u>F</u>ile menu.
2. Select the <u>D</u>isplay icon.

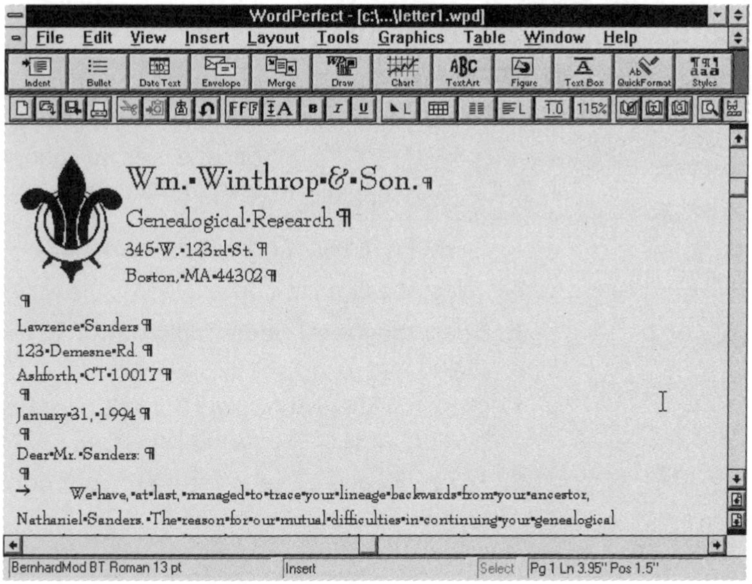

FIGURE 12-1   Showing spaces, tabs, and hard returns

3. Select the Reveal <u>C</u>odes radio button at the top of the dialog box.

4. Select the Show C<u>o</u>des In Detail check box in the Options area of the dialog box.

5. Select OK and <u>C</u>lose to return to your document. From now on, all codes in Reveal Codes will display their full detail all the time, as shown here:

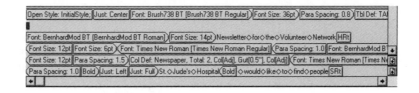

In Reveal Codes, there are diamonds separating my text. What are they and can I get rid of them?

The diamonds mark places where you have pressed the SPACEBAR to insert a space. Reveal Codes displays a diamond for each space in your document, to make locating errant spaces easier. To change this setting so that a space appears instead of diamonds:

1. Select Preferences from the File menu.
2. Select the Display icon.
3. Select the Reveal Codes radio button at the top of the dialog box.
4. Clear the Show Spaces As Bullets check box in the Options area of the dialog box.
5. Select OK and Close to return to your document.

Can I control the amount of space in the application window that Reveal Codes uses?

Yes, you can set the percentage of the window used by Reveal Codes. To do so:

1. Select Preferences from the File menu.
2. Select the Display icon.
3. Select the Reveal Codes radio button.
4. Enter a percentage in the Window Size text box. Reveal Codes will use this percentage of the document window.
5. Select OK, then Close to return to your document.

You can also change the percentage of the window that Reveal Codes uses by dragging the dividing bar between Reveal Codes and the normal document window. However, this setting is only in effect for the current document. The method given above makes a global change for all documents because it actually changes the default setting.

I just switched from WordPerfect for DOS to WordPerfect for Windows. Is there some way to make my function keys work the same way they do in WordPerfect for DOS?

Yes, you can change the function key assignments to match their assignments in WordPerfect for DOS. Changing the function key assignments lets you continue to use the keystrokes you are familiar with. Follow these steps to set WordPerfect to use the same function key assignments as WordPerfect for DOS:

1. Select Preferences from the File menu.
2. Select the Keyboard icon.
3. Highlight <WPDOS Compatible> in the Keyboards list box.
4. Choose Select and Close to return to your document.

Your function keys will now work the way they do in WordPerfect for DOS. If you ever want to switch back to the WordPerfect 6.0 for Windows function key assignments, follow the steps given above but highlight <WPWin 6.0 Keyboard> in the Keyboards list box.

Tech Tip: You can display a template of the function keys for the selected keyboard. From the WordPerfect Help window, select Search, type **keyboard**, select Show Topics, select DOS Keyboard Template from the lower list box, and select Go To. WordPerfect Help displays a template like the one shown in Figure 12-2. From this window, you can select Print Topic from the File menu or select the Print button to print a copy of the template. You can also print the template for the WPWin 6.0 Keyboard by selecting CUA Keyboard Template instead of DOS Keyboard Template. You will want to use the WPWin 6.0 Keyboard if you are using many Windows applications since many of the key combinations are shared by other Windows applications.

At the bottom of the File menu, I see a long list of files that I've worked on recently. How can I get rid of them?

You can use this list of files you've worked on recently to reopen those files quickly. However, if you do not commonly need to work with recently created or opened files or if you want to

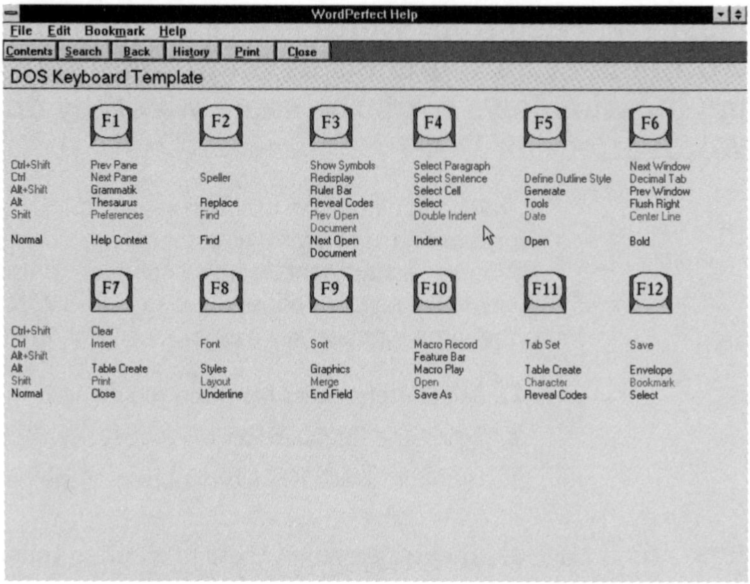

FIGURE 12-2   Keyboard template for the WPDOS-compatible keyboard

delete that listing for confidentiality purposes, you may want to
remove them from the menu. To do so:

1. Select Preferences from the File menu.

2. Select the Environment icon.

3. Clear the Display Last Open Filenames check box in the
   Menu area of the dialog box.

4. Select OK and Close to return to your document. When
   you open the File menu, there will not be a list of files at
   the bottom.

Every time I save a file, I have to switch to the correct subdirectory. Can I set WordPerfect to automatically display my document's directory when I save?

Yes, you can set a default document directory. WordPerfect will then automatically display the chosen default directory when you save files, so you will not need to switch directories or enter a path when saving. To change the default document directory:

1. Select Preferences from the File menu.

2. Select the File icon.

3. Select the Documents/Backup radio button at the top of the dialog box.

4. Enter the directory where you save your documents most often in the Default Directory text box. You can also click the button showing a file folder at the end of the text box to display the Select Directory dialog box, and use it to specify your document directory.

5. Select OK and Close when you have completed your selections.

The icons in the WordPerfect program group in the Program Manager are too close together. Can I change this?

Yes, you can change the spacing between icons in the Windows Program Manager. This is a Windows setting rather than a WordPerfect setting. To change this spacing:

1. Open the Windows Control Panel application. The Control Panel icon is normally found in the Main program group in the Program Manager.

2. Select the Desktop icon or Desktop from the Settings menu.

3. Increase the number in the Spacing text box in the Icons area of the dialog box.

4. Select OK then Exit from the Settings menu when finished.

5. Open the WordPerfect program group.

6. Select Arrange Icons from the Program Manager's Window menu.

How can I get WordPerfect to start up in Draft view every time?

You can choose which view (Page, Two Page, or Draft) WordPerfect will use by default. To choose the view:

1. Select Preferences from File menu.

2. Select the Display icon.

3. Select the View/Zoom radio button at the top of the dialog box.

4. Select the Draft radio button in the Default View area of the dialog box. If you wanted to use a different view as the default, you could select either the Page or Two Page radio button.

5. Select OK and Close to return to your document.

Is there some way to make WordPerfect 6.0 for Windows run faster?

There are several things you can do to help WordPerfect run faster. Try these possibilities:

- Close any other open Windows applications.

- Add more memory to your system. You should have at least 6MB of RAM.

- Close any terminate-and-stay-resident (TSR) programs before running Windows and WordPerfect.

- Use Draft view instead of Page or Two Page view.

- Keep only one document open at a time.

- Create smaller documents or divide larger documents into smaller ones.

- Turn Reveal Codes off.

- Do not display graphics. You can change this setting from the Display Preferences dialog box.

- Do not display comments. You can change this setting from the Display Preferences dialog box.

- Create a permanent Windows swap file. You can change the swap file settings using the Windows Control Panel.

- Make sure your AUTOEXEC.BAT and CONFIG.SYS files are set up so that memory is used efficiently.

- Reduce the size of your SMARTDrive disk cache if you are using SMARTDrive. The SMARTDrive disk cache is usually set up in your AUTOEXEC.BAT or CONFIG.SYS file.

Can I change the colors of the display menu in WordPerfect?

Yes, you can change the colors of the menu, but you do not do this through WordPerfect. Instead, you change the colors using the Windows Control Panel. To do so:

1. Open the Control Panel. Its program icon is usually found in the Main program group in the Program Manager.

2. Select the Color icon or Color from the Settings menu.

3. Select Color Palette to extend the dialog box as shown in Figure 12-3.

4. Select Menu Bar from the Screen Elements drop-down list box, then select a color under Basic Colors. Repeat this step for Menu Text, Disable Text, Highlighted Text, and Highlight.

5. Select OK, then Exit from the Settings menu.

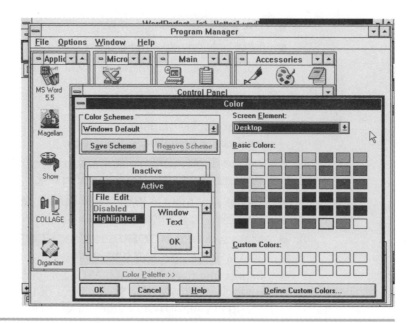

FIGURE 12-3   Windows' Control Panel Color dialog box

When you return to WordPerfect, you will see the new colors. Remember that you have just changed the menu colors in all Windows applications, not just for WordPerfect.

If executing the above steps does not change the menu colors in WordPerfect for Windows, you need to tell WordPerfect to use the colors selected in the Control Panel instead of its own default colors. WordPerfect 6.0 for Windows uses its own default colors for everything except buttons and menus, unless you tell it to use the Windows colors for all display features. To do this:

1. Select Preferences from the File menu.

2. Select the Display icon.

3. Select the Document radio button at the top of the dialog box.

4. Select the Windows System Colors check box in the Show area of the dialog box.

5. Select OK and then Close to return to your document. WordPerfect will now use the colors set using the Windows Control Panel.

How can I change the color of the text that is displayed, without changing the color used to print the text?

You can set the color of text displayed in a document separately from setting the color of text used to print the document. When you change the colors, you are altering the colors Windows applications use. To do so:

1. Open the Windows Control Panel. The Control Panel's icon is normally found in the Main program group of the Program Manager.

2. Select the Color icon or Color from the Settings menu.

3. Select Color Palette to extend the dialog box.

4. Select Windows Text from the Screen Elements drop-down list box.

5. Choose a color under Basic Colors.

6. Select OK, then Exit from the Settings menu.

If executing the above steps does not change the color of text displayed in WordPerfect for Windows, you need to tell WordPerfect to use the colors selected in the Control Panel instead of its own default colors. The steps for changing WordPerfect to use the color settings for Windows applications are described in the previous question.

Tech Tip: Windows includes several predefined color schemes. You can select one of these in place of performing steps 3, 4, and 5 above by selecting one of the options from the Color Schemes drop-down list box. Color schemes affect text, menus, and other parts of the screen.

When I add a macro to a Button Bar button, the button displays the word "Macro." Can I change this text to show which macro the button will start?

You can edit the button so that it displays the name of the macro rather than the word macro. To change the text appearing on a button you have already added to a Button Bar:

1. Open the Button Bar Editor using one of the following methods:

   ■ Right-click the Button Bar and select Edit from the QuickMenu.

   ■ Select Preferences from the File menu, select the Button Bar icon, highlight the Button Bar in the Available Button Bar list box, and select Edit.

2. Double-click the button you want to edit, or right-click it and select Customize.

3. Enter the text you want to appear on the button in the Button Text text box. You can also enter text in the Help Prompt text box that WordPerfect will display in the title bar when you point at the button with the mouse.

4. Select OK twice to return to your document. If you opened the Button Editor using the Button Bar Preferences dialog box, you also need to select Close twice to return to your document.

I've edited my menu. Can I reset it to the default menu?

Yes, you can reset the menu to the default settings. To return to the default menu settings press CTRL+ALT+SHIFT+BACKSPACE. Changing back to the default menu affects only the current session of WordPerfect 6.0 for Windows.

The information about the default menu settings is stored in the Standard template. If you revert to the default menu settings accidentally and want to go back to using the menu settings you defined for this template, you need to edit the current template by following these steps:

1. Select Template from the File menu.

2. Highlight the template you used to create this document in the Document Template to Use list box.

3. Select Edit Template from the Options pop-up list to edit the template.

4. Perform either of the following steps to select the menu the template uses:

   ■ Right-click the menu and select the menu layout from the QuickMenu. This will be the menu layout that documents based on this template will use. You can also select <u>P</u>references to display the Menu Bar Preferences dialog box like the one described in the following option.

   ■ Select Pr<u>e</u>ferences from the <u>F</u>ile menu and the <u>M</u>enu Bar icon to display the Menu Bar Preferences dialog box. Highlight the menu from the <u>M</u>enu Bars list box and choose <u>S</u>elect. Choose <u>C</u>lose to leave the Preferences dialog box.

5. Select <u>E</u>xit Template from the Template Feature Bar and select <u>Y</u>es when prompted if you want to save the file.

How can I display more of my document on the screen?

You can hide the different bars so that there is more space available for displaying your document. To hide the bars:

1. Select <u>H</u>ide Bars from the <u>V</u>iew menu or press ALT+SHIFT+F5. WordPerfect hides the Menu Bar, Scroll Bars, Ruler Bar, Power Bar, Button Bar, and Status Bar.

   Unless you disabled the message, the Hide Bars Information dialog box appears, alerting you to which bars disappear, and how to restore them. Select OK in this dialog box to hide the bars.

To restore the bars:

■ Press ESC.

■ Press ALT+SHIFT+F5.

■ Press ALT+V to open the <u>V</u>iew menu, then select <u>H</u>ide Bars again.

I want to see my labels on the screen arranged the way they will print. Can I do this?

Yes, you can display your labels arranged the same way they will print on your label stock. To do this, select Page or Two Page from the View menu.

 The border around my windows and in the Reveal Codes section looks different on my friend's machine. Is there a way I can change the thickness of my borders?

The thickness of the borders around documents, application windows, and the Reveal Codes separator bar is affected when the border width is changed in the Windows Control Panel. To change your border width to match someone else's or make it more to your liking:

1. Open the Control Panel by double-clicking its program icon, which is located in the Main program group.

2. Select the Desktop icon or Desktop from the Settings menu.

3. Change the entry in the Border Width text box in the Sizing Grid area of the document.

4. Select OK, then Exit from the Settings menu.

Increasing or decreasing the border width creates either a thicker or thinner bar between Reveal Codes and the normal document, and also changes the thickness of the border around all windows.

Can I change the picture on my Button Bar buttons?

Yes, you can change the image on your Button Bar buttons. To do so:

1. Select Preferences from the File menu.

2. Select the Button Bar icon.

3. Highlight the Button Bar that contains the button you want to edit in the Available Button Bars text box.

4. Select Edit.

5. Double-click the button you want to edit in the Button Bar, or right-click it and select Customize. This displays the Customize Button dialog box.

6. Select Edit in the Image area of the dialog box, opening the Button Bar Image Editor.

7. Use the mouse to select different colors, draw a different shape, or cut and paste another graphic image.

8. Select OK twice, then Close twice to return to your document and save the Button Bar button image. You can select Cancel instead of OK in the Button Bar Image Editor dialog box to discard your changes and start again.

Can I change the menus so that some features don't appear and others, that currently reside on submenus, do appear?

Yes, in WordPerfect 6.0 for Windows you can edit the menu layout or create new menus. Menus are saved with templates. If you want to save a specific menu with a specific template, you need to edit the template. Then, follow the steps given here to create a menu that will be saved with that template. If you do not select a specific template, you are saving the new or edited menu in the Standard template, and the menu will be available for all new documents you create. To edit or create a menu:

1. Select Preferences from the File menu.

2. Select the Menu Bar icon.

3. You can either edit an existing menu layout or create a new one:

   ■ Highlight a menu in the Menu Bars list box and select Edit to edit an existing menu layout.

   ■ Select Create, type a menu name, and select OK to create a new menu layout.

4. Use the Menu Bar Editor to choose items you want to add to the menu. You can drag items from the Menu Bar Editor dialog box, or drag items between menus or off menus to move or delete them.

5. When you have finished creating your new menu bar layout, select OK twice, then Close twice to return to your document.

Can I stop WordPerfect from showing the pen graphic when it opens?

Yes, you can prevent WordPerfect from displaying its opening graphic while it is loading. To do so:

1. Highlight the WPWin 6.0 icon in the WPWin 6.0 program group in the Program Manager.

2. Press ALT+ENTER or select Properties from the Program Manager's File menu.

3. Type a space and a colon at the end of the entry in the Command Line text box like this:

```
C:\WPWIN60\WPWIN.EXE :
```

4. Select OK.

From now on, when you start WordPerfect, the opening graphic will not appear.

Tech Tip: There are more options for starting WordPerfect. These other options are described under the question "What startup options does WordPerfect have?" in Chapter 2.

Can network users be prevented from using some of the options in the File Options pop-up list in the Open File dialog box?

Yes. This is how to do it:

1. Start the BIF Editor by selecting <u>R</u>un from the <u>F</u>ile menu, typing **C:\WPC20\BIFED20.EXE**, and selecting OK. Replace the C with the drive letter and WPC20 with the directory where your WordPerfect shared files are stored.

2. Select <u>O</u>pen from the <u>F</u>ile menu and select the WPCNET.BIF file.

3. Double-click on WP Shared Code and Open File.

4. Select <u>I</u>nsert to add another item.

5. Type **Remove File Options** in the <u>I</u>tem text box.

6. Now choose Signed Word from the Item Typ<u>e</u> pop-up list.

7. Type a value from the following list to disable the corresponding option:

File Option	Value
Disable All	-1
Copy	1
Move	2
Rename	4
Delete	8
Create Directory	32
Remove Directory	64
Print	128
Print List	256

To remove multiple items from the list add the items together and insert that number. For instance, if you want to disable Delete, Rename, and Move, type **14**, as shown in Figure 12-4.

8. Select OK to add the item

9. Select <u>C</u>lose and <u>Y</u>es to close the BIF Editor and save the modified file.

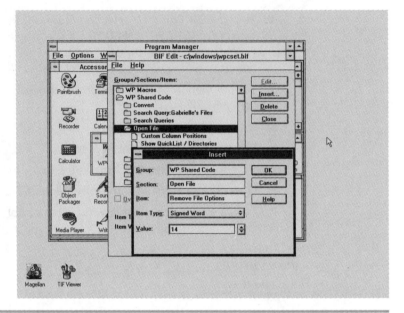

FIGURE 12-4   BIF Editor eliminating options from WordPerfect's File Options
pop-up list

I am trying to edit the WPWin 6.0 Keyboard, but the Edit option is grayed out. What is wrong?

WordPerfect 6.0 for Windows comes with three predefined keyboards: Equation Editor, WPDOS Compatible, and WPWin 6.0 Keyboard. WordPerfect does not let you edit any of these keyboards. Therefore, the Edit option is unavailable when one of these keyboards is selected.

Special Features

WordPerfect offers all of the standard features you have come to expect from word processing applications—and a lot more. WordPerfect 6.0's many special features, such as the new Hypertext feature, will open the door to the latest technology has to offer, while others, such as Abbreviations, will make your day-to-day tasks easier.

Often, the simple things can cause the greatest frustration. You have probably spent time searching for a document that you want to use, or trying to recall the password that you need to open a document. There are some rules you can adopt for organizing your files, filenames, and passwords to prevent these common sources of frustration.

First, make sure that your directory structure offers as much organizing capability as possible. This may mean creating additional directories, since WordPerfect automatically saves all of its files in the \WPWIN60\WPDOCS directory. If you do several different types of work or if you create documents for a number of people, an easy way to organize files is to create subdirectories for each category. For example, a secretary who creates documents for three lawyers might create the directories: \WPWIN60\WPDOCS\SAM, \WPWIN60\WPDOCS\LEE, and \WPWIN60\WPDOCS\CLAIRE. Since all of Sam's files go into his directory, finding his documents is easy.

Second, establish conventions for naming your files. This will make them easier to locate because their names will fit a pattern. For example, if you frequently create sales reports, make sure that the filenames of all the sales reports match. For example, SALESJAN.WPD, SALESFEB.WPD, and SALESMAR.WPD are preferable to SALESJAN.WPD, FEBSLSRP.WPD, and SALESRPT.MAR.

Third, use file extensions. WordPerfect can open files in its format, regardless of the file extension used. You can vary the file extension for different kinds of documents, such as using .RPT for reports, .LTR for letters, and .FRM for forms. Varying the file extension makes it easier for you to make sure you are opening the correct file.

Finally, keep in mind that password protection can cause as many problems as filenames. If you password protect your file, you will need to remember that password again later. If the file is not used frequently, you may forget the password altogether. There are two ways to avoid this:

Use the same password for most documents   For example, password-protect all of your sales reports using the same password. That way, you have only one password to remember. If the security of one set of files, such as payroll information, is more important than that of others, use a different password for that entire set of files. Anyone who learns your usual password will still not be able to open those files.

255

Chapter 13 *Special Features*

Choose a meaningful but obscure password If your password has no meaning for you, it will be hard to remember. However, if it is something people can quickly guess, it will not offer much protection. For example, if you use your own name, your password doesn't offer much security. The best trick is to use a password that is very meaningful to you, but which no one with access to your computer is likely to know. Some suggestions: the name of your favorite uncle, the address of the house where you grew up, or a childhood nickname that you haven't used in decades.

Does WordPerfect have an online tutorial?

WordPerfect 6.0 for Windows does not offer a general tutorial session. However, it does offer the Coach feature. This interactive tutorial can guide users through specific tasks. To access the Coach feature, select Coach from the Help menu, choose the topic you want help on, and select OK. The Coach, as shown in Figure 13-1, will prompt for necessary keystrokes and input information. WordPerfect also includes a Learning WordPerfect manual to help you learn how to use WordPerfect.

What's the difference between timed backups and original backups?

These two backup features can protect your documents from different types of accidents. You should know how to use these different backup features to protect yourself against computer accidents and inadvertent changes to your document.

Timed backups are designed to safeguard your work against power outages and equipment failures. With timed backups, WordPerfect makes a backup copy of your current document every few minutes. Initially, WordPerfect is set to make a backup

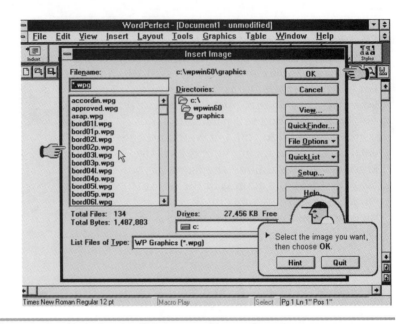

FIGURE 13-1   WordPerfect's Coach will help you with specific tasks

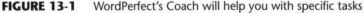

copy of the current document every ten minutes. If you lose power or your computer fails, the next time you use WordPerfect, a dialog box called Timed Backup notifies you of the existence of a backup document. You can then choose to rename, open, or delete that document. If you do not rename the backup copy, save it to a regular file, or open it, that data is lost. You can either disable timed backups, or change the interval between them. To change the timed backup settings:

1. Select Preferences from the File menu.

2. Select the File icon.

3. Select the Documents/Backup radio button at the top of the File Preferences dialog box.

4. Select the Timed Document Backup check box if you want timed backups or clear it if you do not want them.

5. Enter the interval you want between timed backups in the text box after the Timed Document Backup check box.

6. Select OK, then Close to return to your document with the new timed backup settings in effect.

Original document backups save a backup copy of any file that you open, edit, and save. For example, if you retrieve LETTER.DOC, make some changes, then save the document, the previous version of LETTER.DOC would normally be gone. However, when the original document backup is on, WordPerfect changes the name of the old file to LETTER.BK! instead of overwriting it, then saves the edited version with the filename LETTER.DOC. If you later find that you need the original version instead of the edited version, you can simply retrieve LETTER.BK! and edit your document, without your latest changes. To turn original backups on:

1. Select Preferences from the File menu.

2. Select the File icon.

3. Select the Documents/Backup radio button at the top of the dialog box.

4. Select the Original Document Backup check box.

5. Select OK, then Close to return to your document with this new setting in effect.

Please note that these are emergency backup procedures. You should regularly save your work, as often as every five minutes or so, and keep backups of important documents on separate floppy disks. If your hard drive is unreadable or destroyed, or if WordPerfect is corrupted and begins behaving incorrectly, these emergency backup procedures cannot help you. It's also a good idea to keep a copy of important files somewhere away from your computer, in case your computer is stolen, burned, flooded, or otherwise physically damaged. Anything that can damage your computer and hard drive is likely to damage your disks as well.

When I reopen a file, can WordPerfect put me in the same section of a document I was working on previously?

Yes, you can mark your place in your document with WordPerfect, then move to that location in the document quickly after reopening it. To do so:

1. Place your insertion point where you want to go the next time you open the document.

2. Select Bookmark from the Insert menu.

3. Select Set QuickMark to put a placeholder where the insertion point is.

Tech Tip: You can have WordPerfect automatically add the QuickMark placeholder at the insertion point's location when you save a file. To automatically add a QuickMark, select Preferences from the File menu, the Environment icon, then the Save QuickMark on Save check box. Select OK, then Close to return to your document. When the QuickMark placeholder is added automatically, you do not have to follow the steps above.

When you open the document the next time, you can return to this location in one of two ways. To return to this location using Go To from the Edit menu:

1. Select Go To from the Edit menu or press CTRL+G.

2. Select the Bookmark radio button. QuickMark should be selected in the Bookmark drop-down list. If it is not, you need to select it.

3. Select OK. Your insertion point moves to where you inserted the QuickMark.

To move to the QuickMark after reopening the document using Bookmark from the Insert menu:

1. Select Bookmark from the Insert menu.

2. Select Find QuickMark.

What is the Viewer, and how do I use it?

The Viewer displays the contents of a file without opening it. The Viewer is available from directory dialog boxes, such as the Open, Insert File, and Save As dialog boxes that let you specify a file or directory, like the dialog box shown in Figure 13-2. When a Viewer dialog box displays, you can select a filename in the Filename list box, and see the contents of that file. You can use the Viewer to quickly double-check that you are opening the correct document or inserting the correct graphic. Besides letting you see the document you are opening, the Viewer also lets you find specific text within a document and to copy text to the Clipboard.

To view the file currently selected in the File_name list box, select Vie_w to open the Viewer dialog box like the one shown in Figure 13-3. Close the Viewer dialog box by choosing _Close from the dialog box's Control menu, or pressing ESC.

The Viewer can show codes, graphics, and text. It displays the document contents but not all of the document formatting, and therefore does not provide full WYSIWYG viewing of the file. If a file contains text and graphics, only the text displays. If the file contains only graphics, it can be viewed only if it is in a graphics format that WordPerfect supports.

The Viewer can find text within the displayed document. Simply press F2 or select _Find from the QuickMenu in the Viewer. Type the text you want to find and select Find _Next or Find _Prev to move to the next or previous page containing the text. You will notice that every instance of the text is highlighted. You can continue to select Find _Next or Find _Prev from the Find dialog box or you can select Find _Next or Find _Previous from the

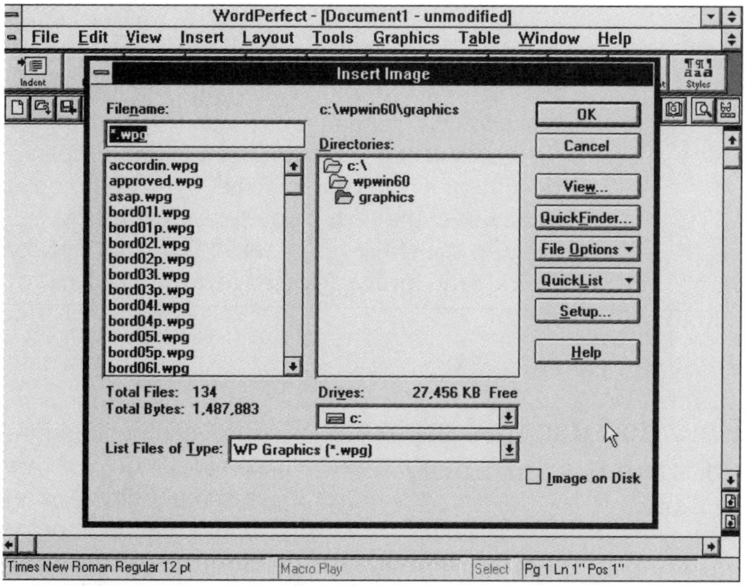

FIGURE 13-2   A directory dialog box with the _View option

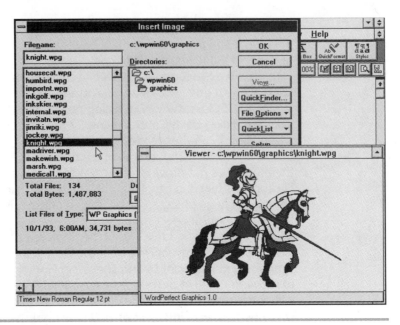

FIGURE 13-3   The Viewer dialog box

Viewer QuickMenu to move between pages containing the selected text. The Find dialog box remains onscreen until you close it.

To copy text from a document without opening it, display the document in the Viewer. Select the text to copy by dragging the mouse over the text. If you select any part of a table, you will be copying the entire table. Select Copy to Clipboard from the QuickMenu for the selected text or press CTRL+C.

How do I use and create a document summary?

The Document Summary feature provides a general overview of a document. It can save a wide variety of information about your documents. You can print the document summary with the document or separately, and can customize the types of information included in the summary.

To create a document summary:

1. Select Document Summary from the File menu.

2. Edit the text box entries to reflect the contents of your document. You are not required to fill in each text box, unless you find it useful.

   You can select Extract Information from Document from the Options pop-up list to have WordPerfect get some information from the document and fill in the text boxes for you.

3. Select OK when you are finished.

To customize the types of information that you want entered in your document summaries:

1. Choose Document Summary from the File menu.

2. Select Configure, opening the Document Summary Configuration dialog box shown here:

```
┌─────────────────────────────────────────────────┐
│ ─           Document Summary Configuration       │
│                                                   │
│  Selected Fields       Available Fields    ┌────┐ │
│ ┌──────────────┐ ┌──────────────────┐ │ OK │ │
│ │Descriptive Name│ │⊠Abstract        ↑│ └────┘ │
│ │Descriptive Type│ │⊠Account          │ ┌──────┐│
│ │Creation Date   │ │☐Address          │ │Cancel││
│ │Revision Date   │ │☐Attachments      │ └──────┘│
│ │Author          │ │⊠Author           │ ┌──────┐│
│ │Typist          │ │☐Authorization    │ │Clear All││
│ │Subject         │ │☐Bill To          │ └──────┘│
│ │Account         │ │☐Blind Copy       │ ┌──────┐│
│ │Keywords        │ │☐Carbon Copy      │ │ Help ││
│ │Abstract        │ │☐Category        ↓│ └──────┘│
│ └──────────────┘ └──────────────────┘         │
│  Drag selected field to order  [Use As Default] │
└─────────────────────────────────────────────────┘
```

The Selected Fields list box displays all of the fields currently included in the document summary. The Available Fields list box shows a list of all fields that can be included in a document summary.

3. To add or remove fields from the Selected Fields list box, select or clear the check box for that field in the Available Fields list box. Select Clear All to clear the check boxes of all the fields in the Available Fields list box.

4. You can change the order in which the fields appear in the Document Summary dialog box by changing their order in the Selected Fields list box. To re-order the fields in this list box, simply drag them to their new position using the mouse.

5. After selecting a set of fields, you can select Use As Default to have WordPerfect use your new selection of fields as the default entries for all document summaries, rather than just this one.

6. Select OK, enter the entries for the document summary fields, then select OK to save the document summary and return to your document.

To print a document summary:

1. Select Document Summary from the File menu.

2. Select Print Summary from the Options pop-up list.

To save your summary as a separate document:

1. Choose Document Summary from the File menu.

2. Select Save Summary As New Document from the Options pop-up list.

3. Enter a filename in the Filename list box and save the document summary as you would a normal document.

To delete a summary saved with a document:

1. Select Document Summary from the File menu.

2. Select Delete Summary from Document from the Options pop-up list.

3. Select Yes in the confirmation dialog box.

Is there some way to make sure that all documents are saved with document summaries?

Yes, you can have WordPerfect prompt you to create a document summary when you save or close a document that does not have one. To have WordPerfect prompt you for a document summary:

1. Select Preferences from the File menu.

2. Select the Summary icon.

3. Select the Create Summary on Save/Exit check box.

4. Select OK, then <u>C</u>lose to return to the current document.

In WordPerfect for DOS, I assigned long filenames to my files to make them easier to identify. Can I still do this in WordPerfect for Windows?

The only way to create long filenames in WordPerfect for Windows is to enter a Descriptive Name in the document summary. To do this:

1. Select Document Summar<u>y</u> from the <u>F</u>ile menu.

2. Enter a description of the file in the Descriptive Name text box.

3. Select OK to return to your document.

Tech Tip: Notice that several files in Figure 13-4 do not have descriptive filenames. This is because the filenames are so meaningful that there is no need for descriptive filenames to clarify their purpose.

To have these descriptive names appear in directory dialog boxes, such as when you are opening or saving files:

1. Select <u>O</u>pen from the <u>F</u>ile menu.

2. Select <u>S</u>etup.

3. Select <u>D</u>escriptive Name, Filename from the <u>S</u>how pop-up list.

4. Select OK to return to the Open File dialog box and Cancel to return to your document without opening any files. From now on, the File<u>n</u>ame list box in the Open File and Save As dialog boxes show both the descriptive name and the actual filename of all files that have both, as shown in Figure 13-4.

How can I use the USPS POSTNET Bar Code Feature?

A POSTNET Bar Code is an encoded representation of a ZIP code, either a 5-digit ZIP Code, a 9-digit ZIP+4 ZIP code, or an 11-digit Delivery Point Code. POSTNET bar codes conform to standards established by the U.S. Postal Service (USPS) for bar-coded ZIP codes and help increase speed and accuracy in

```
┌─────────────────────────────────────────────────────────────────┐
│  ─           WordPerfect - [Document1 - unmodified]      ▼ ▲      │
│  ─  File  Edit  View  Insert  Layout  Tools  Graphics  Table  Window  Help  ▲ │
│  ┌─────────────────────────────────────────────────────────┐     │
│  │  ─                       Open File                        │     │
│  │  Filename:                    c:\wpwin60\wpdocs    ┌──────┐│     │
│  │  ┌──────────────┐                                  │  OK  ││     │
│  │  │ gestlist.wpd │                 Directories:     └──────┘│     │
│  │  └──────────────┘                                  ┌──────┐│     │
│  │  Samples of all available fonts  allfonts.wpd ▲ 🗀 c:\│Cancel││     │
│  │  Membership change       board.wpd      🗀 wpwin60 └──────┘│     │
│  │  Business card master    cards.wpd      🗀 wpdocs  ┌──────┐│     │
│  │  Phone directory         director.wpd             │View..││     │
│  │                          fig03_01.wpd             └──────┘│     │
│  │                          fig03_02.wpd        ┌────────────┐│    │
│  │                          fig03_03.wpd        │QuickFinder.││    │
│  │                          fig03_04.wpd        └────────────┘│    │
│  │                          fig03_06.wpd        ┌───────────┬┐│    │
│  │                          fig07_03.wpd        │File Options│▼│    │
│  │                          fig07_06.wpd        └───────────┴┘│    │
│  │  Wedding guest list      gestlist.wpd        ┌──────────┬┐│     │
│  │  Moving announcement      move.wpd           │QuickList │▼││     │
│  │  Weekly time sheet form   pay.wpd   ▼        └──────────┴┘│     │
│  │                                              ┌──────────┐ │     │
│  │  Total Files:  23           Drives:  27,072 KB Free │Setup..│ │     │
│  │  Total Bytes: 510,197                        └──────────┘ │     │
│  │                             ┌─────────────┬┐ ┌──────────┐ │     │
│  │                             │🖿 c:        │▼│ │   Help   │ │     │
│  │  List Files of Type:┌─────────────────┬┐  └─────────────┘ │    │
│  │                     │All Files (*.*)  │▼│                  │    │
│  │                     └─────────────────┴┘                  │    │
│  │  2/18/94,  9:38AM, 2,307 bytes                            │    │
│  │  Wedding guest list                                       │    │
│  └─────────────────────────────────────────────────────────┘     │
│  Times New Roman Regular 14.4 pt (Tir  Table_A Cell A1   Select Pg 1 Ln 1.08" Pos 2.67" │
└─────────────────────────────────────────────────────────────────┘
```

FIGURE 13-4   Descriptive filenames can help you identify files

the delivery of mail. WordPerfect allows you to place POSTNET bar codes on documents and envelopes.

To include a POSTNET bar code on an envelope:

1. Choose Envelope from the Layout menu.

2. Select the size of the envelopes you are using from the Envelope Definition's drop-down list.

3. Enter the return address in the Return Addresses text box and the mailing address in the Mailing Addresses text box.

Tech Tip: A listing of these Delivery Point Bar Code digits is available from the United States Postal Service.

4. Select Options.

5. Select the Include USPS POSTNET Bar Code check box and OK.

   The ZIP or ZIP+4 Code is placed in the newly displayed POSTNET Bar Code text box. To use an 11-digit Delivery Point Bar Code, you need to type the final 2 digits in this text box.

6. Select Print Envelope to print the envelope with the bar code, or select Append to Doc to add the envelope and bar code to your document, as shown in Figure 13-5.

If you want to insert a POSTNET bar code in a document:

1. Put your insertion point where you want the bar code to appear.

2. Select Other from the Insert menu.

3. Select Bar Code.

4. Enter the ZIP code or Delivery Point Bar Code in the Bar Code Digits text box, and select OK.

You may also insert POSTNET bar codes during a merge, manually, or during an envelope merge. To insert the POSTNET merge code into a form file:

1. Select Merge Codes from the Merge Feature Bar.

2. Highlight POSTNET(string) in the Merge Codes list box.

3. Select Insert, then Close.

4. Put your insertion point between the parentheses in the code and enter the ZIP code.

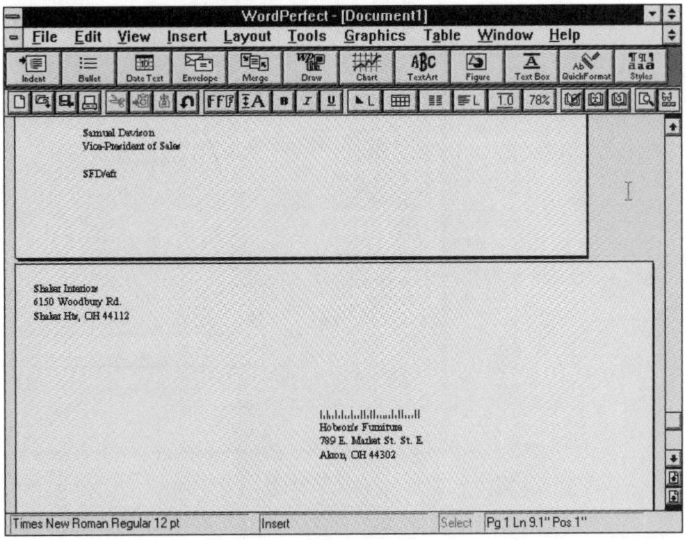

FIGURE 13-5   Document with an appended envelope using the USPS bar code

You can add a POSTNET merge code to an envelope form file by creating an envelope as usual, but inserting a FIELD code in the POSTNET Bar Code text box instead of typing an actual ZIP code.

How do I create a QuickList?

A QuickList defines a list of directories and files you use frequently. QuickLists make it easier for you to locate commonly used files.

To create a QuickList, you must open a directory dialog box, such as the Open File or Save As dialog box. Then:

1. Select Show QuickList or Show Both from the QuickList pop-up list, adding the QuickList list box to the dialog box, as shown in Figure 13-6.

2. Select Add Item from the QuickList pop-up list.

3. Define your new QuickList item using the Directory/Filename text box.

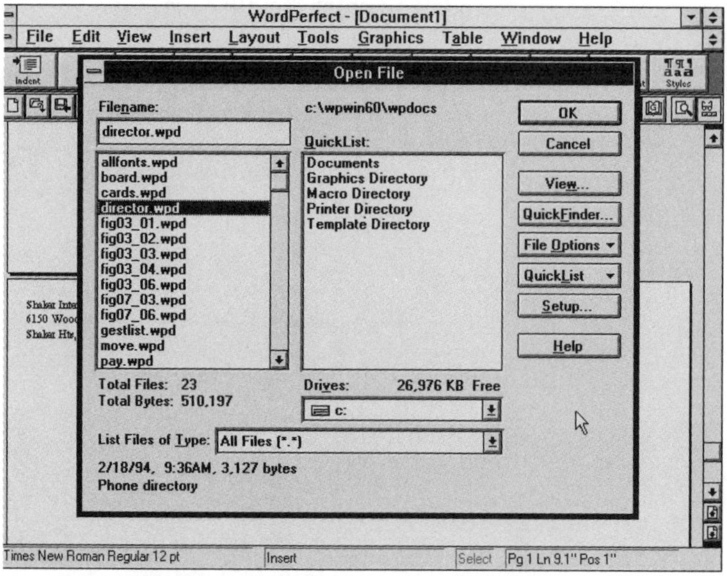

FIGURE 13-6 The QuickList helps you select files quickly

■ To add a new directory to the QuickList item, enter the directory in the Directory/Filename text box.

■ To add a document to the QuickList item, enter its path and filename.

4. Enter a description for the directory or filename in the Description box. This description will appear in the QuickList list box.

5. Choose OK to add the item to the QuickList.

What is the difference between inserting date text and a date code?

When you insert date text, only the actual text for the date is inserted. This date is not automatically updated when the date changes. Instead of a code, you have the actual text, which you can then edit and format as you would any other text. Date codes, on the other hand, cannot be edited the way date text can, but are updated whenever you reopen your document to indicate the current date. Therefore, use date text when you want to refer to a specific date, such as February 2, 1994. Use a date code when you want to indicate the date the document is actually printed or read. To insert either date text or date codes:

1. Select Date from the Insert menu.

2. Select either Date Text or Date Code.

Tech Tip: You can choose the format of the date that you insert into your document. Select Date from the Insert menu, then select Date Format, and select a format, or design a custom date format.

I saved a password-protected document in WordPerfect 5.x format so my assistant could use the file. However, when he opened the file, he was not prompted for the password. Why?

When you save a password-protected WordPerfect 6.0 for Windows file with a different format, using the Save As command from the File menu, the password can be removed from the file or changed. When you select OK to close the Save As dialog box, if you have left the Password Protect check box selected, WordPerfect prompts you for a password. The password that is entered will be the new password for the converted file. If the Password Protect check box is cleared, the converted file will have no password.

Is there a quick way to close my current document?

Yes, you can close your document quickly by pressing CTRL+F4. If the document was already saved, the contents of the current window will clear out and you will have a new document window. If the current document hasn't been saved, a prompt will appear, asking "Save changes to *document name*?". Select Yes or No, depending on whether you want to save the file or discard it before clearing the screen.

Tech Terror: You can also clear the screen by pressing CTRL+SHIFT+F4. However, this clears the screen without prompting you about saving, which could cause you to lose your data.

Tech Tip: The CTRL+F4 and CTRL+SHIFT+F4 key combinations work if you are using the WPWin 6.0 keyboard. If you are using the WPDOS Compatible keyboard, you need to press CTRL+SHIFT+F7.

Can I insert date text and date codes in WordPerfect Draw?

Yes. To insert the date as text or a code when you are in WordPerfect Draw:

1. Create the text area where you want the date.
2. Choose <u>D</u>ate from the <u>T</u>ext menu.
3. Select either Date <u>T</u>ext or Date <u>C</u>ode.

The current date will then appear at the insertion point. If you selected Date <u>T</u>ext, this date will not change unless you edit it manually. If you inserted the date using Date <u>C</u>ode, the current date appears at the insertion point and is updated to the current date each time you print or open the file.

Why won't the math codes in a document I created with WordPerfect 5.1 for DOS work when I open the document in WordPerfect 6.0 for Windows?

WordPerfect for Windows has the ability to perform math calculations, but does not have a Math feature similar to the one in WordPerfect 5.1 for DOS. If you have already inserted math codes in a document, use WordPerfect 5.1 for DOS to do the math calculations. In WordPerfect for Windows, you can use the Tables feature to do automatic math calculations.

How do I mark text that I want to include in a table of contents?

WordPerfect's Table of Contents feature can automatically collect text you have marked throughout your document and use that text to create a table of contents. To mark text for use as a table of contents entry:

1. Select Table of <u>C</u>ontents from the <u>T</u>ools menu, displaying the Table of Contents Feature Bar shown here:

| Table of Contents Level: | Mark <u>1</u> | Mark <u>2</u> | Mark <u>3</u> | Mark <u>4</u> | Mark <u>5</u> | <u>D</u>efine... | <u>C</u>lose | <u>G</u>enerate... |

2. Highlight the word or phrase you want to include as an entry in the table of contents.
3. Choose Mark <u>X</u> from the Table of Contents Feature Bar, where *X* is the level in the table of contents, from one to five, you want for the text entry.

4. Repeat steps 2 and 3 for each entry you want to include in your table of contents.

5. Choose Close from the Table of Contents Feature Bar when finished.

Once you have marked the text, you can define where and how you want the table of contents to appear. To do so:

1. Put the insertion point where you want the table of contents to appear.
   If you want it at the beginning of the document on a page by itself, press CTRL+ENTER to insert a hard page break, then press UP ARROW to move the insertion point back to the first page.

2. Enter any text you want to appear before the table of contents. For example, you could enter **Table of Contents** and press ENTER a few times to add space between this heading and the actual table of contents.

3. Select Table of Contents from the Tools menu to display the Table of Contents Feature Bar.

4. Choose Define from the Table of Contents Feature Bar.

5. Enter the number of levels you want in the table of contents in the Number of Levels text box. You can have up to five levels of entries in your table of contents. As you select a new level, the sample table of contents at the bottom of the dialog box will display how your table might look, using sample data.

6. From the Position pop-up list for each level, select the position where you want the page numbers to appear.

7. Select OK to return to your document and insert the table of contents code.

8. Choose Generate from the Table of Contents Feature Bar to have WordPerfect gather all of the marked text and create the table of contents.

After you select Generate, WordPerfect assembles the marked text and creates a table of contents like the one shown in Figure 13-7.

WordPerfect - [c:\wpwin60\wpdocs\santa]

File   Edit   View   Insert   Layout   Tools   Graphics   Table   Window   Help

Santa's Town Festival

Vendor Information Booklet

What to Expect 3
    History of the Santa Town Festival (3); This
    Year's Expectations (3); Event Publicity (4); What
    You Can Expect (4)
Dates 5
Schedule of Activities 6
Getting a Vendor Location 9
Map 10
Miscellaneous 11
    Bringing Your Children (11); Lost Children (11);
    Lost Belongings (11); Pets (11); Santa's Elves
    (12); Security (12)
Parking .13

CaslonOpnface BT Regular 24 pt (Cooper-WP   Insert   Select   Pg 1 Ln 1" Pos 3.9"

FIGURE 13-7   Tables of contents are easy to create in WordPerfect

What are delay codes and how do they work?

WordPerfect delay codes are signals to WordPerfect to activate formatting and graphics features in your document at a specific point. Delay codes let you select formatting and graphic features to take effect a specified number of pages after the page that contains the delay code. For example, if you want to change the paper definition after a specific page in your document, you can specify the initial paper size at the beginning of the document, then place the second paper size in delay codes. When you use delay codes, you do not have to move to that particular page to change your paper size definition.

You may delay any open code or graphic. Open codes are codes that are not turned off; they affect your document from the point the code is inserted until another similar code is inserted or the document ends. For example, a font code that turns on a larger point size but does not include a paired code to turn it back off, is an open code. Paired codes such as Bold require both a start and a stop code, and cannot be used in delay codes. Also, typing oriented codes such as Center, Indent, and Tab do not work in delayed codes.

You may create a delayed code at any page in your document. To do so:

1. Place the insertion point on the page where you want the delay code.

2. Select Page from the Layout menu.

3. Select Delay Codes.

4. Enter the number of pages after the current page where you want the code to take effect in the Number of Pages to Delay text box. Select OK.

   For example, if you are on page 8 and want the code to take effect at the start of page 12, specify 4. The delay code, [DELAY:12], is placed at the previous hard page break or the beginning of the document if no hard page breaks exist.

5. Choose the codes you want to delay from either the Delay Codes Feature Bar or the regular WordPerfect menus.

6. Once you have inserted your codes, select Close from the Delay Codes Features Bar. Delay codes will appear in Reveal Codes.

How can I delete my delay codes?

To delete your delay codes:

1. Select Reveal Codes from the View menu.

2. Drag the delay code out of Reveal Codes, using the left mouse button.

   Paired [Delay] codes appear on the page where the changes take effect while the main [Delay:#] code is at the top of the document or at a previous hard page break.

Tech Tip: You can also delete delay codes by placing the insertion point immediately before them in Reveal Codes and pressing DEL.

Is it possible to compare two documents and view the differences between them?

Yes, using WordPerfect's Compare Document feature, you can compare the current document to another document file. After the comparison, the current document displays revision marks indicating where text was removed, and where new text was added to the current document. The overstrike format marks deleted text, and red text marks what was added, as shown in Figure 13-8. If you have a monochrome monitor, the colored text displays using shades of gray.

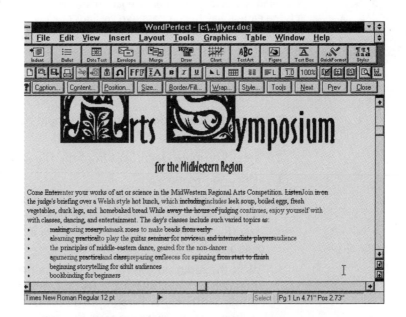

FIGURE 13-8   When you compare documents, overstrikes indicate deleted text and gray text indicates added text

For example, suppose you opened a letter called BLAKE.WPD and did some significant editing on it. You may want to compare this edited copy to the original, saved copy of the letter to see exactly what you changed. You could compare the current edited document to the unedited saved document to have WordPerfect mark all the changes that you made to it. You can also use this method if you have edited and saved a document to a new filename, by opening the edited version and comparing it to the original. Comparing documents is especially useful in reviewing revisions to legal documents or business contracts, where a few minor changes can make a big difference in the meaning of the document. Also, it is a useful tool when you are collaborating on creating a document such as a report, because it makes it easy for one author to quickly discover where the other author made changes.

Tech Note: The process of comparing two documents was once called redlining and was done by careful proofreaders. Redlining is used a great deal in legal circles, because it is the easiest way to compare two versions of a contract or other legal document, and to make sure that no undesired changes were made.

To compare two documents:

1. Open the edited document. This should be the latest, not the original, version of the document.

2. Select Compare Document from the File menu.

3. Select Add Markings.

4. Enter the name of the original document in the Compare Current Document To text box or click the list button after this text box to select the file from a Select File dialog box.

5. Select the radio button for the components of the document you want WordPerfect to compare: Word, Phrase, Sentence, or Paragraph. Select OK.

   When WordPerfect compares the two documents, it will do so using the segments of the documents that you specify. For example, if you select Paragraph, WordPerfect will mark the entire paragraph as changed if a single word in the paragraph has changed. If you selected Word, only that one word is marked as being changed.

The comparison may take some time, depending upon the length and complexity of the files. When it is finished, the document on the screen will show markings for deleted and inserted text. To remove these markings:

1. Select Compare Document from the File menu.
2. Select Remove Markings.

Can I fax a document directly from WordPerfect 6.0 for Windows?

WordPerfect 6.0 for Windows does not support faxing unless a fax modem and its software is already installed in Windows. The fax software must be a Windows fax program and not a DOS application running in Windows. To fax a document:

1. Choose Select Printer from the File menu.
2. Select the fax driver instead of a printer driver from the Printers list box.
3. Select OK to return to your document.
4. Select Print from the File menu, then OK.

The steps from this point on will vary for different fax programs. Consult your fax software's documentation for how to set up the phone call and send the document.

What is Hypertext?

Hypertext creates links that allow you to move from one place to another, either inside a document or to a different document altogether. Hypertext can also launch macros. Hypertext links are meant to connect parts of online documents. These connections, called "jumps," are placed in a document and are linked to additional information that might be of interest to anyone reading the document. Links can be established between documents, bookmarks in the current document or a separate one, or macros. When readers click on a Hypertext jump, they move directly to that information. If the jump is linked to a macro, the macro plays when the reader clicks on the jump. Hypertext links are created and edited using the Hypertext Feature Bar, which can also move between links if you do not have a mouse.

To place a Hypertext link:

1. Create the bookmark, document, or macro that you want the Hypertext jump to move to or play.

2. Open the document that will contain the Hypertext link.

3. Choose Hypertext from the Tools menu, opening the Hypertext Feature Bar, as shown here:

4. Select the words or symbols that will be the link.
   For example, if you want readers to access a description of the Bronx Zoo contained elsewhere by clicking the phrase "Bronx Zoo," highlight the words "Bronx Zoo" at the appropriate place in the document.

5. Select Create from the Hypertext Feature Bar, opening the Create Hypertext Link dialog box shown here:

6. Now you must specify what happens when the Hypertext link is selected, by choosing one of the radio buttons and entering the necessary information. Select:

- *Go To Bookmark* to move to a bookmark in the current document. Enter the bookmark you want the insertion point to move to in the text box.

- *Go To Other Document* to open another document. Enter the document name in the Document text box. If you want to move to a bookmark in that other document, enter the bookmark in the Bookmark text box.

- *Run Macro* to start a macro. Enter the name of the macro in the text box.

7. You can also choose how the Hypertext will appear in this document by selecting either the Text or Button radio button.

Tech Tip: If you select the Text radio button, your Hypertext is automatically formatted with bold and underline. You can remove these font formats and apply whatever formats you desire. Remember to use one consistent format that indicates Hypertext throughout your Hypertext documents, or readers will become very confused about what text they can use to jump to other topics.

8. Select OK to return to your document. When you are done creating Hypertext links, select Close from the Hypertext Feature Bar.

Once the Hypertext links are established, you can either:

- Click the Hypertext text or button to jump to the bookmark or document that the Hypertext is linked to, or to play the Hypertext's macro.

- Move the insertion point to the Hypertext text or button, choose Hypertext from the Tools menu to activate the Hypertext Feature Bar, then select Perform to jump to the bookmark, macro, or document the Hypertext is linked to.

Some other options on the Hypertext Feature Bar are:

- *Back*, which returns you to the place you jumped from
- *Next*, which finds the next Hypertext link after the insertion point
- *Previous*, which finds the last Hypertext link before the insertion point

What is the Abbreviations feature and how would I use it?

WordPerfect's Abbreviations feature lets you quickly insert frequently typed text into documents. For example, if you are constantly typing a long company name in your document, you can use an abbreviation to cut down on the amount of typing that you need to do. Instead of typing the long company name each time, you can type an abbreviation or short form. For example, you could type **Severn&** instead of typing **Severn, Thomas, Winthrop & Delaney, LPA**. Then, you can use the WordPerfect Abbreviations feature to expand the short abbreviation into the longer complete name, instead of having to type it.

To create a WordPerfect abbreviation:

1. Type the complete text, such as **Severn, Thomas, Winthrop & Delaney, LPA**, and select it.
2. Choose <u>A</u>bbreviations from the <u>I</u>nsert menu.
3. Select C<u>r</u>eate.
4. Enter the abbreviation, such as **Severn&**, and choose OK.
5. Select <u>C</u>lose to return to the document.

To expand an abbreviation, move your insertion point to the abbreviation and press CTRL+A.

How can I copy a WordPerfect abbreviation from one template to another?

To copy abbreviations from one template to another:

1. Select <u>A</u>bbreviations from the <u>I</u>nsert menu.

2. Choose C_opy.

3. In the Template to copy _from drop-down list, enter the template the abbreviation is currently located in.

4. Select the abbreviation to copy from the S_elect Abbreviation to Copy list box.

5. Enter the template you want to copy the abbreviation to in the Template to copy _to drop-down list.

6. Choose C_opy, then C_lose to return to your document.

How can I add sound clips to my documents?

Sound clips, which are digitally recorded and stored as .WAV and MIDI files including voice recordings, music, or sound effects, can be added to any WordPerfect document. To hear the sounds, you must have a sound board, a device capable of reproducing the sounds, as well as available sound clips or an application to create them. The Windows Sound Recorder can create .WAV files. To insert a sound clip:

1. Select S_ound from the I_nsert menu.

2. Select I_nsert.

3. Enter the name of the sound clip file in the F_ile text box, or click the List button at the end of the text box and select the file.

4. Select OK, then C_lose to return to your document. The sound clip is marked by a small icon in the margin, like the one shown here:

To hear the sound clip, click this icon.

Tech Tip: Even if you do not have the ability to play sound clips on your system, you can include sound files in your document for use by others who do have the ability to play them.

Is it possible to electronically mail a document directly from WordPerfect 6.0 for Windows?

Yes. WordPerfect 6.0 for Windows supports VIM or MAPI compliant electronic mail programs as well as WordPerfect Office 3.0, 3.1, and 4.0. To electronically mail a file or selected text directly from WordPerfect, select WP Mail from the File menu. Then select the mail options according to your mail systems and choose Send.

If your electronic mail program was installed after WordPerfect 6.0 for Windows, the WP Mail command will not appear on the File menu. To get this command, you need to:

1. Start the WordPerfect 6.0 for Windows Install program using the program icon in the WPWin 6.0 program group in the Program Manager.

2. Select Custom.

3. Select Files.

4. Select Unmark All and OK.

5. Choose Start Installation and follow the prompts.

The next time you start WordPerfect 6.0 for Windows, the WP Mail command will be available in the File menu.

More Tricks and Techniques

While it's useful to find out about all the new bells and whistles that WordPerfect 6.0 for Windows offers, you'll probably find that most of your work involves using basic features. Sometimes you'll find you have questions when you're doing nothing more complicated than moving through your document, changing it, or saving files and leaving the program. This chapter explores the refinements and options that are designed to make your job easier. Once you're acquainted with these often-overlooked shortcuts and small features, you'll become more productive, too.

The Power Bar is designed to make working with WordPerfect easier for you. Rather than memorizing the different menu paths to reach a single option, you can simply click a button to change a font or insert a table. If you're unfamiliar with what the buttons mean, you may ignore them in the daily rush to get work done the way you know how, even if that method is not the most effective. Here you see the default Power Bar buttons and what they do. As you become familiar with the buttons and their use, you can customize the Power Bar to contain the WordPerfect features you frequently use.

Icon	Name	Purpose
	New Document	Opens a new document using the Standard template
	Open	Displays the Open File dialog box
	Save	Displays the Save dialog box or saves a document that already has a filename
	Print	Opens the Print dialog box
	Cut	Cuts the selected text to the Windows Clipboard
	Copy	Copies the selected text to the Windows Clipboard
	Paste	Pastes the contents of the Clipboard at the insertion point
	Undo	Undoes your last action in WordPerfect
	Font Face	Displays a menu of all available fonts
	Font Size	Displays a menu of available font sizes
	Bold Font	Boldfaces the selected text or all subsequent text

Icon	Name	Purpose
I	Italic Font	Italicizes the selected text or all subsequent text
U	Underline Font	Underlines the selected text or all subsequent text
▶ L	Tab Set	Opens the Tab Set dialog box
▦	Table Quick Create	Inserts a table using the number of rows and columns you select
▤	Columns Define	Formats the selected or subsequent text with the number of newspaper columns you select
≡ L	Justification	Sets the justification for the selected or subsequent text
1.0	Line Spacing	Sets the line spacing for the selected or subsequent text
100%	Zoom	Sets how much the document is magnified on the screen
📖	Speller	Starts the Speller to check for spelling in your document
📖	Thesaurus	Starts the Thesaurus to search for alternate words
📖	Grammatik	Starts Grammatik to check grammar in your document
🔍	Page Zoom Full	Zooms the document so you can see the entire page
⊞	View Button Bar	Hides the Button Bar

Are there shortcuts for selecting text in my document?

Yes, WordPerfect offers several shortcuts for selecting the text in a document. Some shortcuts use the mouse (shown in Table 14-1), while others use the keyboard (shown in Table14-2).

Selection	Action
Word	Double-click it.
Sentence	Triple-click it or click once in the left margin beside it.
From the insertion point to the mouse pointer	Hold down SHIFT while you click the document.

TABLE 14-1   Selecting text with the mouse

All keystroke shortcuts for selecting text do so relative to the insertion point's location. For example, if you select to the beginning of the line, you are selecting all text between the insertion point and the beginning of the line containing the insertion point.

Selection	Action
One character to the left	Press SHIFT+LEFT ARROW.
One character to the right	Press SHIFT+RIGHT ARROW.
One line up	Press SHIFT+UP ARROW.
One line down	Press SHIFT+DOWN ARROW.
To the end of the line	Press SHIFT+END.
To the beginning of the line	Press SHIFT+HOME.
To the top of the screen	Press SHIFT+PGUP.
To the bottom of the screen	Press SHIFT+PGDN.
To the beginning of the previous page	Press SHIFT+ALT+PGUP.
To the beginning of the following page	Press SHIFT+ALT+PGDN.
One word to the left	Press SHIFT+CTRL+LEFT ARROW.
One word to the right	Press SHIFT+CTRL+RIGHT ARROW.
One paragraph up	Press SHIFT+CTRL+UP ARROW.
One paragraph down	Press SHIFT+CTRL+DOWN ARROW.
To the top of the document	Press SHIFT+CTRL+HOME.
To the bottom of the document	Press SHIFT+CTRL+END.

TABLE 14-2   Selecting text with the keyboard

WordPerfect also offers a menu shortcut for selecting the entire document at once. Choose Se̲lect from the E̲dit menu, and then select A̲ll.

 Does WordPerfect have an easy way to cut or copy, then paste several different parts of a document?

Yes, you can cut and copy several selections of text, then paste them into a document as a unit. To do this, follow these steps:

1. Select the first section of text.

2. Select C̲opy or Cu̲t from the E̲dit menu to copy the text to the Windows' Clipboard. If you select Cut, the text is deleted from the document as it is copied to the Clipboard.

3. Select the second section of the text.

4. Select Appen̲d from the E̲dit menu. WordPerfect adds the second section of text to the end of the first section of text already stored in the Clipboard. This section of text is not deleted from the document, even if you select Cu̲t with the first section of text.

5. Continue to select and append sections of text until you have copied all of the text you want to the Clipboard.

6. Position your insertion point where you want to insert all of the text you have copied or cut to the Clipboard.

7. Select P̲aste from the E̲dit menu.

 How can I find hard returns or other formatting codes in my document?

In WordPerfect you can search for any formatting code including hard returns, page breaks, tabs, and even font changes. To do so, follow these steps:

1. Select F̲ind from the E̲dit menu or press F2. If you want to replace these codes with other codes, select R̲eplace from the E̲dit menu or press CTRL+F2.

2. Put your insertion point in the F̲ind text box.

Tech Tip: If you want WordPerfect to search the entire document, select Begin Find at Top of Document from the Options menu.

3. Select Codes from the Match menu in the Find dialog box, displaying the Codes dialog box.

4. Choose the code you want to search for in the Find Codes list box and select Insert to enter the code into the Find text box. You can continue to choose and insert codes if you want to search for a combination of codes.

5. When you are finished inserting codes, select the Find Next or Find Prev button. Find Next looks for the first occurrence of these codes after the insertion point, and Find Prev finds the last occurrence of these codes before the insertion point.

6. Select Close to leave the Find Text or the Find and Replace Text dialog box.

I want to sort a list of names by the last name. However, some of the names include more than two words. How can I sort on the last word all the time?

When you sort information and want to sort using a specific word, you specify which word you want to sort by entering a number corresponding to that word's position. For example, to sort by the first word, enter **1**; by the second word, enter **2**; and so on. You can also sort using the last word in a sentence, by entering a negative number. For example, to sort by the last word, enter **-1**; to sort by the next to last word, enter **-2**. To set this up:

1. Select Sort from the Tools menu or press ALT+F9.

2. Enter the document you are going to sort in the Input File text box and where you want to send the sorted data in the Output File text box.

3. Select Line in the Sort By area of the dialog box.

4. Type **-1** in the Word text box for the first key.

5. Select OK.

Since you entered **-1** for the word to sort the lines by, WordPerfect will sort this file by the last word in the line.

I was inserting bullets using the Bullets & Numbers command on the Insert menu and accidentally added extra bullets. I can't move my insertion point to the bullets, so how do I delete them?

WordPerfect offers several different ways to delete extra bullets inserted using the Bullets & Numbers command from the Insert menu, even though you cannot select the bullets. To delete these bullets, follow one of these procedures:

- Put your insertion point at the beginning of the line and press BACKSPACE.

- Put your insertion point at the end of the line before the bullet you want to delete, and press DEL.

- Select Reveal Codes from the View menu or press ALT+F3. Position your insertion point on the bullet that you want to delete in the Reveal Codes screen and press DEL.

- Select the paragraph with the unwanted bullets. Choose Bullets & Numbers from the Insert menu, select <None> from the Styles list box, and select OK.

How do I expand a master document?

When you expand a master document, you are telling WordPerfect to show all of the text in the subdocuments.

Follow these steps to expand a master document:

1. Select Master Document from the File menu.

2. Select Expand Master.

3. Select the check boxes for the subdocuments you want to expand in the Subdocuments list box or choose Mark All or Clear All from the Mark pop-up list. By default, all subdocuments are selected.

4. Choose OK.

Tech Tip: You can use the subdocument icon and your mouse to work with a subdocument. You can expand a subdocument by double-clicking the subdocument icon to display the Expand Master Document dialog box. You can also change which document a master document uses as a subdocument by displaying the icon's QuickMenu and selecting Subdocument. You can click the icon once to see a comment that displays the document name that the icon represents.

Can I insert a table into my comments?

Yes, you can insert a table into a comment. WordPerfect's comments are sections of text that are not actually part of the document, but which are displayed as icons in the margins. When you select a comment icon, the comment is displayed. Comments in WordPerfect documents are used like sticky notes on your printed documents. Follow these steps to insert a table into a comment:

1. Select Co<u>m</u>ment from the <u>I</u>nsert menu, then <u>C</u>reate to begin creating your comment.

2. Select <u>C</u>reate from the T<u>a</u>ble menu or press F12 to insert the table.

3. Enter the number of columns and rows for the table, then select OK.

4. Enter the table's contents and any other text to appear in the comment.

5. Choose <u>C</u>lose from the Comment Feature Bar to insert the comment into your document.

In your document, your comment looks like the one displayed in Figure 14-1. To display the comment, click it. To edit the comment, double-click it, or choose Co<u>m</u>ment from the <u>I</u>nsert menu, then <u>E</u>dit.

Is there an easy way to flip through the pages of a document?

If you add the Page item to your Status Bar, as shown below, you can click its arrows to move forward or backward through your document a page at a time. You can also double-click the Page item to display the same Go To dialog box that the <u>G</u>o To command in the <u>E</u>dit menu displays.

| Times New Roman Regular 12 pt | | Insert | Select | Pg 1 Ln 1" Pos 1" | Page 1 | | 10:36 AM |

To add the Page item, follow these steps:

1. Right-click the Status Bar.

WordPerfect - [c:\...\board.wpd - unmodified]

File   Edit   View   Insert   Layout   Tools   Graphics   Table   Window   Help

BRRTA

The Board of Directors of BRRTA has decided to raise the cost of membership to $20.00, and require membership for attendance at conferences and other group events. While this

Do we really want to bring up the issue of the polling we did last year? This action is going to be hard enough to sell to the membership without reminding them that they've already turned it down once.

	For	Against	Undecided/No Response
Members	45%	50%	5%
Active Non-Members	14%	80%	6%

have grown by over 50%. This means that a smaller proportion of those involved in our activities are actually paying to make those activities feasible.

Lucida Calligraphy Italic 6 pt   Insert   Select   Pg 1 Ln 0.75" Pos 1.92"

FIGURE 14-1   A comment added to a document

2. Select <u>P</u>references from the Status Bar's QuickMenu.
3. Select the Page check box in the S<u>t</u>atus Bar Items list box and select OK.

Tech Tip: If the left arrow in the Page item is gray, you are on the first page of the document. If the right arrow is gray, you are on the last page of the document.

I'm new to Windows applications, and all the buttons and icons on top of my screen are overwhelming. Is there a quick way to find out what each one does?

Yes, WordPerfect can offer a quick hint about the purpose of each of the buttons and icons that appear at the top of your WordPerfect for Windows application window. To see these hints, position the mouse pointer on the button or icon you want to know about. A brief description of the icon or button's function displays in the title bar of your application window, as shown here:

> Speller - Check for misspelled words, double words, irregular capitalization - Ctrl+F1
>
> File Edit View Insert Layout Tools Graphics Table Window Help
>
> Indent Bullet Date Text Envelope Merge Draw Chart TextArt Figure Text Box QuickFormat Styles

Tech Tip: The title bar is the solid color bar across the very top of the screen which displays the name of your application, which is, in this case, WordPerfect.

If these descriptions do not appear, this option is turned off. To turn this option back on, follow these steps:

1. Select Preferences from the File menu.

2. Select the Environment icon by double-clicking it, or highlighting it and pressing ENTER.

3. Select the Show Help Prompts check box in the Menu area of the dialog box.

4. Select OK and Close to return to your document. The descriptions should now appear in the Title Bar.

My Button Bar is displayed but I do not have a mouse. Can I select the Button Bar buttons with the keyboard?

No, you cannot select the buttons on the Button Bar with a keyboard. You must use a mouse. Since you cannot use the Button Bar without a mouse, you may want to remove it from the screen. To do so, select Button Bar in the View menu so it no longer has a check mark. This menu command is a toggle switch. If you select it again, you will display the Button Bar.

In previous versions of WordPerfect for Windows, I used the WordPerfect File Manager to make copies and backups of files. Can I still do this without exiting WordPerfect 6.0 for Windows?

While WordPerfect 6.0 for Windows does not include the WordPerfect File Manager, you can still carry out file operations from within WordPerfect. To use WordPerfect to create backup copies of your files, follow these steps:

1. Select <u>O</u>pen from the <u>F</u>ile menu.

2. Select the file to copy.

3. Select <u>C</u>opy from the File <u>O</u>ptions pop-up list, which displays the Copy File dialog box.

4. Enter the path (drive and directory) you want the file copied to in the <u>T</u>o text box.

   Instead of typing the full path, you can click the button that looks like a file folder after the <u>T</u>o text box to display the Select Directory dialog box. You can use this dialog box to specify the destination for the copied file.

5. Select <u>C</u>opy, then Cancel to return to your document without opening the file you just copied.

After I exit WordPerfect, Windows tells me I don't have enough memory to start another application. Why?

When you exit WordPerfect for Windows, WordPerfect keeps control of some memory to contain the program files so that reloading WordPerfect won't take as long. To free up those remaining system resources, exit Windows, then restart it.

How do I switch between open documents in WordPerfect?

Switching between open documents is very easy. To do so:

1. Open your <u>W</u>indow menu.

   The <u>W</u>indow menu lists all currently open documents at the bottom, with a check mark beside the currently active document.

2. Select the document you want to become the currently active document.

You can also switch between documents using the keyboard:

1. Press CTRL+SHIFT+F6 to switch to the next open document.

2. Press CTRL+F6 to switch to the previous open document.

Why doesn't WordPerfect 6.0 for Windows ask me for my user initials, as previous network versions of WordPerfect did?

WordPerfect can now detect automatically which network you are on and what your user name is on that network. You do not need to supply your initials when you start WordPerfect. Then WordPerfect creates a file with an eight-character filename using the extension .BIF. The first four characters in the filename are the first four characters of your user name on your network. The second four characters are a hashed value of the first four characters. This file, a binary information file, contains your user settings, such as file locations and other preference settings. Each user has his or her own .BIF file so that WordPerfect can be customized for each user. .BIF files are stored by default in the \WINDOWS directory, unless they are redirected to a different directory specified by the /pi switch in the WP_WP_.ENV file.

My computer stops responding when I try saving my WordPerfect document to a floppy disk. What can I do?

You may encounter this error because of a memory allocation error. If your computer locks up when saving a file to a disk drive, you may need to edit the SYSTEM.INI file. To do so, follow these steps:

1. Select Open from the File menu.

2. Select the SYSTEM.INI file in your \WINDOWS directory, then choose OK.

3. Select OK in the Convert File Format dialog box to convert the file from ANSI text format into WordPerfect.

4. Select Find from the Edit menu.

5. Type **[386Enh]** in the Find text box, then select Find Next and Close.

6. Add the following lines to this section:

```
IRQ9GLOBAL=YES
EMMEXCLUDE=E000-FFFF
VIRTUALHDIRQ=OFF
```

7. Select <u>S</u>ave from the <u>F</u>ile menu.

8. In the Save Format dialog box, choose the ANSI Text (Windows) radio button and choose OK.

Can I rescue data that I accidentally deleted from my document?

WordPerfect 6.0 for Windows has two features for restoring deleted information: Undelete and Undo.

- *Undelete* restores information at the insertion point. Use Undelete by selecting U<u>n</u>delete from the <u>E</u>dit menu or by pressing CTRL+SHIFT+Z.

Tech Tip: If the text was cut to the Clipboard instead of being deleted, this command does not work. However, you can select <u>P</u>aste from the <u>E</u>dit menu to paste it from the Clipboard back to the document.

- *Undo* restores deleted information to the location from where it was deleted. Use Undo by selecting <u>U</u>ndo from the <u>E</u>dit menu or by pressing CTRL+Z.

Tech Terror: You cannot restore all information. Undelete only stores the last three deletions, so if you have deleted text more than three times, you cannot restore more than the last three deletions. Undo only remembers the last action that you did, so you can only use Undo to restore text if you do so immediately, before you move onto another task.

How can I make a file a hidden file?

A hidden file is one that has the hidden file attribute assigned to it by DOS. You can set file attributes from within WordPerfect. To apply the file attributes, follow these steps:

1. Select Open from the File menu.
2. Select the filename.
3. Select Change Attributes from the File Options pop-up list or from the QuickMenu that appears when you right-click a filename.
4. Select the Hidden check box and choose OK. You will not see the filename in the Filename list box.
5. Select Cancel to return to your document without opening a document.

If you want to retrieve this file later, you need to remember the document name, or use the Windows File Manager to find it. WordPerfect does not list the filename in the Filename list box if you try to open it in WordPerfect. To find the file using the File Manager:

1. Open the File Manager. The File Manager icon should appear in the Main program group in the Program Manager.
2. Select By File Type from the File Manager's View menu.
3. Select the Show Hidden/System Files check box unless it is already selected.
4. Select OK.

Changing this setting causes the File Manager to display hidden files in the selected directories.

You can remove the hidden attribute from a file using the Windows File Manager. Use the following steps:

1. Select the file in the directory listing.
2. Select Properties from the File menu or press ALT+ENTER.
3. Clear the Hidden check box and select OK.

After removing this attribute, the file will again appear in the Filename list box in WordPerfect.

How can I assign a password to a document?

Assigning a password to a document prevents unauthorized users from reading or making changes. To save a file with a password, follow these steps:

1. Select Save As from the File menu.

2. Enter the name of the file in the Filename text box as you normally do when saving files.

3. Select the Password Protect check box, then select OK.

4. Type your password in the Type Password for Document text box shown here, then select OK:

Tech Tip: Use the same password for all of your documents to make it easier to remember.

5. Type the password again and select OK. This step ensures that you typed the correct password, since you do not see what you typed, only a series of asterisks.

Each time you open this file, WordPerfect will prompt you to enter the password. If you forget the password, you will not be able to open the document.

Tech Terror: If you forget your password, WordPerfect Corporation cannot provide it to you. You may be able to open these files using a third-party utility program.

How can I keep the asterisks from appearing when I enter passwords for my files?

Use the BIF Editor to set the Don't Echo Password Asterisks setting to True. To make this change, follow these steps:

1. Start the BIF Editor by selecting Run from the Program Manager's File menu, typing **\WPC20\BIFED20.EXE**, and selecting OK.

2. Select Open Private BIF from the File menu.

3. Double-click WP Shared Code in the Groups/Sections/Items list box or highlight it and press ENTER.

4. Double-click Open File below WP Shared Code or highlight it and press ENTER.

5. Highlight Don't Echo Password Asterisks and select Edit.

6. Select True and OK.

7. Select Close to save the change and close the BIF Editor.

To make the asterisks appear again, set the same flag to False. This information is available in the README.NET file that is installed when WordPerfect is installed on a network.

Index

X, Y, Z